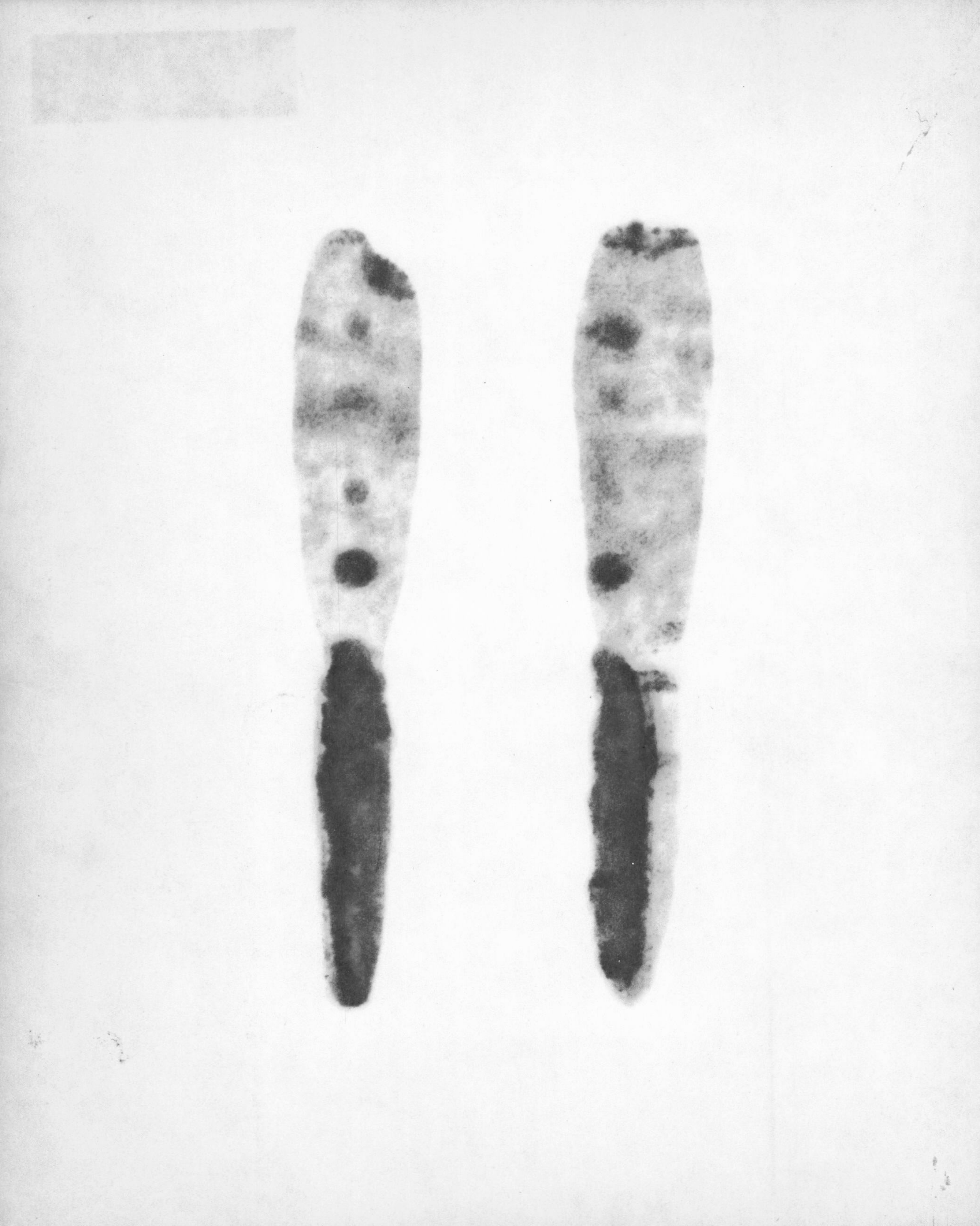

GREGG *Shorthand*

Shorthand written
by Charles Rader

Diamond Jubilee Series
Second Edition

John Robert Gregg

Louis A. Leslie

Charles E. Zoubek

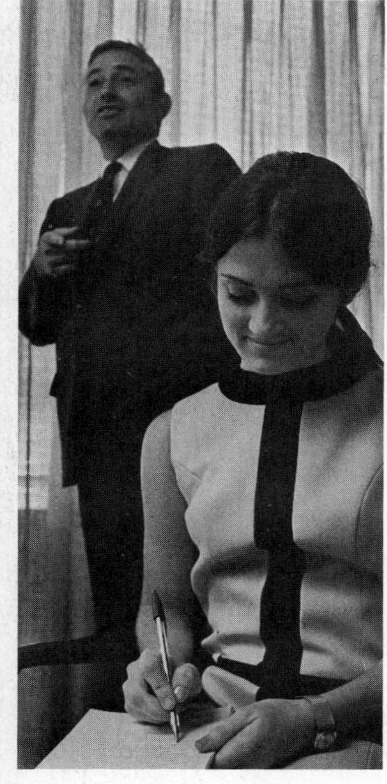

GREGG Shorthand

Gregg Division
McGraw-Hill Book Company

New York
St. Louis
Dallas
San Francisco
Düsseldorf
Johannesburg
Kuala Lumpur
London
Mexico
Montreal
New Delhi
Panama
Rio de Janeiro
Singapore
Sydney
Toronto

ACKNOWLEDGMENTS

The authors wish to express their appreciation to the following people for their valuable assistance in the preparation of *Gregg Shorthand, Diamond Jubilee Series, Second Edition*:

The teachers who have shared with the authors their experience with the first edition.

Mr. Charles Rader, for the beautiful shorthand and for the supervision of the production of the book.

Betty Binns, the designer, who was responsible for the physical attractiveness of the book.

Mrs. Mary Louise Intorrella and Mr. Jerome Edelman, members of the Gregg staff, who contributed so much to the production of the book.

Mr. Martin Bough of *Fundamental Photographs*, who took the cover, title, and chapter photographs.

Miss Bambi Hammil, who directed the taking of the pictures.

Mr. Syd Karson of *McGraw-Hill, Inc.*, who took the photographs for "Your Shorthand Practice Program" on pages 10, 11, and 12.

King Typographic Service Corp., which set the type, and R. R. Donnelley and Sons Company, which printed the book.

GREGG SHORTHAND, DIAMOND JUBILEE SERIES, SECOND EDITION

11 *DODO* 0 9 8 7

ISBN 07-024625-4

Preface

Gregg Shorthand, the universal system

Since its publication in 1888, Gregg Shorthand has been learned and used by millions of writers throughout the world not only in English but in many foreign languages as well. To most people the terms "shorthand" and "Gregg" are synonymous. Gregg Shorthand is truly the universal system of shorthand.

Gregg Shorthand is used by stenographers and secretaries as a vocational tool that enables them to obtain and hold interesting and rewarding positions in business. It is used by business and professional men and women who are relieved of the burden of writing cumbersome longhand when they must make notes, prepare important memoranda, and draft speeches and reports.

The success of any system of shorthand rests on the merits of its alphabet. The Gregg alphabet is the most efficient shorthand alphabet devised in more than 2,000 years of shorthand history. The fact that this alphabet, virtually without change, has been the basis of Gregg Shorthand for more than 80 years is indeed a tribute to the genius of its inventor, John Robert Gregg.

Diamond Jubilee Series, Second Edition

Objectives Gregg Shorthand, Diamond Jubilee Series, issued in 1963, the seventy-fifth anniversary of its invention, has been well received by the shorthand teaching profession. Teachers found the system changes to be logical and the new teaching and learning devices helpful. The major objectives of that edition were:

1 To teach the student to read and write Gregg Shorthand rapidly and accurately in the shortest time possible.

2 To provide the student with transcription readiness by building his vocabulary and developing his ability to spell and punctuate accurately—all concurrently with the teaching of shorthand.

The objectives of *Gregg Shorthand, Diamond Jubilee Series, Second Edition,* remain the same as those of the First Edition.

Organization

In *Gregg Shorthand, Diamond Jubilee Series, Second Edition,* no word-building principles or outlines have been changed; nor have the organization of the textbook and the order of presentation of shorthand principles been changed.

Like the First Edition, the Second Edition is divided into three parts—Principles, Reinforcement, and Shorthand and Transcription Skill Building. These parts are subdivided into 10 chapters and 70 lessons. The last new theory is presented in Lesson 47.

New format

The first thing that will immediately impress the student and teacher is the new, modern format of the Second Edition. This Second Edition is without doubt the most attractive, eye-appealing shorthand textbook ever published.

This format makes it possible to present the shorthand practice material in two columns that are approximately the width of the columns of the student's shorthand notebook. The shorter lines make reading easier, for the eye does not have to travel so far from the end of one line of shorthand to the beginning of the next. The new format also makes it possible to highlight the words from the Reading and Writing Practice that are singled out for spelling attention. The words are placed in the margins rather than in the body of the shorthand.

Building transcription skills

This Second Edition continues to place great stress on the nonshorthand elements of transcription, which are taught concurrently with shorthand. It retains all the helpful transcription exercises of the First Edition, with slight, but very helpful, modifications. These include:

Business Vocabulary Builders Beginning with Chapter 2, each lesson contains a Business Vocabulary Builder consisting of several business words or expressions for which meanings are provided. The words and expressions are selected from the Reading and Writing Practice. The Business Vocabulary Builders help to overcome a major transcription handicap — a limited vocabulary.

Spelling—Marginal Reminders Words singled out from the Reading and Writing Practice for special spelling attention appear in the margins of the shorthand. Usually each word appears on the same line as its shorthand outline. These words appear in a second color in the shorthand so that they are easy to spot.

In the Second Edition, spelling is introduced in Chapter 4 rather than in Chapter 6, as in the First Edition.

Spelling—Families An effective device for improving spelling is to study words in related groups, or spelling families. In the Second Edition, the student studies six spelling families.

Similar-Words Drills These drills teach the student the difference in meaning between similar words that stenographers often confuse—*it's, its; accept, except; there, their.*

Punctuation Beginning with Lesson 31, nine frequent usages of the comma are introduced. Only one comma usage is presented in any given lesson. The commas appear in a square in the shorthand, and the reason for the use of the comma is shown above the square.

Common Prefixes An understanding of the meaning of common English prefixes is an effective device for developing the student's understanding of words. In the Second Edition, the student studies five common English prefixes.

Grammar Checkup In a number of lessons, drills are provided on rules of grammar that students often apply incorrectly.

Transcription Quiz Beginning with Lesson 57, each lesson contains a Transcription Quiz consisting of a letter in which the student has to supply internal punctuation. This quiz provides him with a daily test of how well he has mastered the punctuation rules presented in earlier lessons.

Reading and writing practice

In this Second Edition there are 31,378 words of shorthand practice material in the Reading and Writing Practice exercises. Much of the material is new. That which has been retained from the First Edition has been revised and brought up to date.

A new feature is the inclusion of a brief-form letter in *every* lesson of Part 1 (except the review lessons) beginning with Lesson 5. In the First Edition brief-form letters were provided only in those lessons in which a new group of brief forms was introduced.

Other features

Shorthand spelling helps When a new shorthand letter or abbreviating device is presented, the shorthand spelling is given. Formerly, this information had to be provided by the teacher.

Chapter openings Each chapter is introduced by a beautifully illustrated spread that not only paints for the student a vivid picture of the life and duties of a secretary but also inspires and encourages him in his efforts to acquire the necessary skills.

Student helps To be sure that the student gets the greatest benefit from each phase of his shorthand study, he is given step-by-step suggestions on how to handle it when it is first introduced.

Reading scoreboards At various points in the text, the student is given an opportunity to determine his reading speed by means of a scoreboard. The scoreboard enables him to calculate the number of words a minute he is reading. By comparing his reading speed from scoreboard to scoreboard, he sees some indication of his shorthand reading growth.

Recall charts In the last lesson of each chapter in Part 1, a unique recall chart is provided. This chart contains illustrations of all the theory taught in the chapter. It also contains illustrations of all the theory the student has studied up to that lesson.

Check lists To keep the student constantly reminded of the importance of good practice procedures, occasional check lists are provided. These check lists deal with writing shorthand, reading shorthand, homework, proportion, etc.

Acknowledgments

Gregg Shorthand, Diamond Jubilee Series, Second Edition, is published with pride and with the confidence that it will help teachers of Gregg Shorthand do an even more effective job of training rapid and accurate shorthand writers and transcribers.

The Publishers

Contents

Your shorthand practice program

How rapidly you develop skill in reading and writing shorthand will depend largely on two factors—the amount of time you devote to practice and the *efficiency* with which you practice. You will derive the greatest benefit from the material on which you practice if you practice efficiently. You will also be able to complete each lesson in the shortest possible time—a consideration that is no doubt of importance to you. The suggestions given here will help you to get the maximum benefit from the time you invest in shorthand practice.

Before you begin, select a quiet place in which to practice—and resist the temptation to turn on the radio or television set. Then follow the steps outlined below for each part of your shorthand practice.

Reading word lists

In each lesson there are a number of word lists that illustrate the principles introduced in the lesson. As part of your home practice, read these word lists in this way:

1 *With the type key exposed,* spell—aloud if possible—the shorthand characters in each outline in the list, thus: *"see, s-e; fee, f-e."* Reading aloud will help to impress the shorthand outlines firmly on your mind. Read all the shorthand words in the list in this way—with the type key exposed—until you feel you can read the shorthand outlines without referring to the type key.

2 Then *cover the type key* with a card or a piece of paper and read aloud from the shorthand, thus: *"s-e, see; f-e, fee."*

3 If the spelling of a shorthand outline does not immediately give you the meaning, move the card or piece of paper to expose the key and determine the meaning of the outline you cannot read. *Important:* Do not spend more than a few seconds trying to decipher an outline.

4 After you have read all the words in the list, read them a second time—perhaps even a third.

Note: In reading brief forms for common words and phrases, which first occur in Lesson 3, you need not spell the shorthand outlines.

The student studies the word lists by placing a card or a slip of paper over the type key and reading the shorthand words aloud.

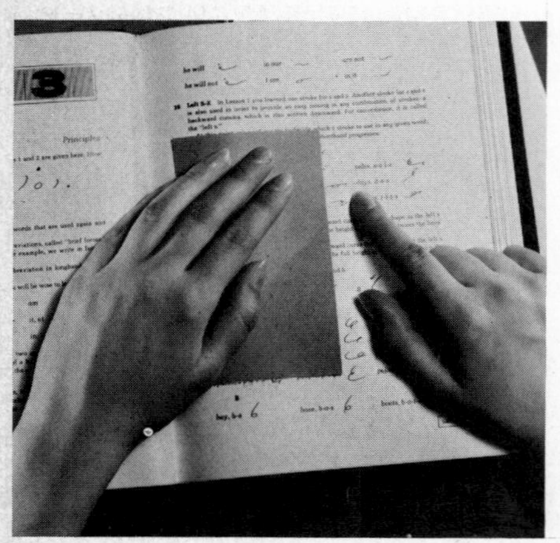

Reading sentences, letters, and articles

Each lesson contains a Reading Practice (Lessons 1-6) or a Reading and Writing Practice (Lessons 7-70) in which sentences, letters, or articles are written in shorthand. Your practice on this material will help you develop your shorthand vocabulary. The first thing you should do is *read* the material. Two procedures are suggested for reading shorthand—one with a Student's Transcript and one without a Student's Transcript.

Procedure With Student's Transcript If you have been supplied with a Student's Transcript to the shorthand in this textbook, you should follow this procedure:

1 Place the Student's Transcript to the right of your textbook and open it to the key to the Reading Practice or the Reading and Writing Practice you are about to read.

2 Place your left index finger under the shorthand outline that you are about to read and your right index finger under the corresponding word in the Student's Transcript.

3 Read the shorthand outlines aloud until you come to a word you cannot read. Spell the shorthand strokes in that outline. If this spelling does not *immediately* give you the meaning, anchor your left index finger on the outline and look in the transcript, where your right index finger is resting near the point at which you are reading.

4 Determine the meaning of the outline you cannot read and place your right index finger on it.

5 Return to the shorthand from which you are reading—your left index finger has kept your place for you—and continue reading in this manner until you have completed the material.

6 If time permits, read the material a second time.

By following this procedure, you will lose no time finding your place in the shorthand and in the transcript when you cannot read an outline.

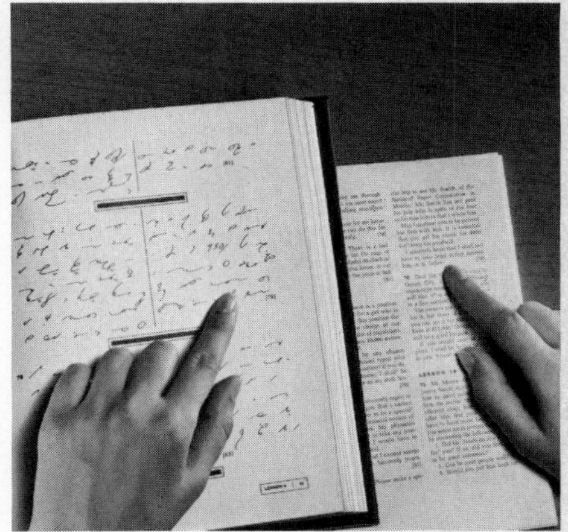

Refer to your Transcript whenever you cannot read an outline. Keep your left index finger anchored in the shorthand; the right index finger on the corresponding place in the Transcript.

Procedure Without Student's Transcript If you have not been supplied with a Student's Transcript, you should follow this procedure:

1 Before you start reading the shorthand, have a blank piece of paper or a blank card handy.

2 Read the shorthand aloud.

3 When you come to a shorthand outline that you cannot read, spell the shorthand strokes in the outline. If the spelling gives you the meaning, continue reading. If it does not, write the outline on your sheet of paper or card and continue reading. Do not spend more than a few seconds trying to decipher the outline.

4 After you have gone through the entire Reading and Writing Practice in this way, repeat this procedure if time permits. On this second reading you may be able to read some of the outlines

The student reads the Reading and Writing Practice, writing on the card any outlines that she cannot read after spelling them.

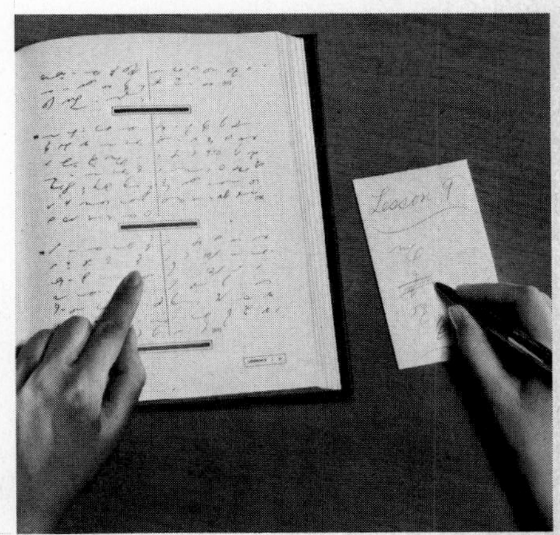

that escaped you on your first time through. When that happens, cross those outlines off your sheet or card.

5 Finally—and very important—at the earliest opportunity ask your teacher or a classmate the meaning of the outlines that you could not read.

Remember, during the early stages your shorthand reading may not be very rapid. That is only natural, as you are, in a sense, learning a new language. If you do each day's lesson faithfully, however, you will find your reading rate increasing almost from day to day.

When copying, the student reads a convenient group of words aloud and then writes that group in her notebook. Notice how she keeps her place in the shorthand with her left index finger.

Writing the Reading and Writing Practice

Before you do any writing of shorthand, you should give careful consideration to the tools of your trade—your notebook and your writing instrument.

Your notebook The best notebook for shorthand writing is one that measures 6 x 9 inches and has a vertical rule down the center of each page. If the notebook has a spiral binding, so much the better, as the spiral binding enables you to keep the pages flat at all times. The paper should, of course, take ink well.

Your writing instrument A fountain pen is the most satisfactory instrument for writing Gregg Shorthand, but a fine ball-point pen will also do nicely. *A pencil is not recommended.* Because writing with a pen requires little pressure, you can write for long periods of time without becoming fatigued. A pencil, however, requires considerable pressure. In addition, the point quickly becomes blunt; and the blunter it gets, the more effort you have to expend to write with it. Pen-written notes remain legible almost indefinitely; pencil notes become blurred and hard to read. Pen-written notes are also easier to read under artificial light.

Having selected your writing tools, follow these steps in writing the Reading and Writing Practice:

1 Read the material you are going to copy, following the suggestions for reading shorthand on page 11. *Always* read the Reading and Writing Practice before copying it.

2 When you are ready to start writing, read a convenient group of words from the printed shorthand; then write the group, reading aloud as you write. Keep your place in the shorthand with your left index finger if you are right-handed or with your right index finger if you are left-handed.

In the early stages your writing may not be very rapid, nor will your notes be as well written as those in the book. With regular practice, however, you will soon become so proud of your shorthand notes that you won't want to write any more longhand!

Good luck with your study of Gregg Shorthand.

1
PRINCIPLES

Chapter 1

Shorthand—stepping-stone to a career

There are many reasons why people decide to learn shorthand. No doubt you have your reasons. Perhaps the title of secretary appeals to you, and you realize that shorthand is a "must" if you are to earn that title. Perhaps you wish to acquire a skill that will help you earn your way through college. Or perhaps you have some personal reason for wanting to learn shorthand.

One very big reason why many people study shorthand is that they know that it opens doors to positions of responsibility that might otherwise be closed to them. In other words, they use shorthand as a stepping-stone to an interesting and profitable career.

How does shorthand open doors? How does it serve as a stepping-stone to a career? Let's cite the case of Janet Greene, a young lady who has considerable talent in art and is anxious to use this talent in the field of advertising.

Upon graduation from school Janet applied to several advertising agencies for a position in their art departments. She quickly found out that competition in this field is keen and that agencies were reluctant to hire young artists who have had no experience.

After being told by several personnel directors that they had no openings in which they could use her talent, Janet asked one of them, "How can

I get into the advertising field? I have my heart set on becoming a commercial artist." The personnel director's answer was direct: "Study shorthand and develop a good stenographic skill. You can always get a job as a stenographer—a well-paying job, too. Get your foot in the door of an advertising agency by working there as a stenographer. Then when you have made a niche for yourself, let it be known that you have artistic talents and ambitions. The chances are that you will be given an opportunity to demonstrate your talents." Good advice!

Every year countless young women—and many men—use their shorthand skill to open doors to varied and interesting careers. They may be careers in publishing, in advertising, in television, or in management. Competition is keen in these fields, and often the only way for a beginner to get into them is through the back door —the stenographic door!

Even the young lady who isn't really interested in a career—only in the title of "Mrs."—finds shorthand and stenographic training valuable. Thousands of young women continue to work after they are married to help earn money for a new home, to save for vacation travel, or to help meet unexpected expenses.

You have made a wise decision to learn shorthand!

GREGG SHORTHAND IS EASY TO LEARN

Anyone who has learned to read and write longhand can learn to read and write Gregg Shorthand—it is as simple as that. The strokes you will write in Gregg Shorthand are the same strokes you are accustomed to writing in longhand.

Learning to write Gregg Shorthand is actually easier than learning to write longhand. Skeptical? Well, the following illustration should convince you of the truth of that statement.

In longhand, *f* may be expressed in many ways, all of which you had to learn. Here are six of them:

In addition, in many words the sound of *f* is expressed by combinations of other letters of the alphabet; for example, *ph,* as in *phase; gh,* as in *rough.*

In Gregg Shorthand there is only one way to express the sound of *f,* as you will learn later in this lesson.

With regular practice, your skill in Gregg Shorthand will develop rapidly.

Principles

GROUP A

1 **S-Z** The first stroke you will learn is the shorthand *s,* which is one of the most frequently used letters in the English language. The shorthand *s* is a tiny downward curve that resembles the longhand comma in shape.

Because in English *s* often has the sound of *z,* as in *saves,* the same downward curve is used to express *z.*

S-Z

2 A The next stroke you will learn is the shorthand *a*, which is simply the longhand *a* with the final connecting stroke omitted.

A

3 Silent Letters Omitted Many words in the English language contain letters that are not pronounced. In shorthand, these silent letters are omitted; only the sounds that are actually pronounced in a word are written. Examples:

The word *say* would be written *s-a;* the *y* would not be written because it is not pronounced. The word *face* would be written *f-a-s;* the *e* would not be written because it is not pronounced and the *c* would be represented by s because it is pronounced s.

What letters in the following words would not be written in shorthand because they are not pronounced?

day	*same*	*mean*	*tea*
save	*steam*	*dough*	*snow*

4 S-A Words With the strokes for *a* and s, you can form the shorthand outlines for two words.

say, s-a *ace, a-s*

▶ Notice that the *c* in *ace* is represented by the shorthand s because it has the s sound.

5 F, V The shorthand stroke for *f* is a downward curve the same shape as s except that it is larger—about half the height of the space between the lines in your shorthand notebook.

The shorthand stroke for v is also a downward curve the same shape as s and *f* except that it is very large—almost the full height of the space between the lines of your shorthand notebook. Note the difference in the sizes of s, *f*, v.

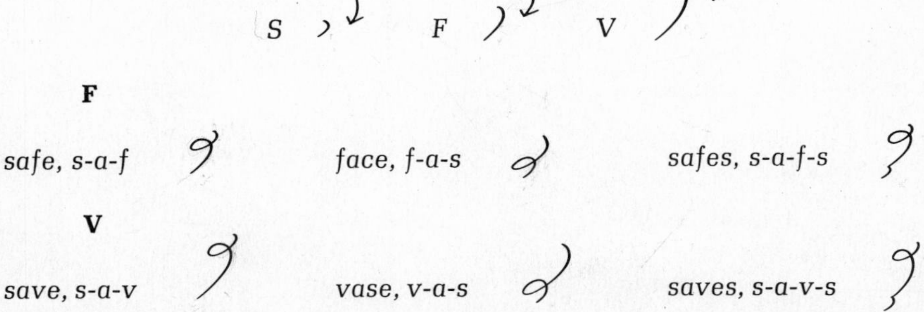

▶ Notice that the final s in *saves* has the z sound, which is represented by the s stroke.

6 **E** The shorthand stroke for *e* is a tiny circle. It is simply the longhand *e* with the two connecting strokes omitted.

E

Be sure to make the *e* circle tiny and the *a* circle large.

Compare: E A

see, s-e	sees, s-e-s	ease, e-s
fee, f-e	fees, f-e-s	easy, e-s-e

▶ Notice that the *y* in *easy* is pronounced *e;* therefore, it is represented by the *e* circle.

> *Suggestion:* At this point take a few moments to read the procedures outlined for practicing word lists on page 10. By following those procedures, you will derive the greatest benefit from your practice.

GROUP B

7 **N, M** The shorthand stroke for *n* is a very short forward straight line.
The shorthand stroke for *m* is a longer forward straight line.

N M

N

see, s-e	say, s-a	vain, v-a-n
seen, s-e-n	sane, s-a-n	knee, n-e

▶ Notice that the *k* in *knee* is not written because it is not pronounced.

M

may, m-a	mean, m-e-n	same, s-a-m
main, m-a-n	name, n-a-m	seem, s-e-m
me, m-e	aim, a-m	fame, f-a-m

8 T, D The shorthand stroke for *t* is a short upward straight line. The shorthand stroke for *d* is a longer upward straight line.

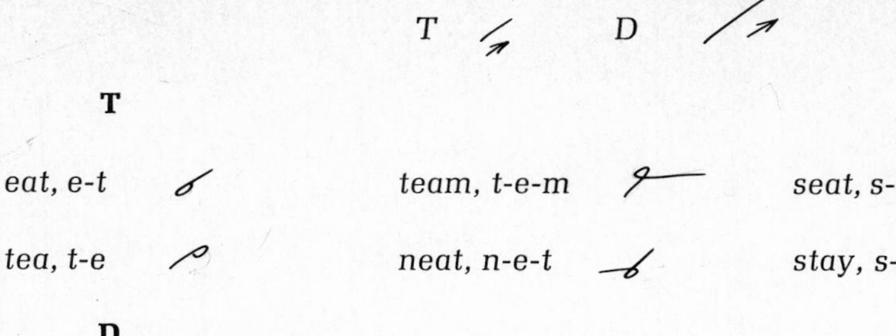

T　　D

T

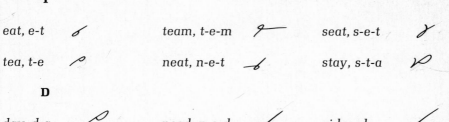

eat, e-t	*team, t-e-m*	*seat, s-e-t*
tea, t-e	*neat, n-e-t*	*stay, s-t-a*

D

day, d-a	*need, n-e-d*	*aid, a-d*
date, d-a-t	*made, m-a-d*	*saved, s-a-v-d*

9 Punctuation and Capitalization

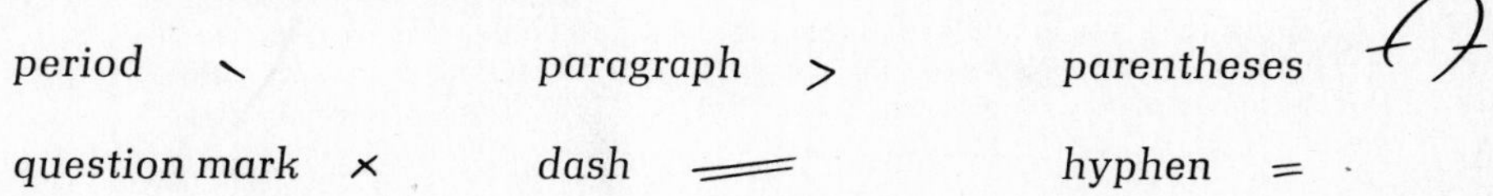

period	*paragraph*	*parentheses*
question mark	*dash*	*hyphen*

For all other punctuation marks, the regular longhand forms are used.

Capitalization is indicated by two upward dashes placed underneath the word to be capitalized.

Dave　　*Fay*　　*May*

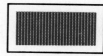

Reading practice

With the help of an occasional longhand word, you can already read complete sentences.

Read the following sentences, spelling each shorthand outline aloud as you read it, thus: *D-a-v-s, Dave's; f-e-t, feet.* If you cannot read a shorthand outline after you have spelled it, refer to the key.

1 hurt 2 on 25 a with 3

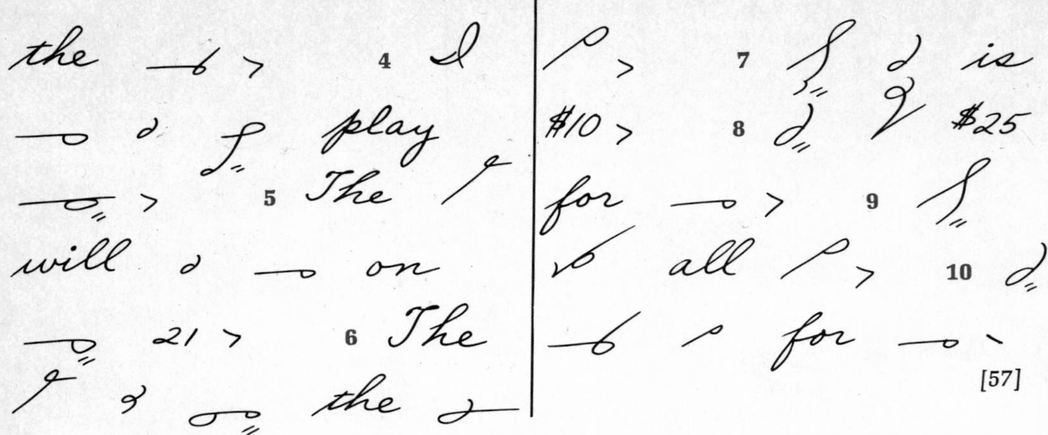

1. Dave's feet hurt. 2. Fay made a date with Dean on May 25. 3. Amy made me eat the meat. 4. I may see Navy play Maine. 5. The dean will see me on May 21. 6. The dean sees Amy the same day. 7. Dave's fee is $10. 8. Fay saved $25 for me. 9. Dave stayed all day. 10. Fay made tea for me.

Principles

10 Alphabet Review In Lesson 1 you studied the following nine shorthand strokes. How quickly can you read them?

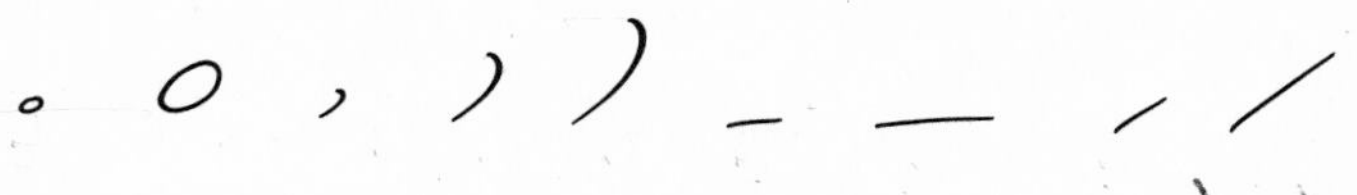

11 O, R, L The shorthand stroke for *o* is a small deep hook.

The shorthand stroke for *r* is a short forward curve.

The shorthand stroke for *l* is a longer forward curve about three times as long as the stroke for *r*.

▶ Note how these shorthand strokes are derived from their longhand forms.

O R L

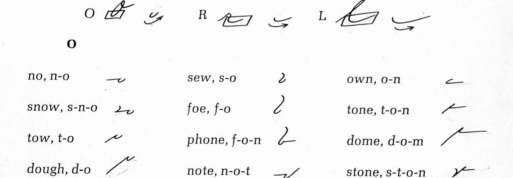

O

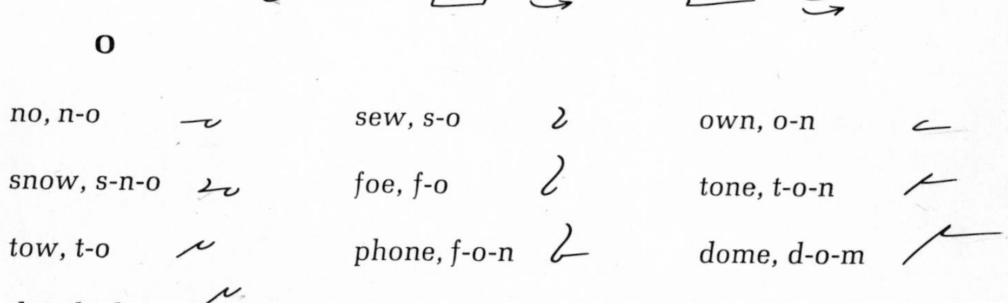

no, n-o	*sew, s-o*	*own, o-n*
snow, s-n-o	*foe, f-o*	*tone, t-o-n*
tow, t-o	*phone, f-o-n*	*dome, d-o-m*
dough, d-o	*note, n-o-t*	*stone, s-t-o-n*

▶ Notice that in the words in the third column the *o* is placed on its side. By placing *o* on its side before *n* and *m* in these and similar words, we obtain smoother joinings than we would if we wrote the *o* upright.

R

ray, r-a	*raid, r-a-d*	*ear, e-r*
rate, r-a-t	*trade, t-r-a-d*	*dear, d-e-r*

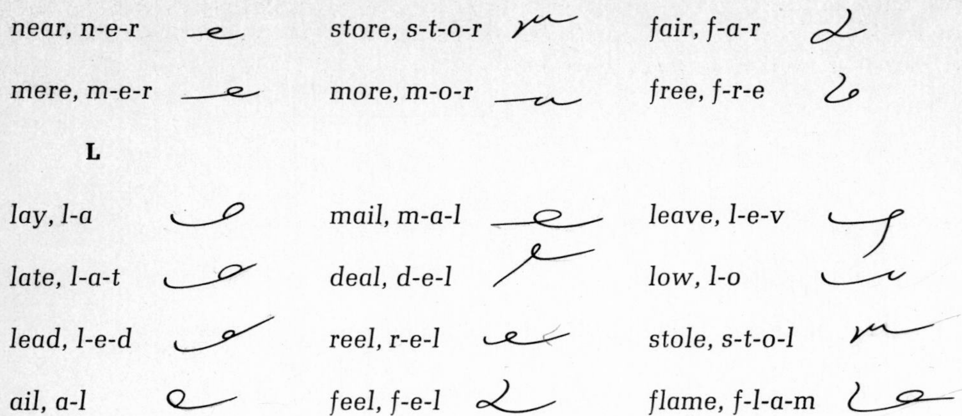

near, n-e-r	store, s-t-o-r	fair, f-a-r
mere, m-e-r	more, m-o-r	free, f-r-e

L

lay, l-a	mail, m-a-l	leave, l-e-v
late, l-a-t	deal, d-e-l	low, l-o
lead, l-e-d	reel, r-e-l	stole, s-t-o-l
ail, a-l	feel, f-e-l	flame, f-l-a-m

▶ Notice that *fr*, as in *free*, and *fl*, as in *flame*, are written with one sweep of the pen, with no stop between the *f* and the *r* or *l*.

free *flame*

12 **H, -ing** The letter *h* is simply a dot placed above the vowel. With few exceptions, *h* occurs at the beginning of a word.

Ing, which almost always occurs at the end of a word, is also expressed by a dot.

H

he, h-e	hair, h-a-r	hole, h-o-l

-ing

heating, h-e-t-ing	heeding, h-e-d-ing	hearing, h-e-r-ing

13 **Long Ī** The shorthand stroke for the long sound of ī, as in *my*, is a large broken circle.

I

my, m-ī	fine, f-ī-n	right, write r-ī-t
might, m-ī-t	vine, v-ī-n	light, l-ī-t
tire, t-ī-r	line, l-ī-n	side, s-ī-d

14 Omission of Minor Vowels Some words contain vowels that are either not pronounced or are slurred in ordinary speech. For example, the word *even* is really pronounced *e-vn*; the word *meter* is pronounced *met-r*. These vowels may be omitted in shorthand.

reader, r-e-d-r *total*, t-o-t-l *later*, l-a-t-r

meter, m-e-t-r *heater*, h-e-t-r *even*, e-v-n

Reading practice

With the aid of a few words written in longhand, you can now read the following sentences. Remember to spell each shorthand word aloud as you read it and to refer to the key when you cannot read a word.

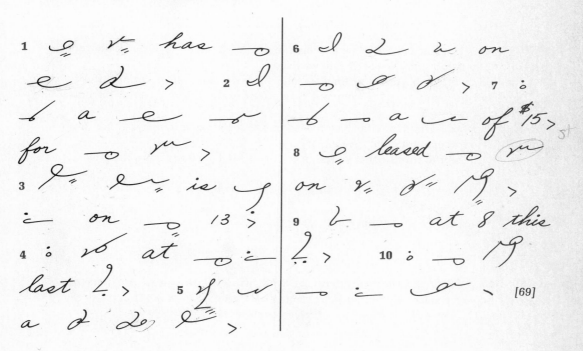

[69]

1. Ray Stone has my nail file. 2. I need a mail meter for my store. 3. Dale Taylor is leaving home on May 13. 4. He stayed at my home last evening. 5. Steven wrote a fine fairy tale. 6. I feel sore on my right side. 7. He made me a loan of $15. 8. Ray leased my store on East Side Drive. 9. Phone me at eight this evening. 10. He may drive me home later.

Principles

15 Alphabet Review The strokes you studied in Lessons 1 and 2 are given here. How fast can you read them?

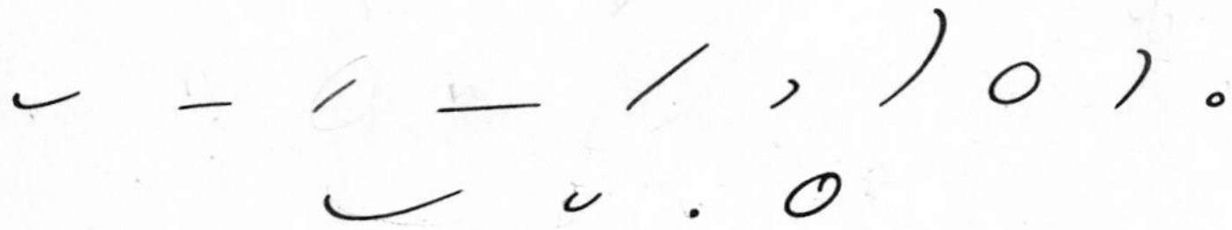

16 Brief Forms The English language contains many words that are used again and again in all the writing and speaking that we do.

As an aid to rapid shorthand writing, special abbreviations, called "brief forms," are provided for many of these common words. For example, we write *m* for *am*, *v* for *have*.

You are already familiar with the process of abbreviation in longhand—*Mr.* for *Mister, memo* for *memorandum, Ave.* for *Avenue.*

Because these brief forms occur so frequently, you will be wise to learn them well!

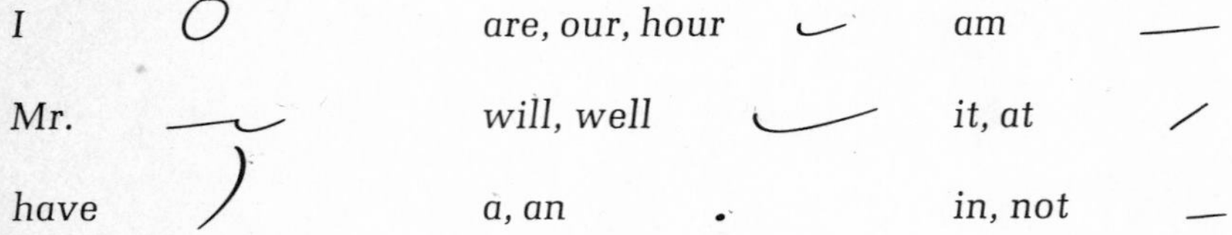

I
are, our, hour
am
Mr.
will, well
it, at
have
a, an
in, not

▶ Notice that some of the shorthand outlines have two or more meanings. You will have no difficulty selecting the correct meaning of a brief form when it appears in a sentence. The sense of the sentence will give you the answer.

17 Phrases By using brief forms for common words, we are able to save writing time. Another device that helps save writing time is called "phrasing," or the writing of two or more shorthand outlines together. Here are a number of useful phrases built with the brief forms you have just studied.

I have   *I have not*   *I will*

he will	*in our*	*are not*
he will not	*I am*	*in it*

18 Left S-Z In Lesson 1 you learned one stroke for s and z. Another stroke for s and z is also used in order to provide an easy joining in any combination of strokes—a backward comma, which is also written downward. For convenience, it is called the "left s."

At this point you need not try to decide which s stroke to use in any given word; this will become clear to you as your study of shorthand progresses.

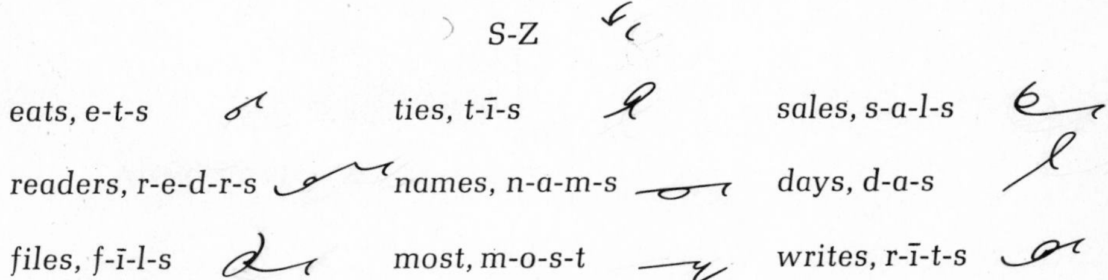

S-Z
eats, e-t-s
ties, t-ī-s
sales, s-a-l-s
readers, r-e-d-r-s
names, n-a-m-s
days, d-a-s
files, f-ī-l-s
most, m-o-s-t
writes, r-ī-t-s

19 P, B The shorthand stroke for p is a downward curve the same shape as the left s except that it is larger—approximately half the height of the space between the lines in your shorthand notebook.

The shorthand stroke for b is also a downward curve the same shape as the left s and p except that it is much larger—almost the full height of the space between the lines in your shorthand notebook.

▶ Notice the difference in the sizes of left s, p, and b.

S P B

P

pay, p-a	price, p-r-ī-s	hopes, h-o-p-s
pays, p-a-s	please, p-l-e-s	opens, o-p-n-s
pairs, p-a-r-s	plane, p-l-a-n	paid, p-a-d
spares, s-p-a-r-s	people, p-e-p-l	pains, p-a-n-s

B

bay, b-a	base, b-a-s	boats, b-o-t-s

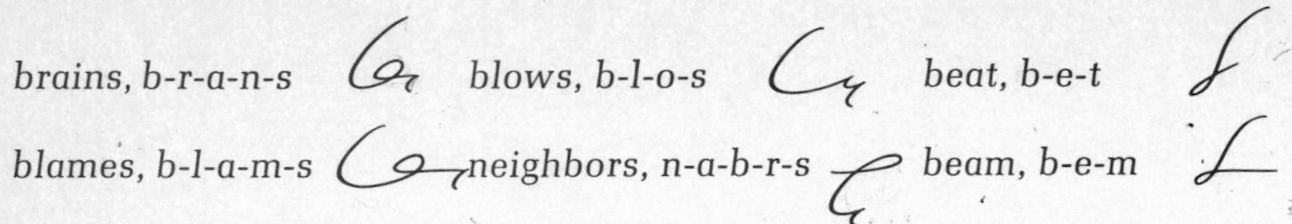

brains, b-r-a-n-s blows, b-l-o-s beat, b-e-t

blames, b-l-a-m-s neighbors, n-a-b-r-s beam, b-e-m

▶ Notice that the combinations *pr,* as in *price; pl,* as in *please; br,* as in *brains;* and *bl,* as in *blames,* are written with one sweep of the pen without a pause between the *p* or *b* and the *r* or *l.*

price please brains blames

Reading practice

You have already reached the point where you can read sentences written entirely in shorthand.

> *Suggestion:* Before you start your work on this Reading Practice, read the practice procedures for reading shorthand on page 10. By following those procedures, you will obtain the most benefit from your reading.

GROUP A

1

2

3

4

5

6

7

[60]

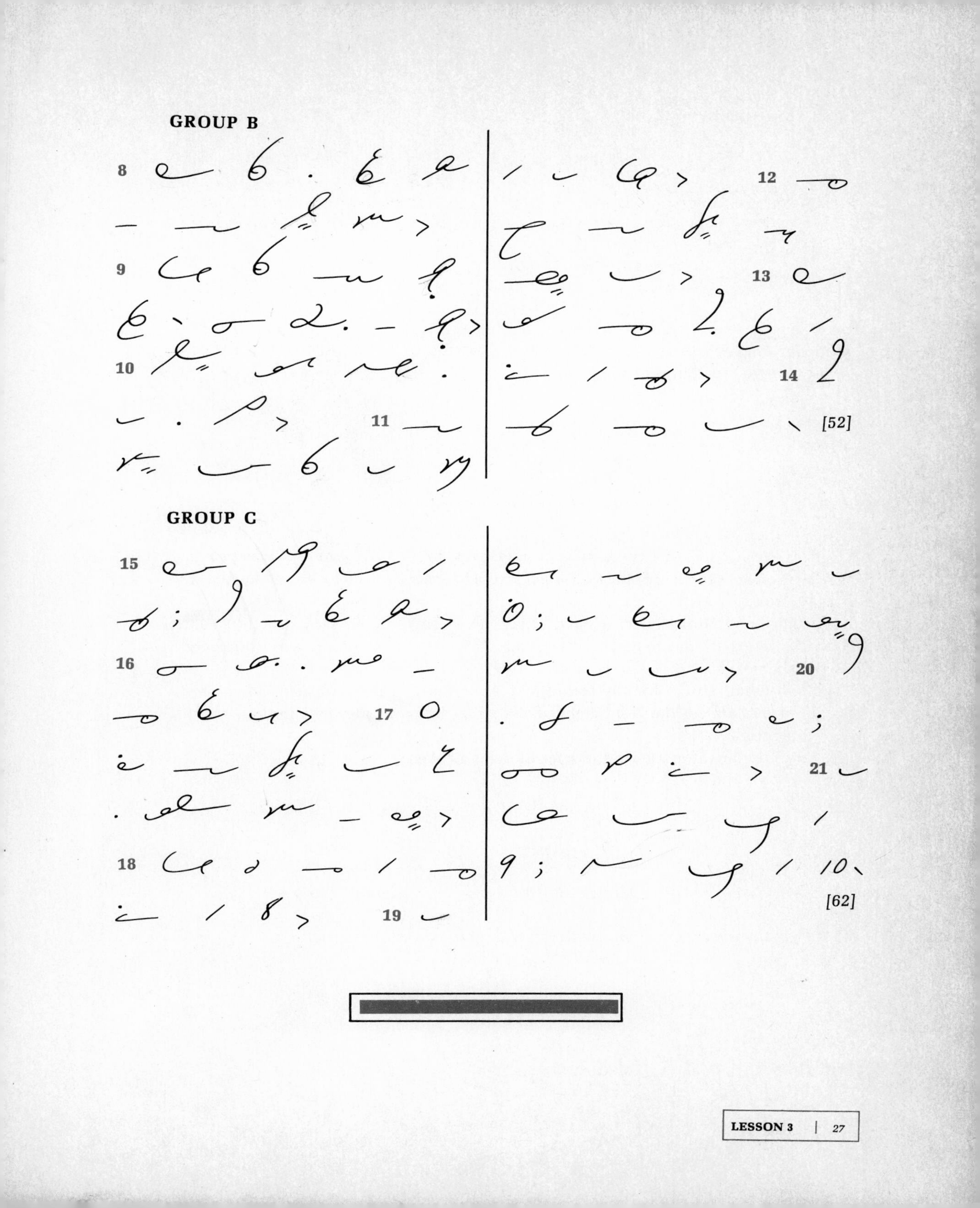

GROUP B

8

9

10

11

12

13

14

[52]

GROUP C

15

16

17

18

19

20

21

[62]

Principles

20 Alphabet Review In Lessons 1 through 3, you studied 17 shorthand strokes. How rapidly can you read these strokes?

21 Sh, Ch, J The shorthand stroke for *sh* (called "ish") is a very short downward straight stroke.

The shorthand stroke for *ch* (called "chay") is a longer downward straight stroke approximately half the height of the space between the lines in your shorthand notebook.

The shorthand stroke for the sound of *j*, as in *jail* and *age*, is a long downward straight stroke almost the full height of the space between the lines in your shorthand notebook.

▶ Note carefully the difference in the sizes of these strokes.

Sh Ch J

Sh

she, ish-e *shows, ish-o-s* *shades, ish-a-d-s*

showing, ish-o-ing *showed, ish-o-d* *shaped, ish-a-p-t*

Ch

each, e-chay *reached, r-e-chay-t* *chairs, chay-a-r-s*

teach, t-e-chay *chains, chay-a-n-s* *cheaper, chay-e-p-r*

J

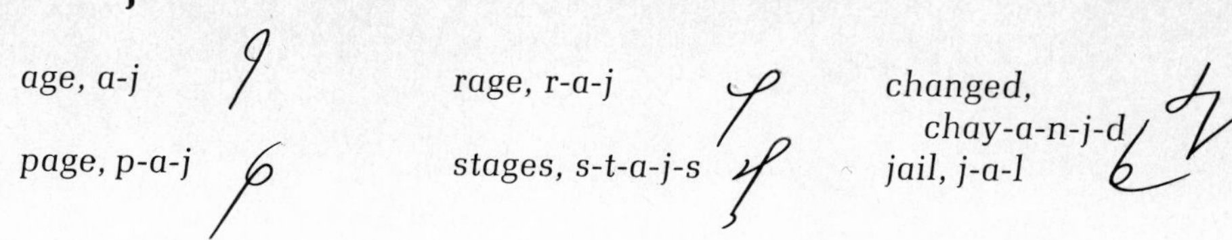

22 OO, K, G The shorthand stroke for the sound of *oo,* as in *to,* is a tiny upward hook.

The shorthand stroke for *k* is a short forward curve.

The shorthand stroke for the hard sound of *g,* as in *gain,* is a much longer forward curve. It is called "gay."

OO

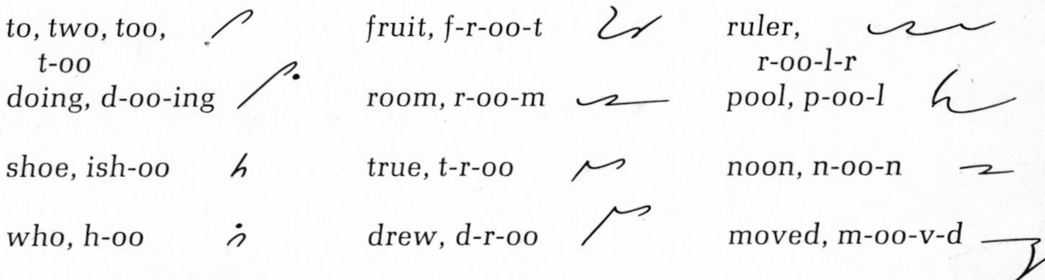

to, two, too, t-oo
doing, d-oo-ing
shoe, ish-oo
who, h-oo
fruit, f-r-oo-t
room, r-oo-m
true, t-r-oo
drew, d-r-oo
ruler, r-oo-l-r
pool, p-oo-l
noon, n-oo-n
moved, m-oo-v-d

▶ Notice that the *oo* is placed on its side when it follows *n* or *m,* as in *noon* and *moved.* By placing the *oo* hook on its side in these combinations rather than writing it upright, we obtain smooth joinings.

K

ache, a-k

take, t-a-k

make, m-a-k

liked, l-ī-k-t

came, k-a-m

care, k-a-r

keeps, k-e-p-s

claims, k-l-a-m-s

maker, m-a-k-r

G

gain, gay-a-n

game, gay-a-m

gave, gay-a-v

goals, gay-o-l-s

gale, gay-a-l

gear, gay-e-r

going, gay-o-ing

grade, gay-r-a-d

gleam, gay-l-e-m

▶ Notice that *kr,* as in *maker,* and *gl,* as in *gleam,* are written with a smooth, wavelike motion. But *kl,* as in *claims,* and *gr,* as in *grade,* are written with a hump between the *k* and the *l* and the *g* and the *r.*

maker  *gleam*  *claims*  *grade*

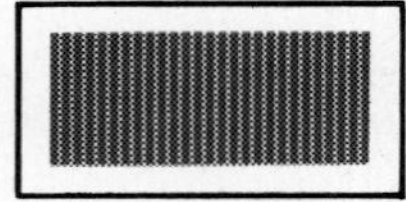

Reading practice

The following sentences contain many illustrations of the new shorthand strokes you studied in Lesson 4. They also review all the shorthand strokes, brief forms, and phrases you studied in Lessons 1 through 3.

Read these sentences aloud, spelling each shorthand outline that you cannot read immediately.

GROUP A

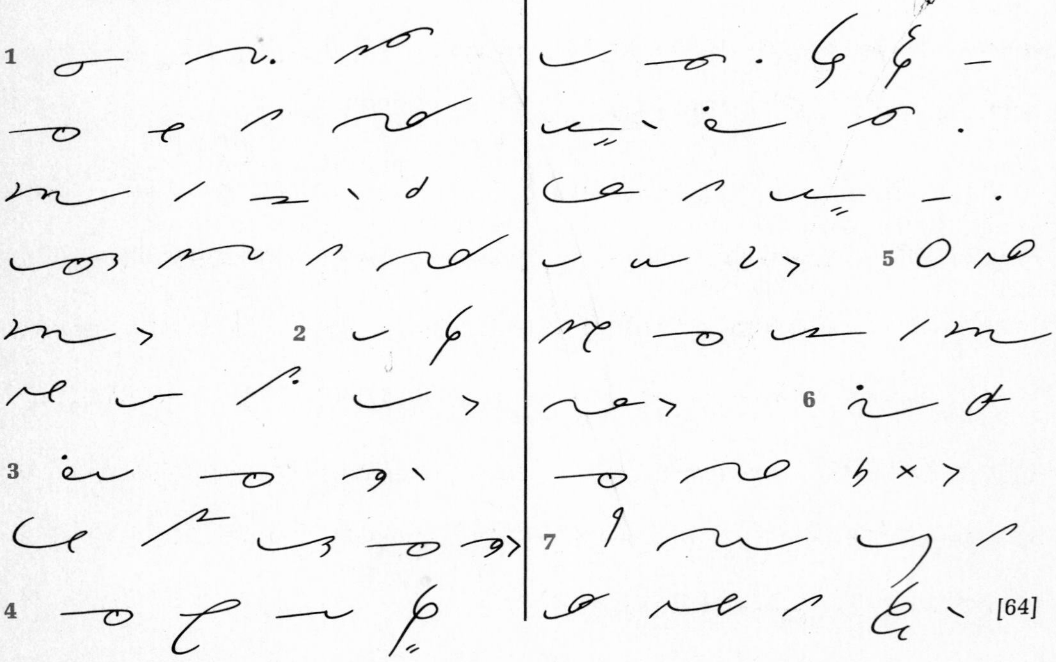

[64]

GROUP B

11

12

13

14

[58]

GROUP C

15

16

17

18

19

20

21

22

23

24

[85]

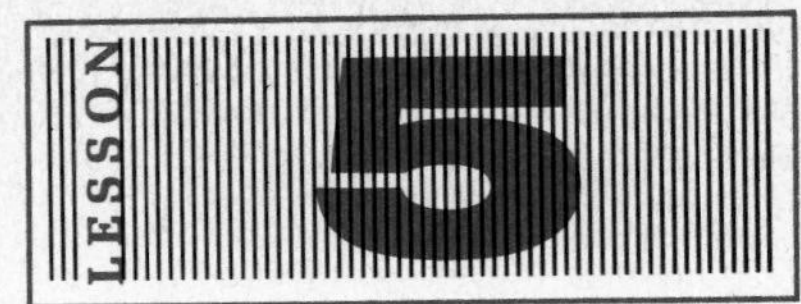

Principles

23 Alphabet Review Here are all the shorthand strokes you have studied in Lessons 1 through 4. See how rapidly you can read them.

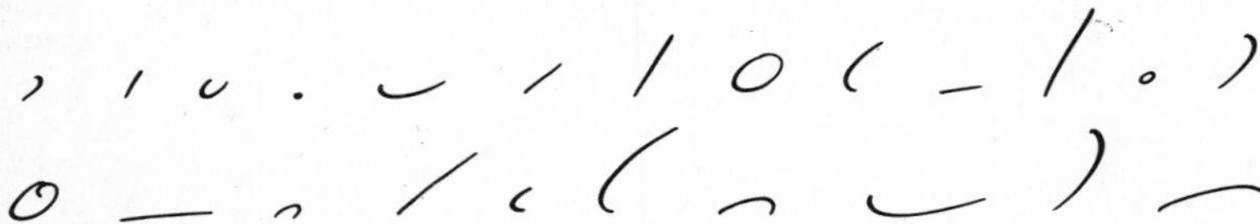

24 A, Ä The large circle that represents the long sound of ā, as in *main,* also represents the vowel sounds heard in *act* and *arm.*

A

has, h-a-s | *acting, a-k-t-ing* | *fast, f-a-s-t*
had, h-a-d | *facts, f-a-k-t-s* | *past, p-a-s-t*
man, m-a-n | *matters, m-a-t-r-s* | *last, l-a-s-t*

Ä

mark, m-a-r-k | *far, f-a-r* | *calm, k-a-m*
parked, p-a-r-k-t | *farms, f-a-r-m-s* | *arm, a-r-m*
large, l-a-r-j | *cars, k-a-r-s* | *start, s-t-a-r-t*

25 E, I, Obscure Vowel The tiny circle that represents the sound of ē, as in *heat,* also represents the vowel sounds heard in *let* and *trim,* as well as the obscure vowel heard in *her, church.*

E

let, l-e-t | *telling, t-e-l-ing* | *test, t-e-s-t*

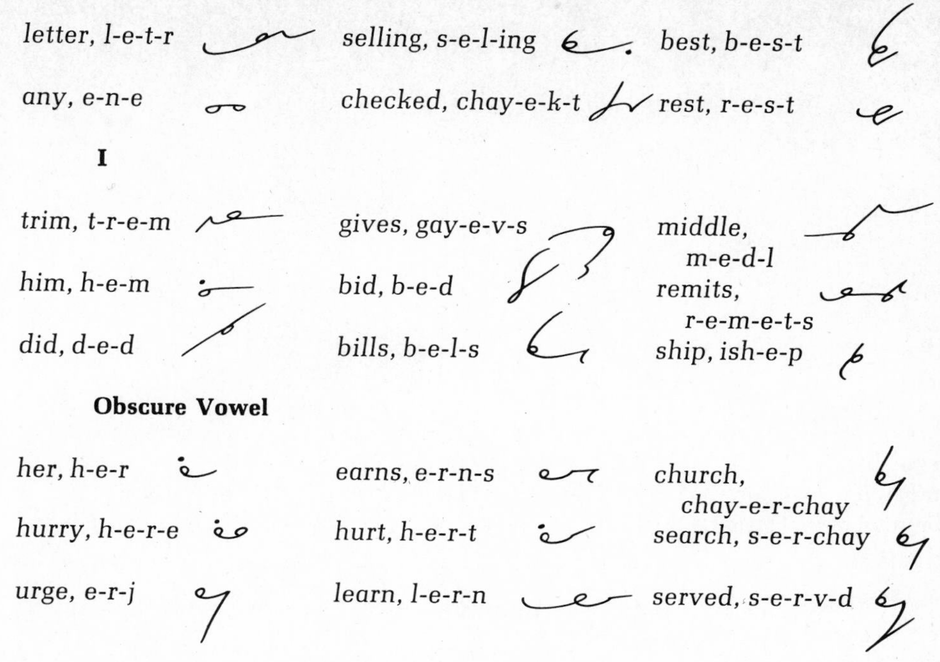

letter, l-e-t-r
selling, s-e-l-ing
best, b-e-s-t
any, e-n-e
checked, chay-e-k-t
rest, r-e-s-t
I
trim, t-r-e-m
gives, gay-e-v-s
middle, m-e-d-l
him, h-e-m
bid, b-e-d
remits, r-e-m-e-t-s
did, d-e-d
bills, b-e-l-s
ship, ish-e-p
Obscure Vowel
her, h-e-r
earns, e-r-n-s
church, chay-e-r-chay
hurry, h-e-r-e
hurt, h-e-r-t
search, s-e-r-chay
urge, e-r-j
learn, l-e-r-n
served, s-e-r-v-d

26 **Th** Two tiny curves, written upward, are provided for the sounds of *th*. These curves are called "ith."

At this time you need not try to decide which *th* stroke to use in any given word; this will become clear to you as your study of shorthand progresses.

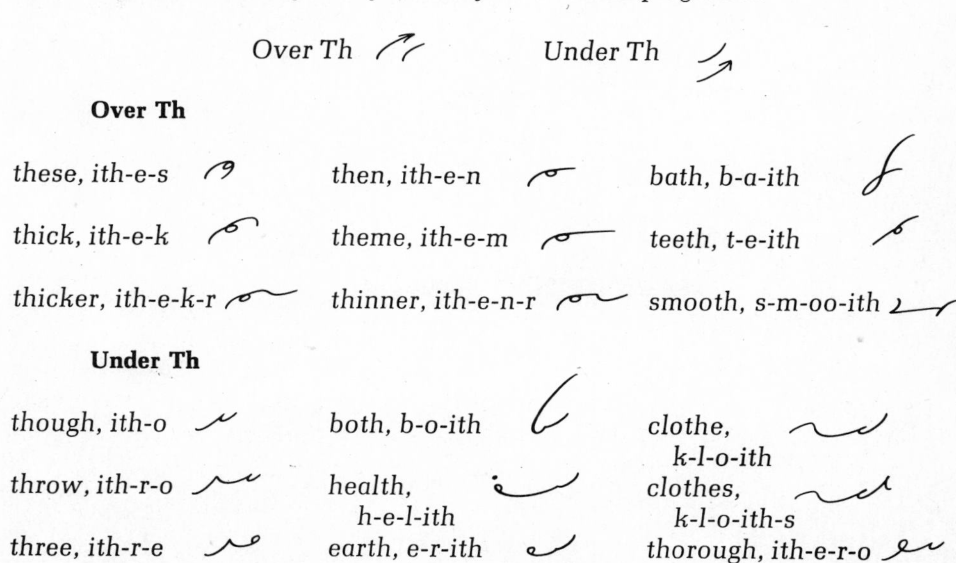

27 Brief Forms Here is another group of brief forms for very frequently used business words. Learn them well.

is, his	can	of
the	you, your	with
that	Mrs.	but

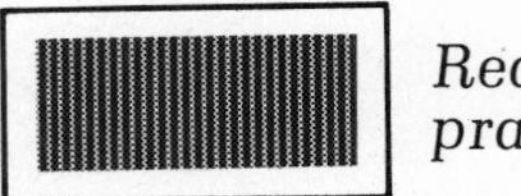

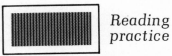

Reading practice

Your progress has been so rapid that you can already read business letters written entirely in shorthand.

28 Brief-Form Letter This letter contains one or more illustrations of all the brief forms you studied in this lesson.

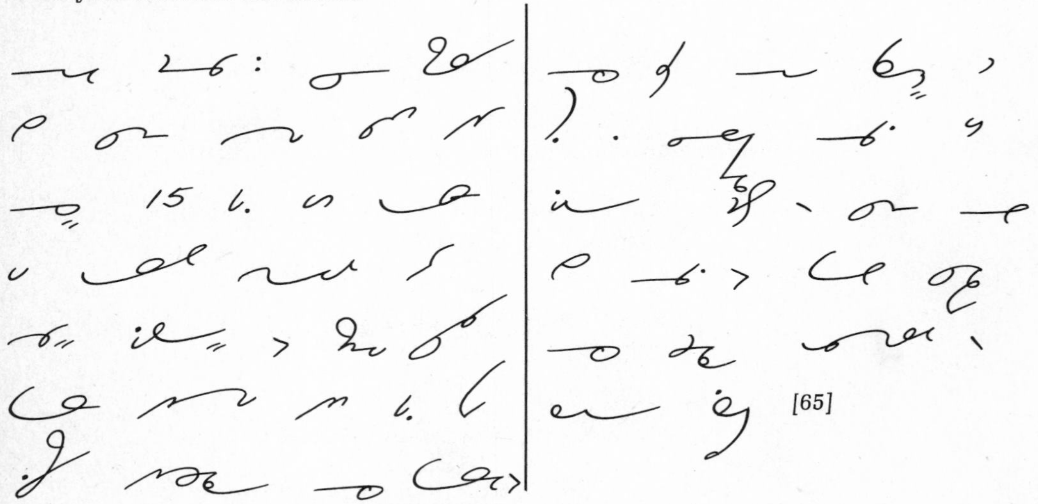

[65]

29

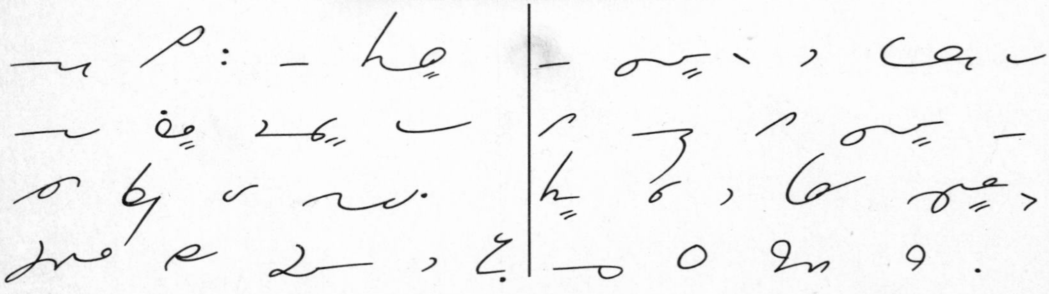

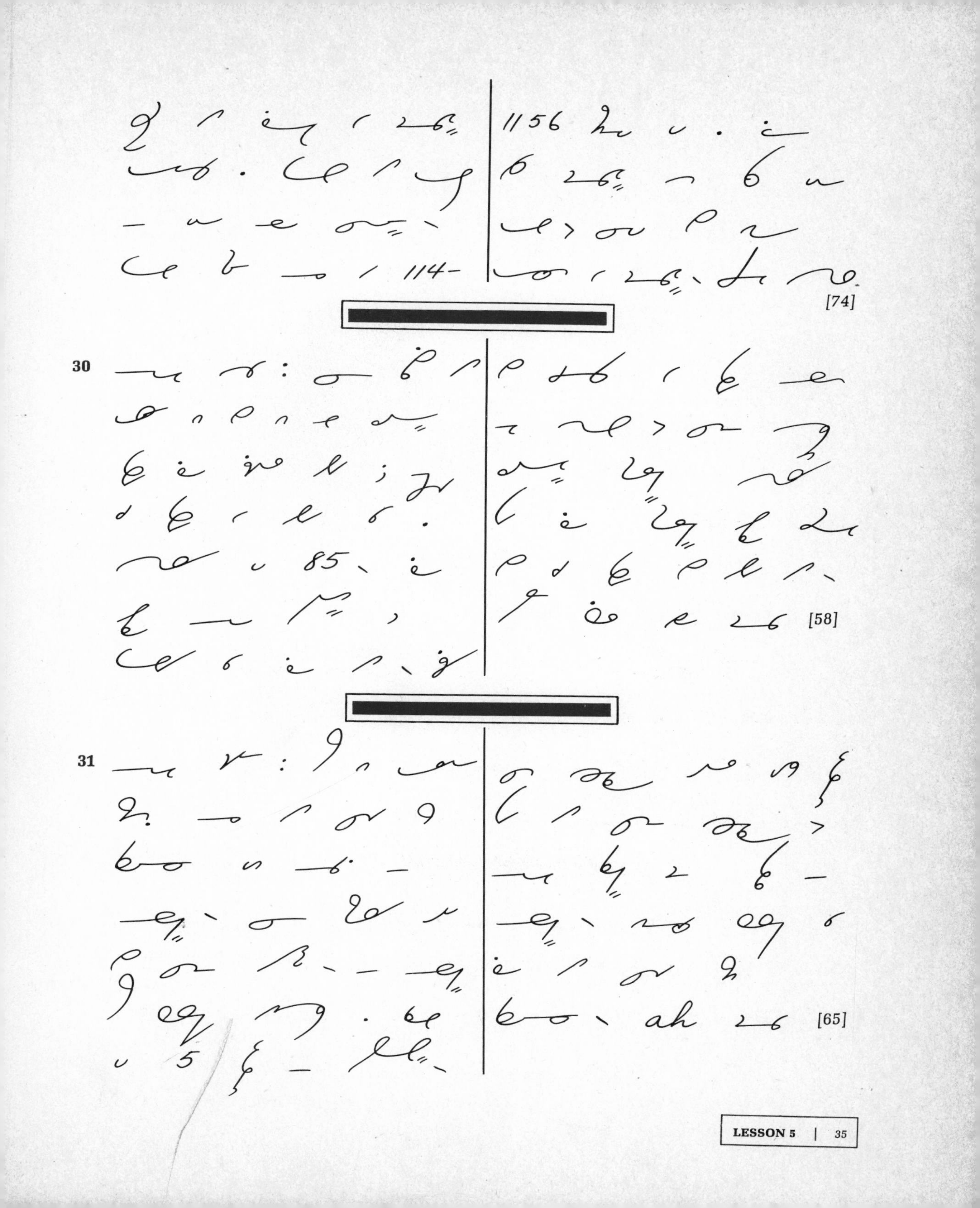

[74]

30

[58]

31

[65]

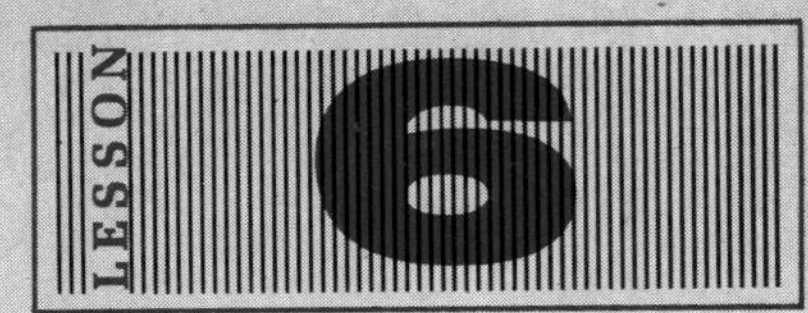

Recall

Lesson 6 contains no new strokes for you to learn. In this lesson you will find an alphabet review, a simple explanation of the principles that govern the joining of the strokes you studied in Lessons 1 through 5, a Recall Chart, and a Reading Practice employing the shorthand devices of Lessons 1 through 5.

32 **Alphabet Review** Here are all the shorthand strokes you studied thus far. Can you read them in 20 seconds or less?

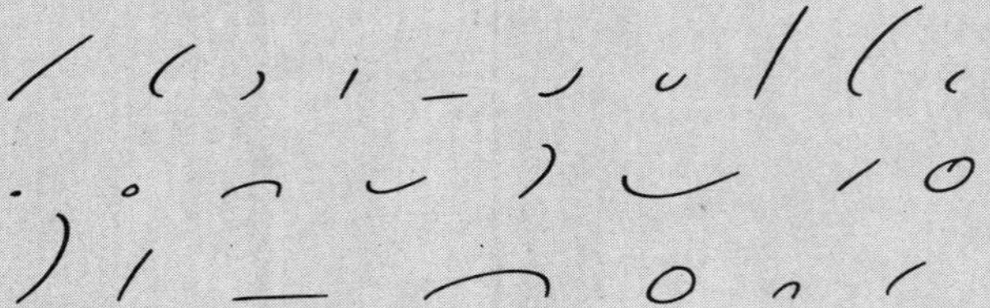

Principles of joining

As a matter of interest, you might like to know the principles by which the words you have already learned are written. Notice the groups into which the joinings naturally fall.

33 Circles are written inside curves and outside angles.

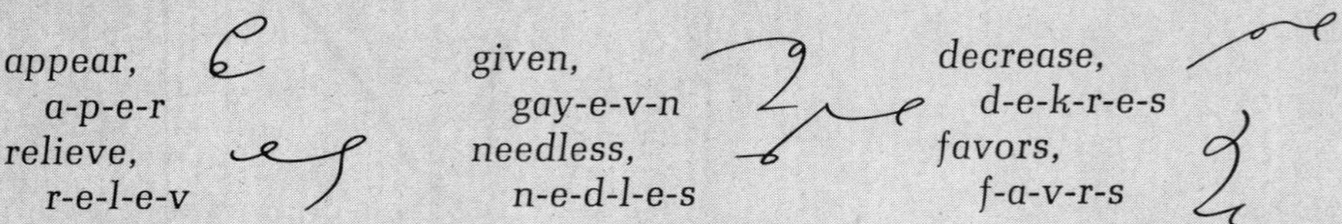

34 Circles are written clockwise (in this direction ↻) on a straight line or between two straight strokes in the same direction.

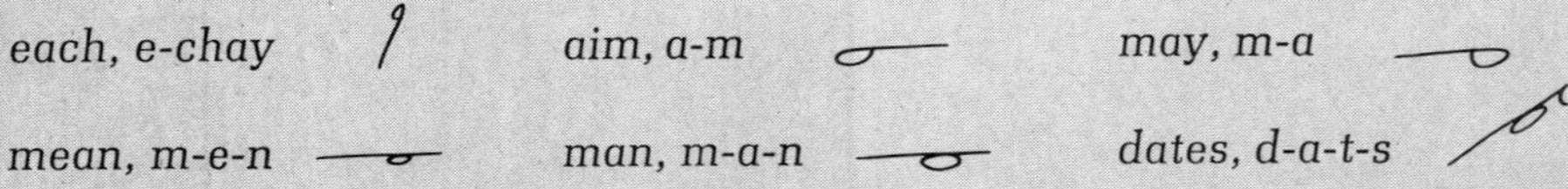

35 Between two curves written in opposite directions, the circle is written on the back of the first curve.

gear, gay-e-r rack, r-a-k paved, p-a-v-d

carriage, k-a-r-j leak, l-e-k vapor, v-a-p-r

36 The *o* hook is written on its side before *n, m* unless a downward character comes before the hook.

owns, o-n-s loan, l-o-n homes, h-o-m-s

but

bone, b-o-n zone, s-o-n shown, ish-o-n

37 The *oo* hook is written on its side after *n, m.*

noon, n-oo-n moon, m-oo-n moved, m-oo-v-d

38 The over *th* is used in most words, but when *th* is joined to *o, r, l,* the under *th* is used.

these, ith-e-s both, b-o-ith threads, ith-r-e-d-s

39 **Recall Chart** The following chart, which reviews the shorthand devices you studied in Lessons 1 through 5, is divided into three parts: (1) words that illustrate the principles, (2) brief forms, (3) phrases.

Spell out each word aloud, thus: *a-k-t, act.* You need not spell the brief forms and phrases.

The chart contains 84 words and phrases. Can you read the entire chart in 9 minutes or less? If you can, you are making good progress.

WORDS

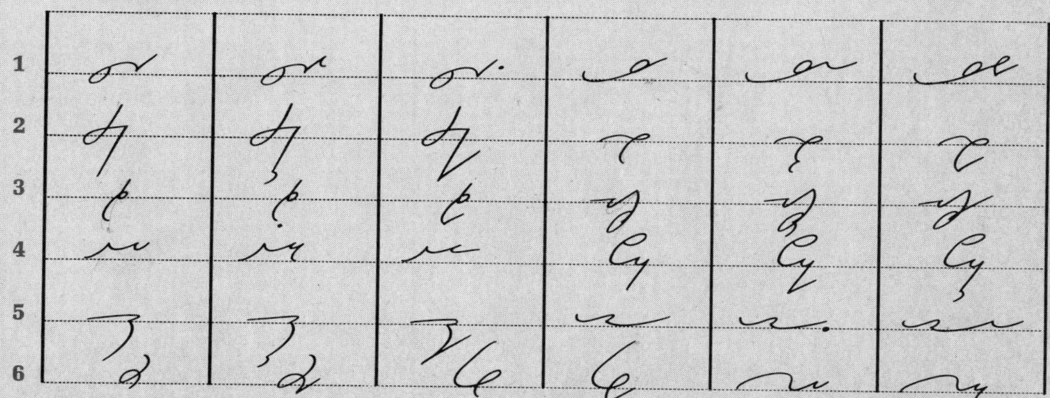

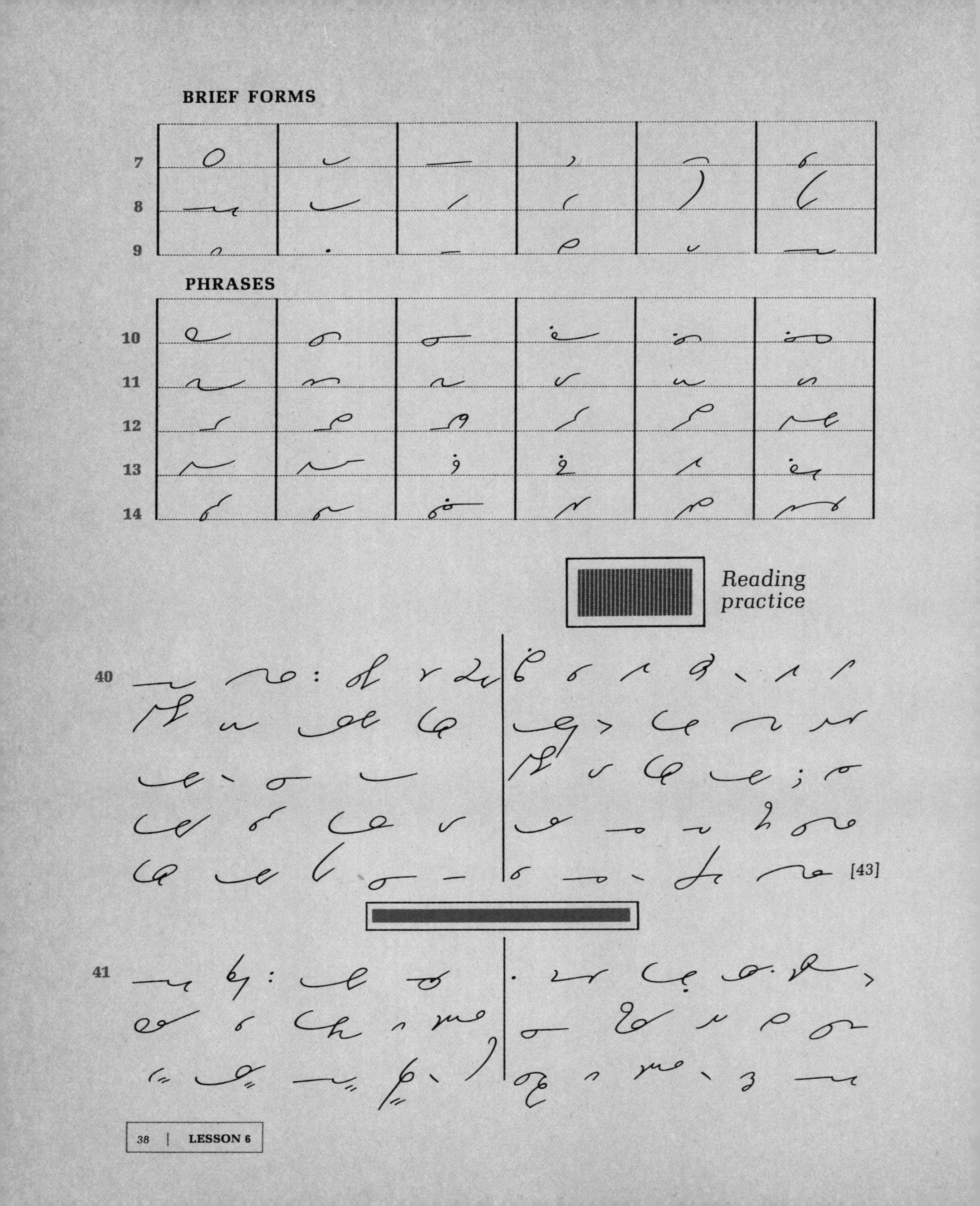

BRIEF FORMS

7

8

9

PHRASES

10

11

12

13

14

Reading practice

40

[43]

41

[76]

42

116-1151 [56]

43

15

[73]

Chapter 2
Shorthand in the business office

Mr. Harding is general manager of a large manufacturing plant. If you were a fly on the wall in his office on a regular business day, this is what you might be likely to hear:

"Miss Phillips, please bring in your notebook. I want to dictate some letters . . . ."

". . . and, John, be sure to send a copy of that report to Mr. Castle in Denver and two copies to Ed Smith in Toledo—no, better send him three. By the way, when you send Smith's copies, include a list of our recent price changes. A copy of the report should go to Alison, too; I think he is in Miami this week. Be sure that everything goes airmail special. . . ."

"When Mrs. Cochran calls, tell her our group will meet her at the National Airport, South Terminal, at 3:30. Ask her to bring along the photographs and news releases on the Wilson project. Tell her she should plan to stay over in Wichita an extra day or two. Fred Toffi wants her to see the public relations people at Boeing. . . ."

If the employees to whom these instructions are directed

are to carry them out fully and accurately, they must listen carefully—and write the instructions down! Only if these employees can write shorthand rapidly can they be sure of getting all the facts on paper.

Studies show that almost half of our communicating time in the office is spent listening to others, and much of what the business employee hears must be recorded if he is to recall and act on it later.

Nearly all business employees have occasional need for a fast writing ability. For the stenographer or secretary, however, such a skill is a constant need. Shorthand is as important to her (or him) as the ability to type. Taking things down in shorthand is so much a part of her daily routine that when she is summoned by her boss—either directly or by buzzer or telephone—she automatically picks up her notebook and pen.

Every year hundreds of thousands of people in all parts of the world learn shorthand. Most of them study shorthand because they want to become secretaries. Secretarial work is perhaps the most popular—and frequently the most important—career in the world for young women.

More and more young men are learning shorthand, too. Some executives in such fields as transportation, engineering, and manufacturing hire men exclusively as secretaries. Frequently men who do not intend to become secretaries learn shorthand and find it a valuable skill in helping them to advance more rapidly in their chosen field. Thousands have found shorthand the open-sesame to administrative positions.

And speaking of business offices, the United States Government runs perhaps the largest "business office" in the world. The armed services alone need thousands of stenographers to record the many details of military activities. Many of these stenographers are civilians employed in the different branches of the armed forces. Other government installations, in Washington and throughout the free world, employ hundreds of thousands of civilian office personnel and offer an almost unlimited choice of fields of work for the skilled shorthand writer. The work is interesting and challenging.

Principles

44 **O, Aw** The small deep hook that represents ō, as in *row,* also represents the sounds heard in *hot* and *drawing.*

O

Spell: *h-o-t, hot*

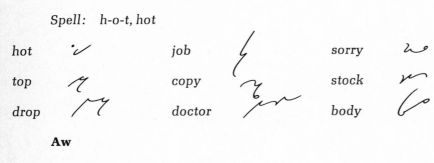

hot	*job*	*sorry*
top	*copy*	*stock*
drop	*doctor*	*body*

Aw

Spell: *d-r-o-ing, drawing*

drawing	*ought*	*all*
law	*taught*	*call*
cause	*brought*	*small*

45 **Common Business-Letter Salutations and Closings**

Dear Sir	*Yours truly*	*Yours very truly*
Dear Madam	*Sincerely yours*	*Very truly yours*

▶ Note: While the expressions *Dear Sir, Dear Madam,* and *Yours truly* are considered too impersonal by experts in letter writing, they are still used by many businessmen. Therefore, special abbreviations are provided for them.

Building transcription skills

46 BUSINESS VOCABULARY BUILDER

Words are the stenographer's tools of her trade. The more words she knows and understands, the easier her task of taking dictation and transcribing will be.

To help you increase your knowledge and understanding of words, each lesson hereafter will contain a Business Vocabulary Builder consisting of words or expressions, selected from the Reading and Writing Practice, that should be part of your everyday vocabulary. A brief definition, as it applies in the sentence in which it occurs, will be given for each word or expression.

Before you begin your work on the Reading and Writing Practice, be sure that you understand the meaning of the words and expressions in the Business Vocabulary Builder.

Business vocabulary builder

marketing All activities involved in getting goods from the producer to the user.

semester A school term consisting, usually, of eighteen weeks.

abroad Outside the country.

bursar A treasurer of a school, such as a college.

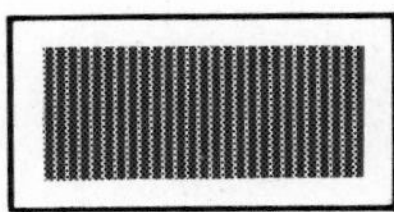

Reading and writing practice

Suggestion: Before you begin your work on the letters that follow, turn to page 10 and read the procedures outlined there for reading and writing shorthand. To make the most rapid progress, follow those procedures carefully.

47 Brief-Form Review Letter This letter reviews all the brief forms presented in Lesson 5 as well as many presented in Lesson 3.

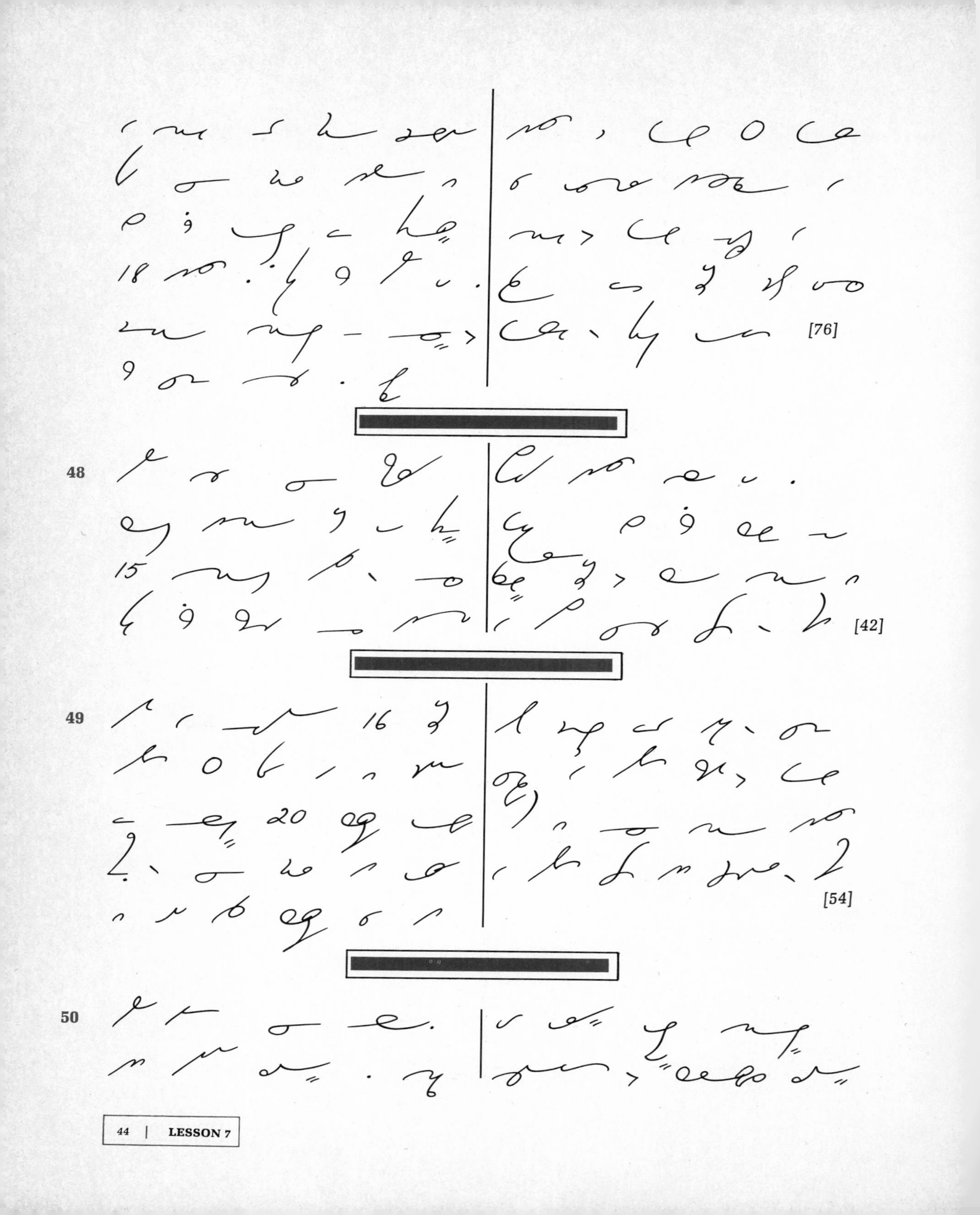

[76]

48

[42]

49

[54]

50

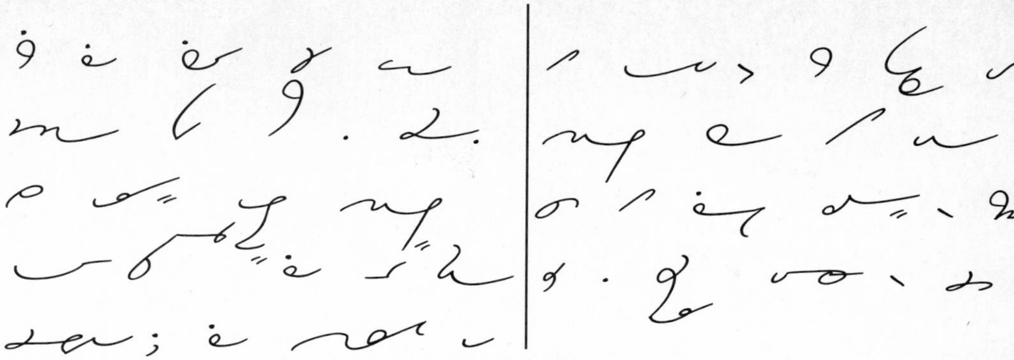

[71]

51

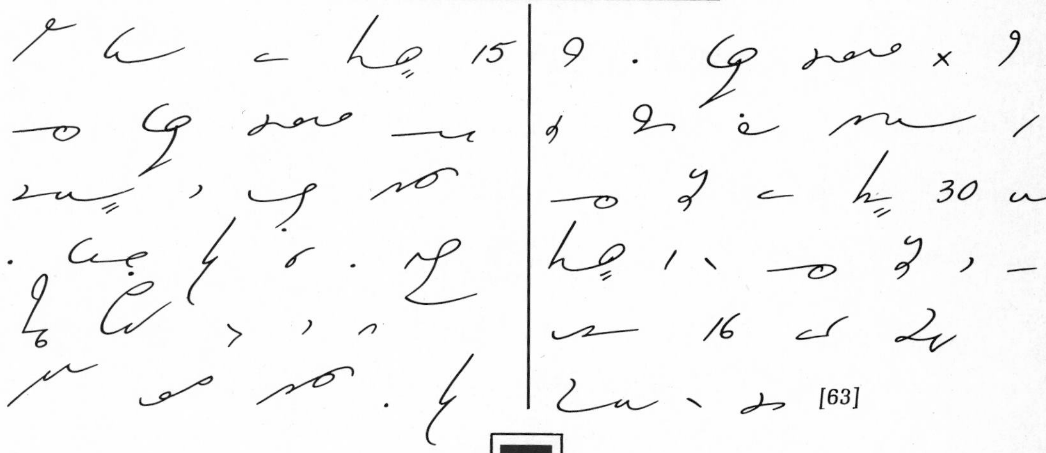

[63]

52

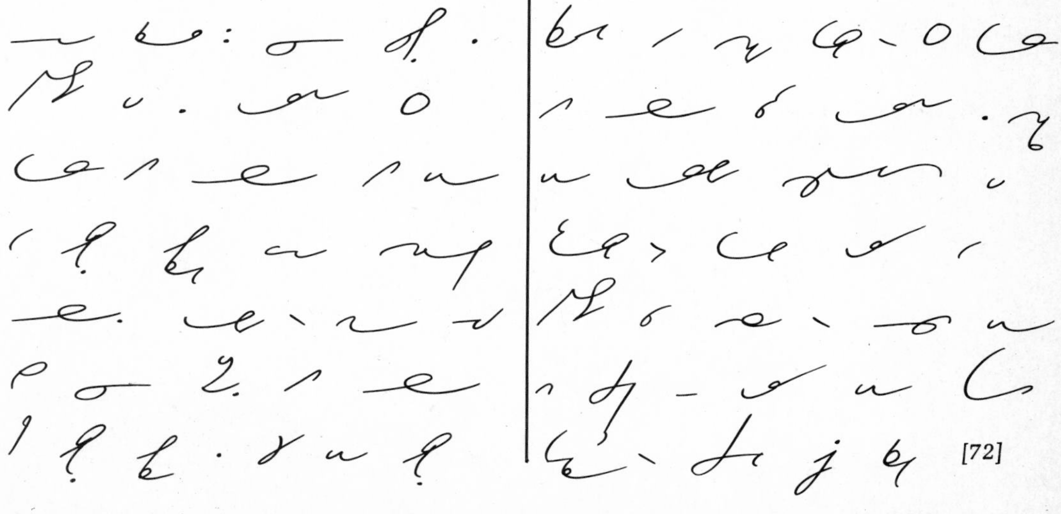

[72]

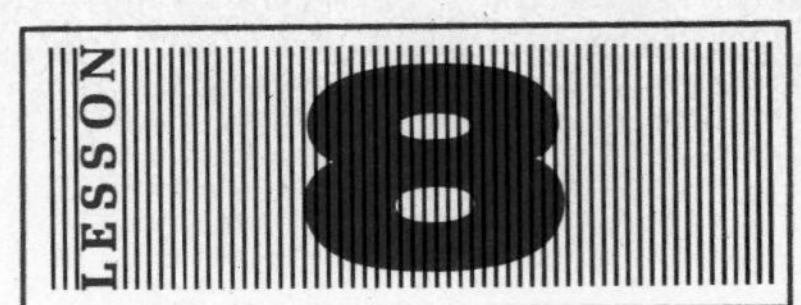

Principles

53 **Brief Forms** Here is the third group of brief forms for frequently used words.

for	*be, by*	*their, there*
shall	*put*	*this*
which	*would*	*good*

54 **Word Ending -ly** The very common word ending *-ly* is expressed by the *e* circle.

Spell: b-r-e-f-le, *briefly*

briefly	*nearly*	*highly*
only	*merely*	*totally*
mostly	*properly*	*daily*

▶ Notice how the circle for *-ly* in *daily* is added to the other side of the *d* after the *a* has been written.

55 **Amounts and Quantities** In business you will frequently have to take dictation in which amounts and quantities are used. Here are some devices that will help you write them rapidly.

400	$4	4 o'clock
4,000	$4,000	$4.50
400,000	$400,000	4 percent

▶ Notice that the *n* for *hundred* and the *th* for *thousand* are placed underneath the figure.

56

Business vocabulary builder	
	goods Merchandise.
	earnestly Sincerely.
	billing machines Machines used in the preparation of bills and invoices.
	observe Inspect; watch.

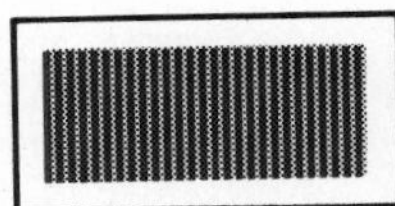

Reading and writing practice

57 **Brief-Form Letter** This letter contains one or more illustrations of the brief forms presented in this lesson.

[103]

58

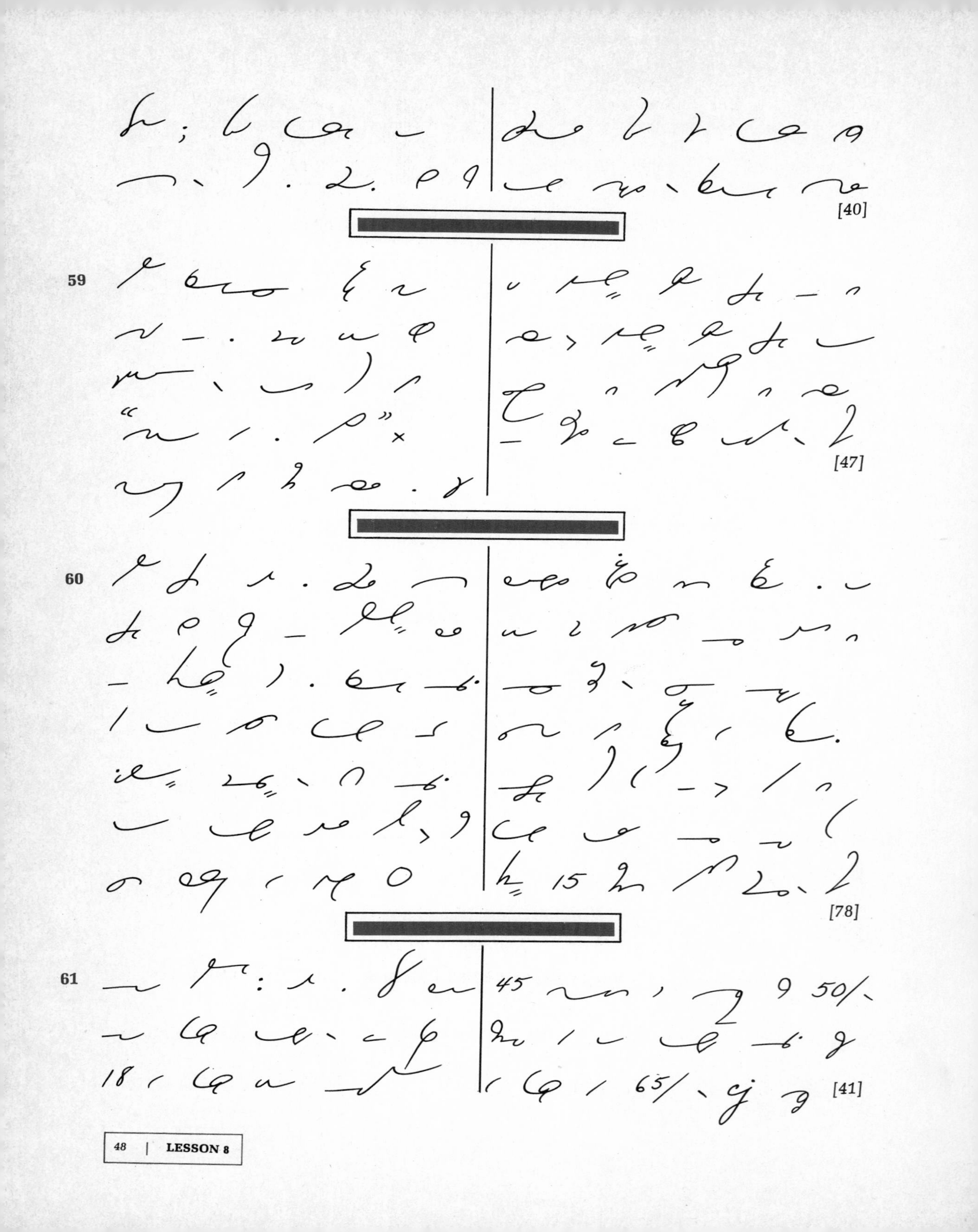

[40]

59

[47]

60

[78]

61

[41]

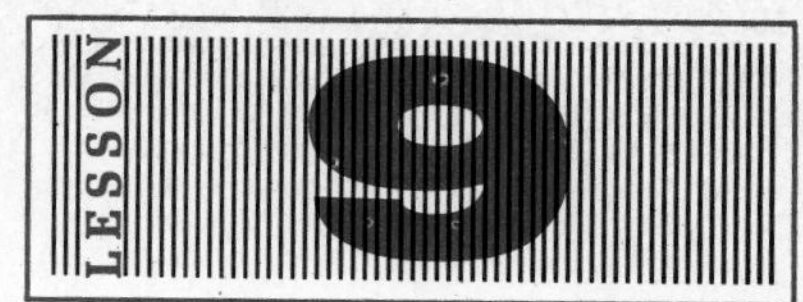

Principles

62 **Word Ending -tion** The word ending *-tion* (sometimes spelled *-sion, -cian,* or *-shion*) is represented by *sh.*

Spell: a-k-shun, action

action	*occasion*	*nation*
portions	*physician*	*national*
position	*fashions*	*cautioned*

63 **Word Endings -cient, -ciency** The word ending *-cient* (or *-tient*) is represented by *sh-t; -ciency,* by *sh-s-e.*

Spell: p-a-shun-t, patient; e-f-e-shun-s-e, efficiency

patient	*efficient*	*efficiency*

64 **Word Ending -tial** The word ending *-tial* (or *-cial*) is represented by *sh.*

Spell: o-f-e-shul, official

official	*financial*	*special*
social	*initialed*	*specially*

65 **T for To in Phrases** In phrases, *to* is represented by *t* when it is followed by a downstroke.

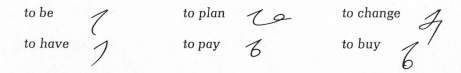

to be	*to plan*	*to change*
to have	*to pay*	*to buy*

to see | to show | to feel

Building transcription skills

66

Business vocabulary builder

financial Having to do with money.

corporation A type of business organization that is owned by stockholders.

essential Necessary.

take legal action Sue; take to court.

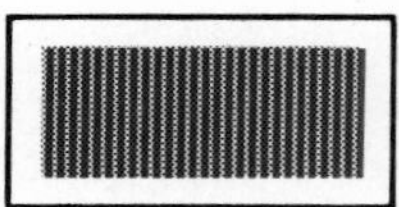

Reading and writing practice

67 **Brief-Form Review Letter** The following letter reviews the brief forms presented in Lesson 8.

[70]

68

[61]

69

950

ab

[79]

70

10

12

12

[83]

Principles

71 **Nd** The shorthand strokes for *n-d* are joined without an angle to form the *nd* blend, as in *lined.*

Nd

Compare: *line* *lined*

Spell: *l-ī-end, lined; l-a-end, land*

trained *signed* *mind*

strained *friendly* *find*

planned *kind* *spend*

72 **Nt** The stroke for *nd* also represents *nt*, as in *sent.*

Spell: *s-e-ent, sent; ent-oo, into*

sent *renting* *agent*

events *painted* *into*

prevent *parent* *entirely*

73 **Ses** The sound of *ses*, as in *senses*, is represented by joining the two forms of *s*. The similar sounds of *sis*, as in *sister*, and *sus*, as in *versus*, are represented in the same way.

Compare: *sense* *senses*

face *faces*

Spell: s-e-n-sez, senses

addresses	causes	passes
promises	places	sister
offices	necessary	basis
cases	losses	versus

Building transcription skills

74

Business vocabulary builder

firm (*noun*) Company.

vacancy Opening.

mailing pieces Usually such items as circulars, booklets, and other advertising matter that are mailed to customers or possible customers.

current Belonging to the present time.

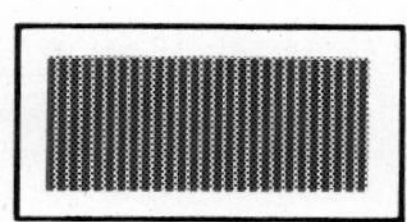

Reading and writing practice

75 **Brief-Form Review Letter** This letter reviews all the brief forms you studied in Lesson 8.

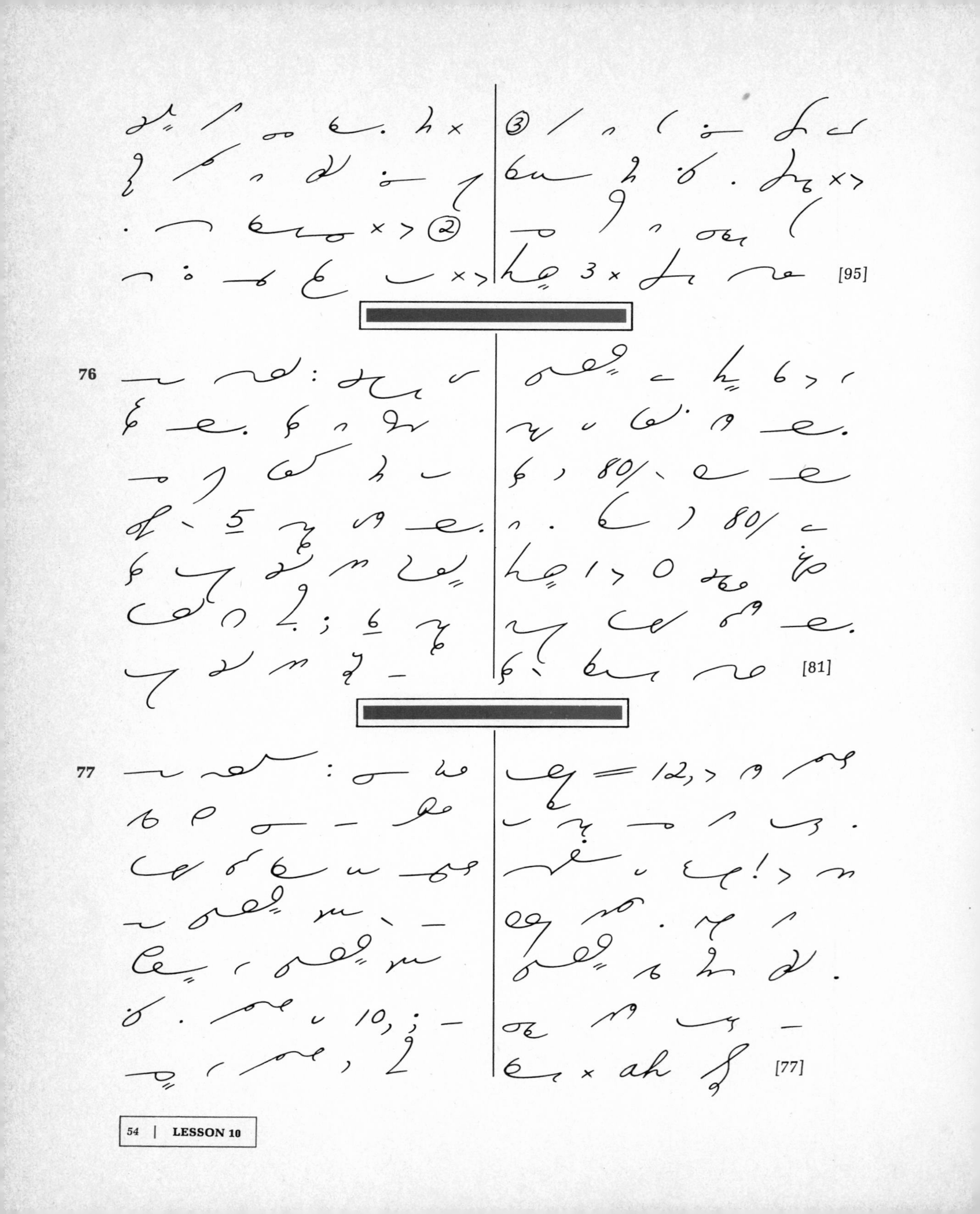

[95]

76

[81]

77

[77]

78

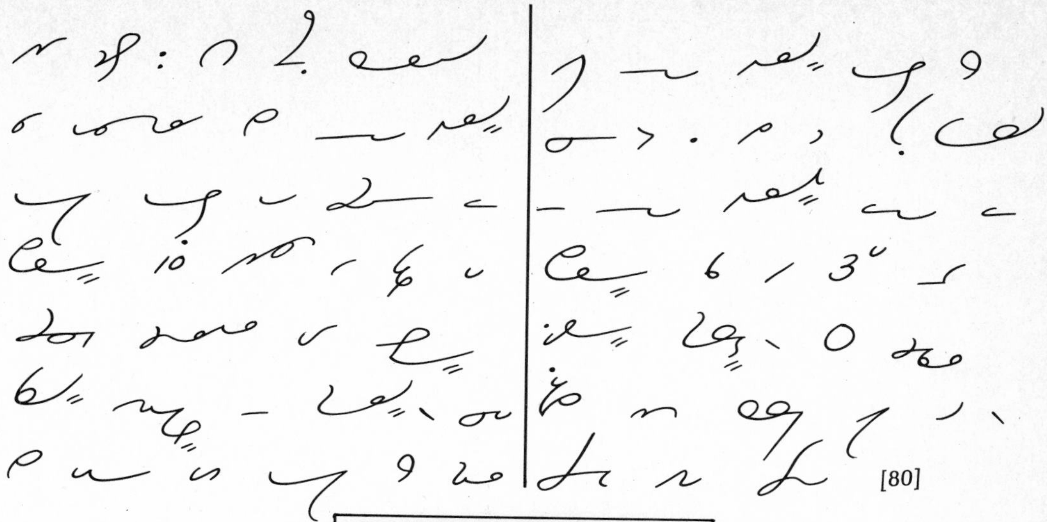

[80]

79

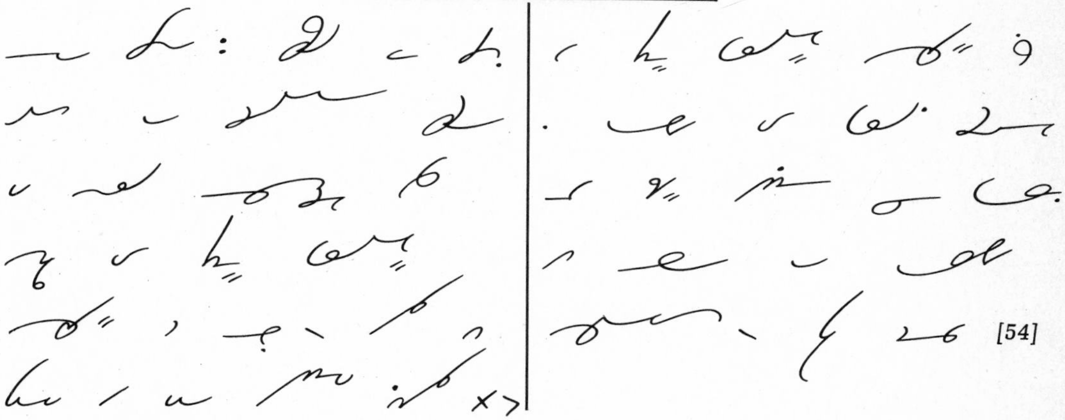

[54]

SHORTHAND READING CHECK LIST

When you read shorthand, do you—

☐ **1** Read aloud so that you know that you are concentrating on each outline that you read?

☐ **2** Spell each outline that you cannot immediately read?

☐ **3** Reread each Reading and Writing Practice a second time?

☐ **4** Occasionally reread the suggestions for reading shorthand given on pages 10 and 11?

Principles

80 Brief Forms

and		*was*		*should*	
them		*when*		*could*	
they		*from*		*send*	

81 Rd The combination *rd* is represented by writing *r* with an upward turn at the finish.

Compare: fear   *feared*

Spell: f-e-ärd, feared; h-e-ärd, heard

stored		appeared		heard	
tired		guarded		toward	
hired		record		harder	

82 Ld The combination *ld* is represented by writing the *l* with an upward turn at the finish.

Compare: nail   *nailed*

Spell: n-a-eld, nailed; o-eld, old

failed		mailed		billed	
old		child		held	
settled		folded		told	

83 **Been in Phrases** The word *been* is represented by *b* after *have, has, had.*

had been	*you have been*	*it has been*
have been	*I have not been*	*there has been*
I have been	*has been*	*should have been*

84 **Able in Phrases** The word *able* is represented by *a* after *be* or *been.*

have been able	*has been able*
I have been able	*I should be able*
you have not been able	*to be able*
had been able	*you will be able*

Building transcription skills

85

Business vocabulary builder

parcel post A department of the post office that collects and delivers packages.

ignored Paid no attention to.

air travel card A card that enables a traveler to purchase a plane ticket on credit.

Reading and writing practice

86 **Brief-Form Letter** The following letter contains at least one illustration of every brief form in paragraph 80.

[104]

87

[61]

88

[64]

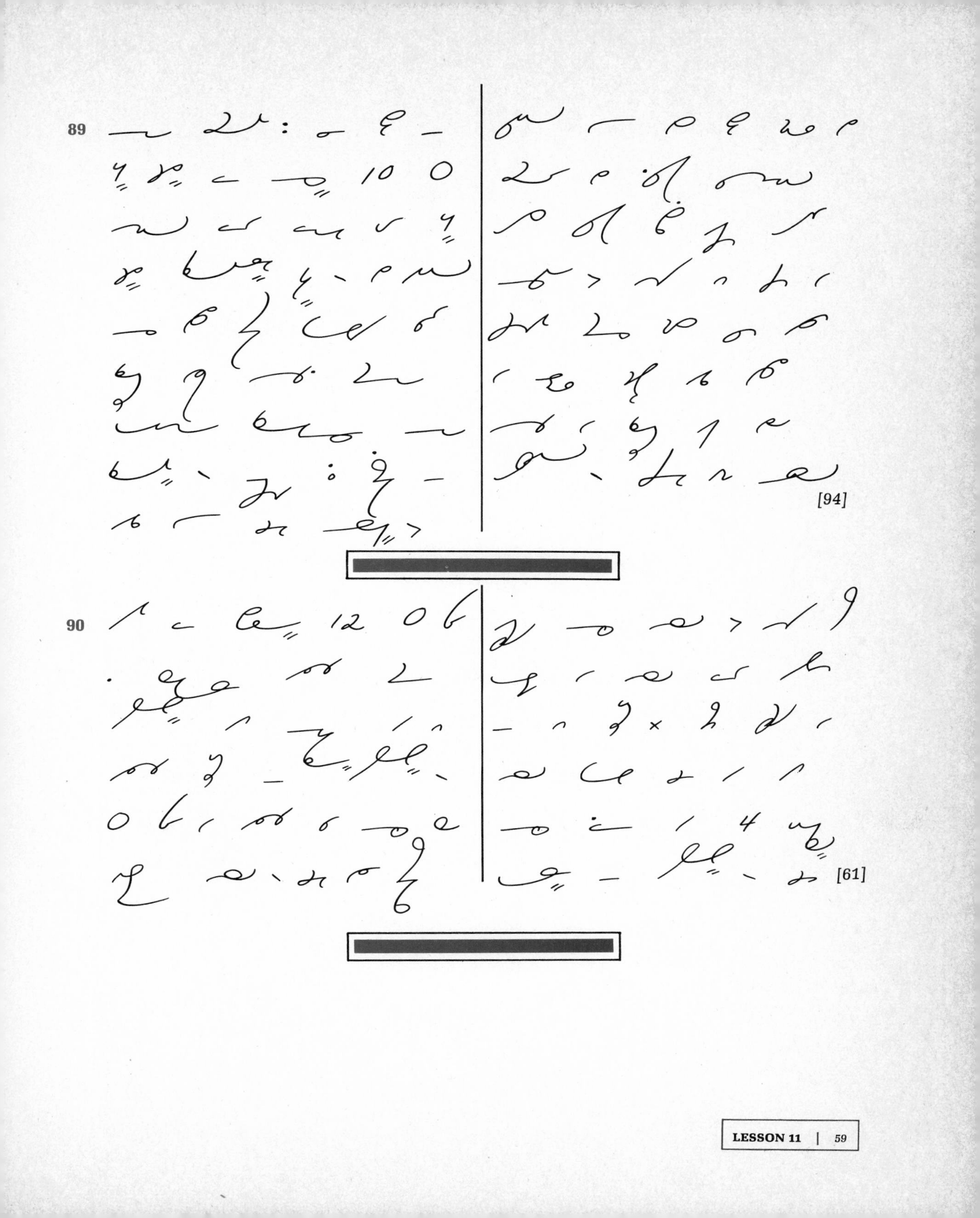

89

[94]

90

[61]

Recall

Lesson 12 is a "breather" for you; it presents no new shorthand devices for you to learn. It contains a number of principles of joining, a helpful Recall Chart, and several short letters that you should have no difficulty reading.

Principles of joining

91 At the beginning and end of words, the comma *s* is used before and after *f, v, k, g;* the left *s*, before and after *p, b, r, l.*

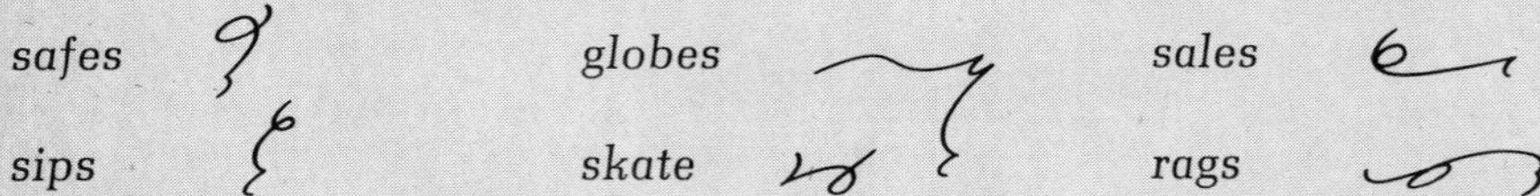

92 The comma *s* is used before *t, d, n, m, o;* the left *s* is used after those characters.

stones *solos* *needs*

93 The comma *s* is used before and after *sh, ch, j.*

sashes *reaches* *stages*

94 The comma *s* is used in words consisting of an *s* and a circle vowel or *s* and *th* and a circle vowel.

see *these* *seethe*

95 Gregg Shorthand is equally legible whether it is written on ruled or on unruled paper; consequently, you need not worry about the exact placement of your outlines on the printed lines in your notebook. You will be able to read your outlines regardless of their placement on the printed line. The main purpose that the printed lines in your notebook serve is to keep you from wandering uphill and downhill as you write.

However, so that all outlines may be uniformly placed in the shorthand books from which you study, this general rule has been followed:

The base of the first consonant of a word is placed on the line of writing. When s comes before a downstroke, however, the downstroke is placed on the line of writing.

dome	*names*	*pace*
save	*shave*	*space*

96 Recall Chart The following chart contains all the brief forms in Chapter 2 and one or more illustrations of all the shorthand devices you have studied in Chapters 1 and 2.

Can you read the entire chart in 9 minutes or less?

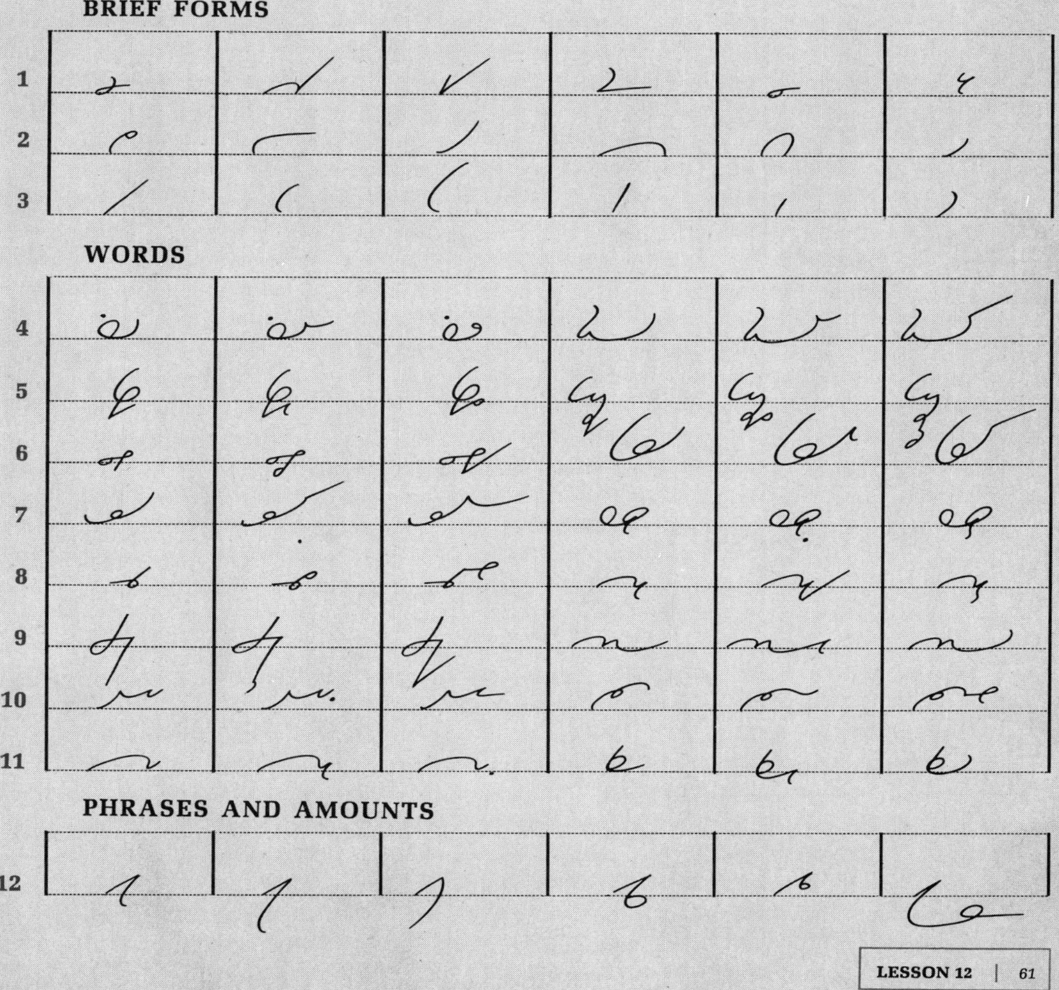

13						
14						
15	4/	4	4	4	5,	6

Building transcription skills

97

Business vocabulary builder	
	initial First.
	vacant Empty.
	admit Let in.

Reading and writing practice

98

16

[84]

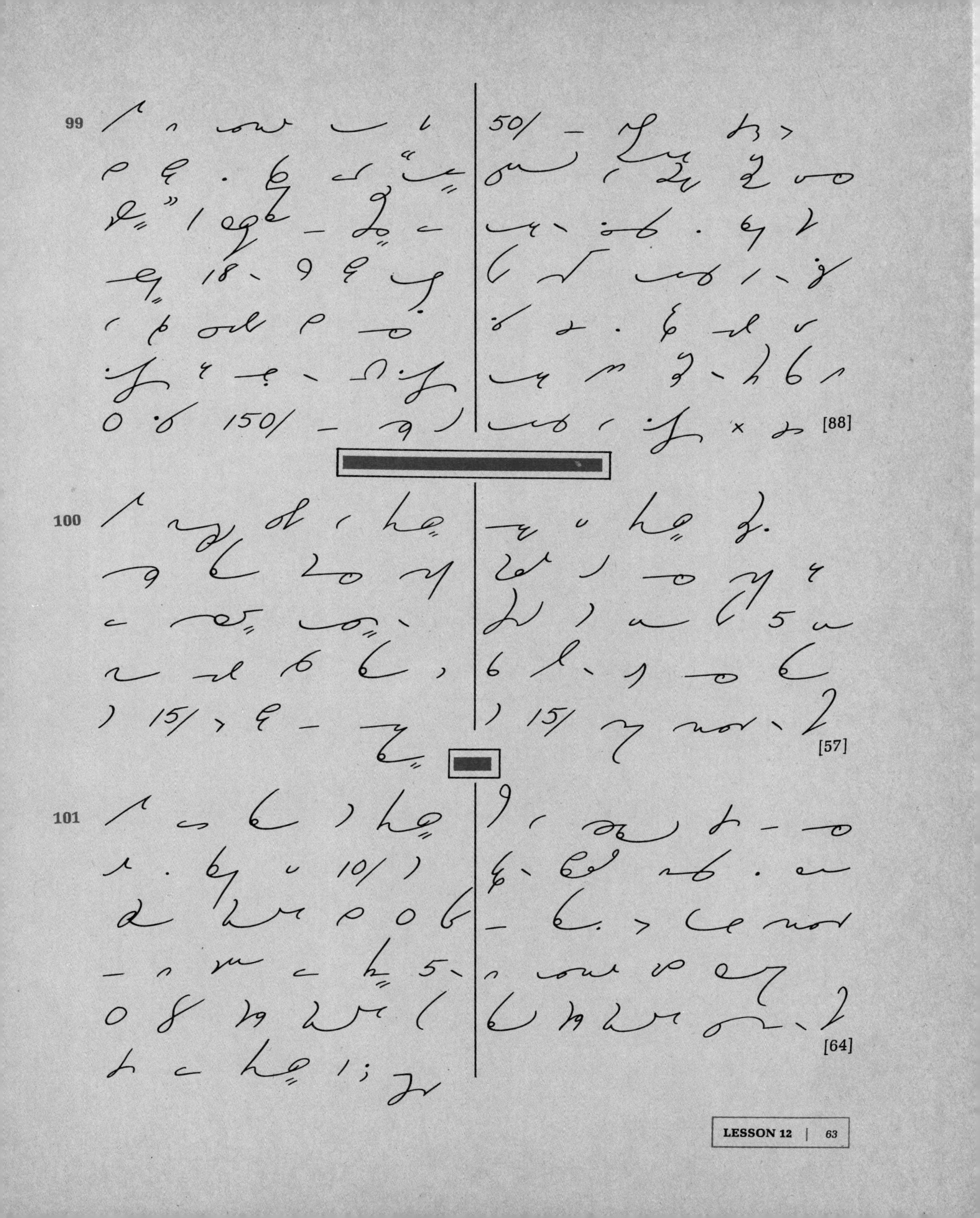

99

[88]

100

[57]

101

[64]

Chapter 3
Why be a secretary?

If you were to ask ten successful secretaries what they like about their jobs, you would no doubt obtain ten different answers. These answers, however, could be "capsuled" into five primary reasons why secretaries like their jobs:

1. "The work is interesting." The secretary in a travel-agency office gave this reason. Would you find it exciting to work in an organization that makes and sells phonograph records? broadcasts radio and television programs? produces advertisements for radio, TV, magazines, and newspapers?

operates an airline? These are only a few of the types of firms that need secretaries.

2. "A secretary often has dealings with important people." This was the reason given by a secretary to a lawyer. Secretaries do work for and with important people. These important people, and those with whom they come in contact, make the decisions that turn the wheels of industry, of business, of the professions, and of the arts. The secretary is brought into the "inner circle" of management, where she can observe big things happening.

3. "An office is a pleasant place in which to work." Does this sound like a strange reason for choosing secretarial work? Not if you consider the fact that more of a secretary's waking hours are spent in the office than at home. The important people in an office rate the best accommodations. If the executive for whom the secretary works has a choice location, she is likely to have one, too.

4. "The salary is good." The secretary who gave this reason works in an engineering firm that manufactures electronic devices for rockets. In comparison with general office employees the secretary receives excellent pay. Often the magic word "shorthand" makes the difference between a medium-paying job and a well-paying one!

5. "The work has variety." Most secretaries won't argue with the one who gave that reason. The secretary has dozens of opportunities for variety every day. The alert secretary will find all the variety she can possibly want; one day is never like another! In most business offices there is never a dull moment.

Principles

102 Brief Forms

glad		*very*		*soon*	
work		* *thank*		*enclose*	
yesterday		*order*		*were, year*	

*In phrases, the dot is omitted from *thank*. *Thanks* is written with a disjoined left s in the dot position.

thank you		*thank you for*		*thanks*	

103 U, OO The hook that expresses the sound of *oo*, as in *to*, also represents the vowel sounds heard in *does* and *foot*.

U

Spell: *d-oo-s, does*

does		*none*		*us*	
dozen		*number*		*precious*	
above		*enough*		*just*	

▶ Notice that the *oo* in *none, number, enough* is turned on its side; that *oo-s* join without an angle in *us, precious, just.*

OO

Spell: *f-oo-t, foot*

foot		*looked*		*took*	

book		pulled		pushed	
full		stood		cooked	

104 W, Sw At the beginning of words, the sound of *w* is represented by the *oo* hook; *sw*, by s-oo.

Spell: *oo-e, we; s-oo-e-t, sweet*

we		*wash*		*sweet*	
way		*wanted*		*swim*	
wait		*wood*		*swell*	
week, weak		*wool*		*swear*	

Building transcription skills

105

Business vocabulary builder	
	dealers Those who sell or distribute goods.
	copy (*noun*) Matter, usually typewritten, to be set up for printing.
	wearing apparel Clothing.
	cruise A pleasure trip by boat.

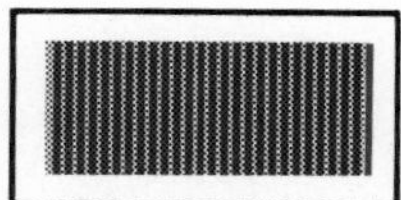

Reading and writing practice

106 Brief-Form Letter In the following letter all the brief forms presented in this lesson are used at least once.

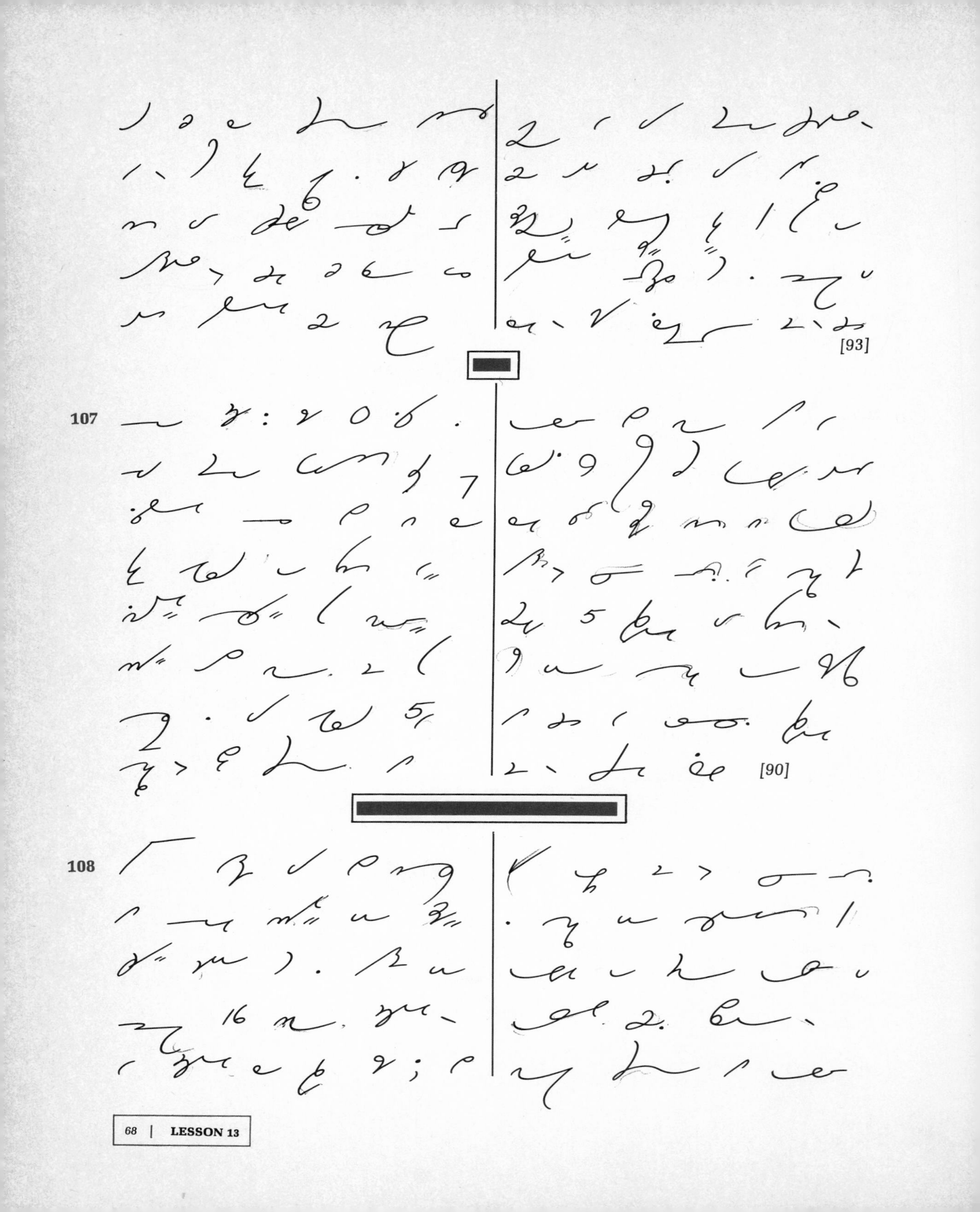

[93]

107

[90]

108

[88]

109

[83]

110

[95]

LESSON 14

Principles

111 **Wh** *Wh,* as in *white,* is pronounced *hw*—the *h* is pronounced first. Therefore, in shorthand, we write the *h* first.

Spell: *h-oo-ī-t, white*

white	*wheel*	*whip*
while	*whale*	*wheat*

112 **W in the Body of a Word** When the sound of *w* occurs in the body of a word, as in *quick,* it is represented by a short dash underneath the vowel following the *w* sound. The dash is inserted after the rest of the outline has been written.

Spell: *k-oo-e-k, quick*

quick	*twice*	*always*
quit	*liquid*	*roadway*
quite	*equipped*	*Broadway*

113 **Ted** The combination *ted* is represented by joining *t* and *d* into one long upward stroke.

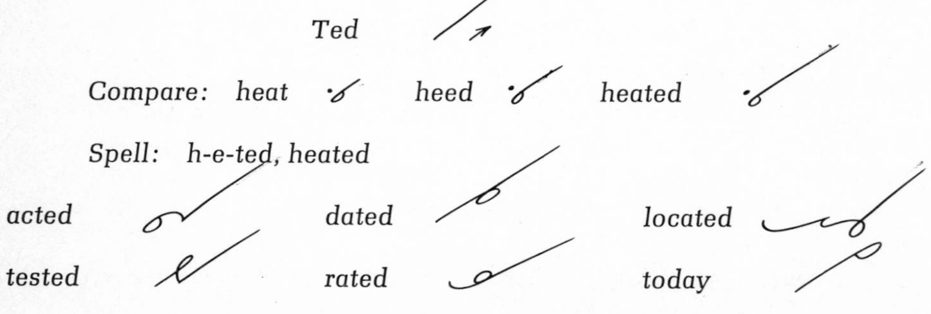

Ted

Compare: *heat* *heed* *heated*

Spell: *h-e-ted, heated*

acted	*dated*	*located*
tested	*rated*	*today*

rested seated steady

114 **Ded, Dit, Det** The long stroke that represents *ted* also represents *ded, dit, det.*

Spell: *t-r-a-ded, traded; o-ded, audit; ded-a-l-s, details*

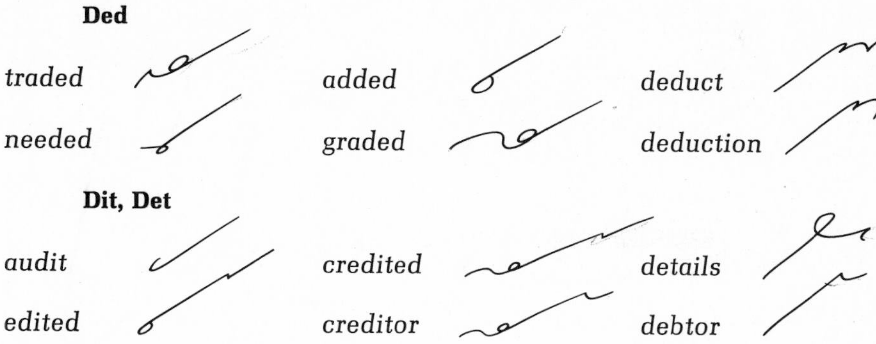

Ded

traded added deduct

needed graded deduction

Dit, Det

audit credited details

edited creditor debtor

Building transcription skills

115

Business vocabulary builder	**frosted glasses** Glasses having a slightly roughened surface. **quote** Give a price on. **authorized** Having permission to. **survey** (*noun*) Inspection.

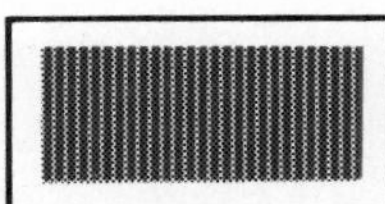

Reading and writing practice

116 **Brief-Form Review Letter** The following letter reviews the brief forms you studied in Lesson 13.

[84]

117

[118]

118

[73]

119

[63]

UP AND DOWN CHECK LIST

Do you always write the following strokes upward?

☐ **1** and their-there ☐ **2** it-at would

Do you always write the following strokes downward?

☐ **1** is-his for have ☐ **2** shall which

Principles

120 Brief Forms

value *what* *thing, think*

than *about* *why*

one, won *great* *business*

121 Brief-Form Derivatives

once *things, thinks* *businessman*

greater *thinking* *businesses*

▶ Notice that a disjoined left *s* is used to express *things, thinks;* that the plural of *business* is formed by adding another left *s*.

122 Word Ending -ble The word ending *-ble* is represented by *b*.

Spell: *p-a-bul, payable*

payable *sensible* *tables*

available *terrible* *troubled*

reliable *possible* *cabled*

123 Word Beginning Re- The word beginning *re-* is represented by *r*.

Spell: *re-s-e-v-d, received*

received *receipted* *resisted*

revise	*referring*	*reappear*
repaired	*research*	*reopen*

Building transcription skills

124

Business vocabulary builder	
	racks Equipment on which clothes are hung.
	sites Places; locations.
	strive Try hard.

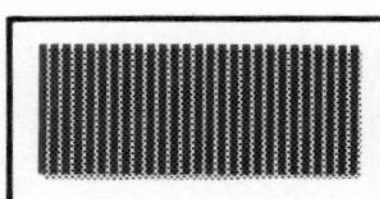

Reading and writing practice

125 **Brief-Form Letter** All the brief forms presented in this lesson are used at least once in this letter.

[121]

126

[88]

127

[95]

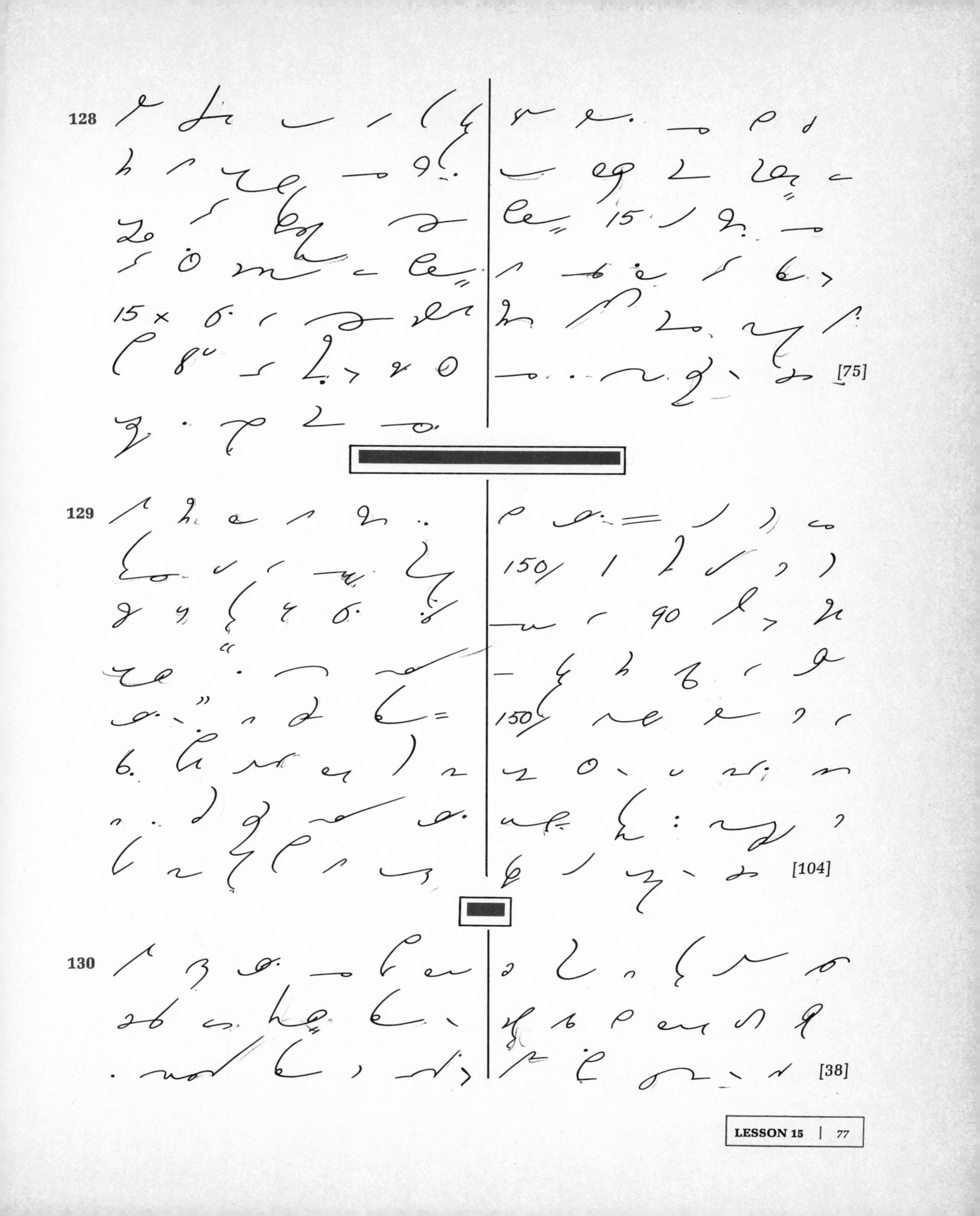

128

[75]

129

[104]

130

[38]

Principles

131 **Oi** The sound of *oi*, as in *toy*, is represented by .

Spell: *t-oi, toy*

toy		*annoy*		*appoint*	
boy		*oil*		*noise*	
join		*spoil*		*voice*	

132 **Men, Mem** The combinations *men, mem* are represented by joining *m* and *n* into one long forward stroke.

Men, Mem

Compare: *knee* *me* *many*

Men

Spell: *men-t, meant*

men		*meant*		*mended*	
mentioned		*mentally*		*amend*	
menace		*mends*		*women*	

Mem

Spell: *mem-b-r, member*

member		*remember*		*memory*	

133 **Min, Mon, Mun, etc.** The long forward stroke used for *men, mem* also represents *min, mon, mun,* etc.

Spell: *men-e-t, minute; men-r, manner*

minute	*monthly*	*managed*
month	*money*	*manner*

134 **Word Beginning Be-** The word beginning *be-* is represented by *b.*

Spell: *be-k-a-m, became*

became	*belief*	*because*
begin	*believed*	*below*

Building transcription skills

135

Business vocabulary builder	
	asset Anything of value owned by a company—cash, equipment, etc.
	immensely Very much; greatly.
	treasurer An official in charge of the funds of a company or organization.
	succeeding Filling a job left by someone.

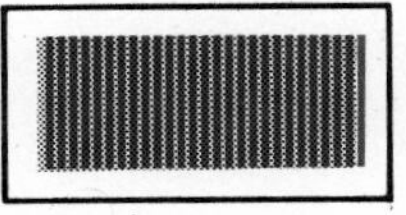

Reading and writing practice

136 **Brief-Form Review Letter** This letter reviews the brief forms you studied in Lesson 15.

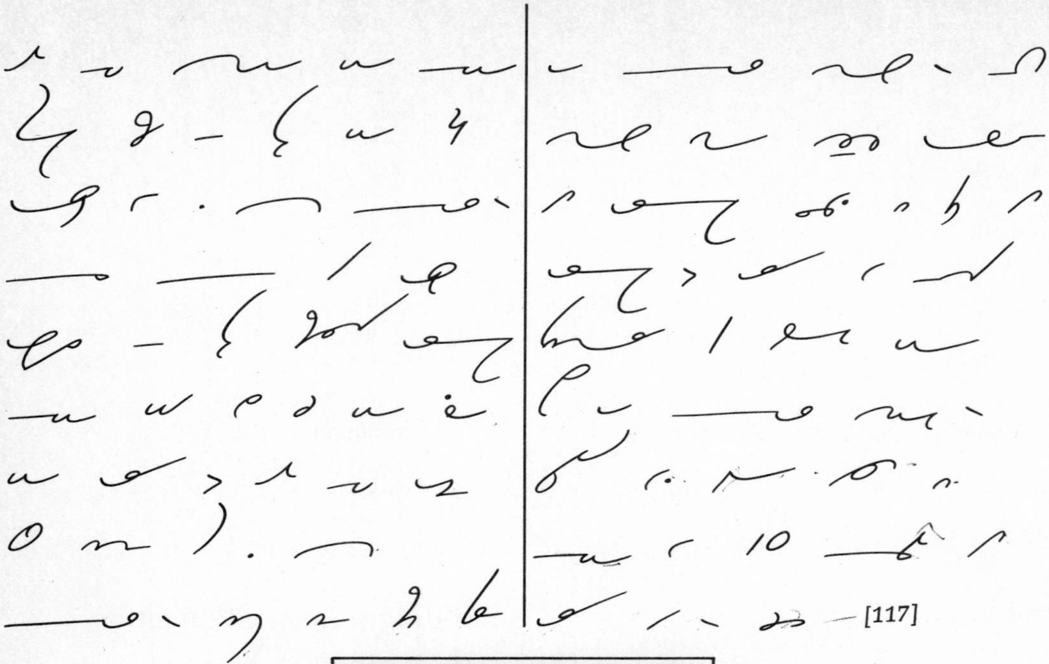

[117]

137

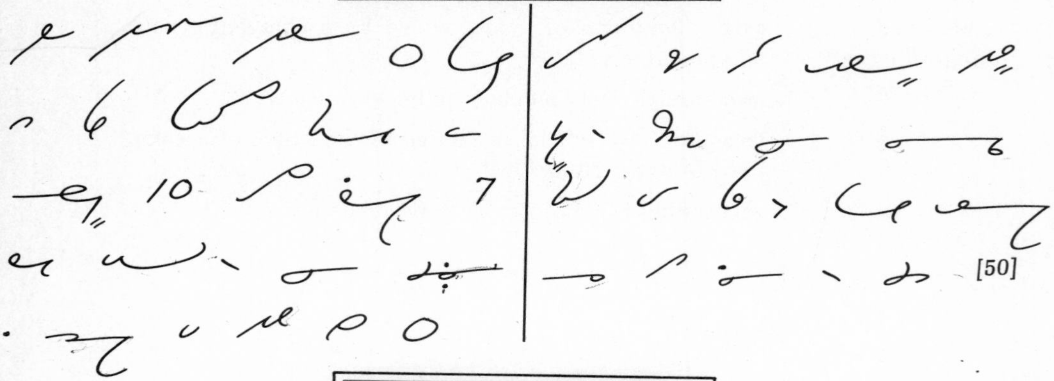

[50]

138

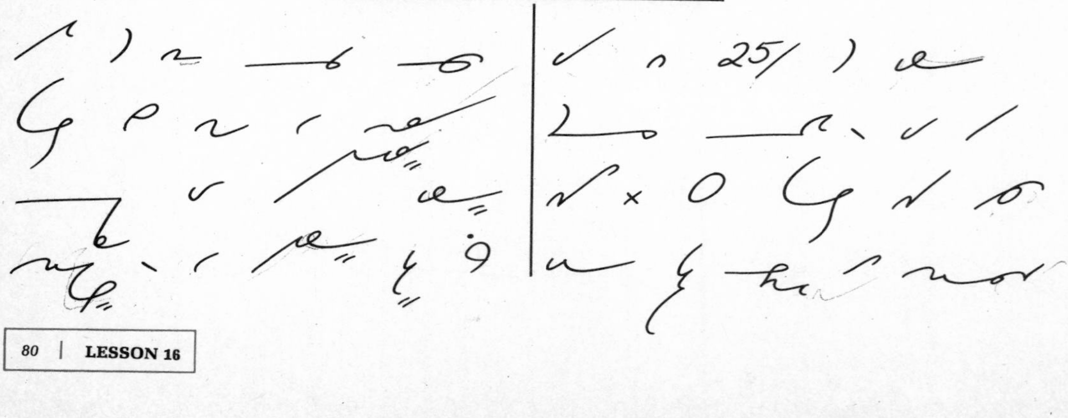

[86]

139

[83]

140

[76]

Principles

141 **Brief Forms** When you have learned the following six brief forms, you will have learned more than half the brief forms of Gregg Shorthand.

gentlemen	*important, importance*	*where*
morning	*those*	*manufacture*

142 **Word Beginnings Per-, Pur-** The word beginnings *per-, pur-* are represented by *pr.*

Spell: *pur-s-n, person; pur-chay-a-s, purchase*

Per-

person	*perfect*	*personal*
permit	*persisted*	*perhaps*

Pur-

purchase	*purple*	*purse*

143 **Word Beginnings De-, Di-** The word beginnings *de-, di-* are represented by *d.*

Spell: *de-s-ī-d, decide; de-r-e-k-t, direct*

De-

decide	*desired*	*derive*
delay	*deserve*	*deposit*

Di-

direct	*direction*	*diploma*

144 **SIMILAR-WORDS DRILL**

In the English language there are many groups of words that sound or look alike, but each member of the group is spelled differently and each has its own meaning.

Example: **sent** (dispatched), **scent** (a smell), **cent** (a coin).

There are many other groups of words that sound or look *almost* alike.

Example: **area** (space); **aria** (a melody).

The stenographer who is not careful will sometimes select the wrong member of the group when transcribing, with the result that her transcript makes no sense.

From time to time in the lessons ahead you will be given a similar-words exercise designed to help you select the correct word, so that when you become a stenographer you will not suffer the embarrassment of having your letters returned for correction.

Read carefully the definitions and the illustrative sentences in each similar-words exercise.

SIMILAR-WORDS DRILL | **it's, its**

it's The contraction of *it is*.

It's *a fine day.*

its (*no apostrophe*) Possessive form meaning *belonging to it.*

Its *operating efficiency has been proven.*

145

Business vocabulary builder	
	board of directors A group of people who run a company or organization.
	minimum The least (*maximum,* the most).
	personnel records Information concerning the people who work for a company.
	proceed Go ahead (do not confuse with *precede,* which means "come before").

Reading and writing practice

146 **Brief-Form Letter** This letter contains one or more illustrations of all the brief forms you studied in this lesson.

213-116-1185 [107]

147

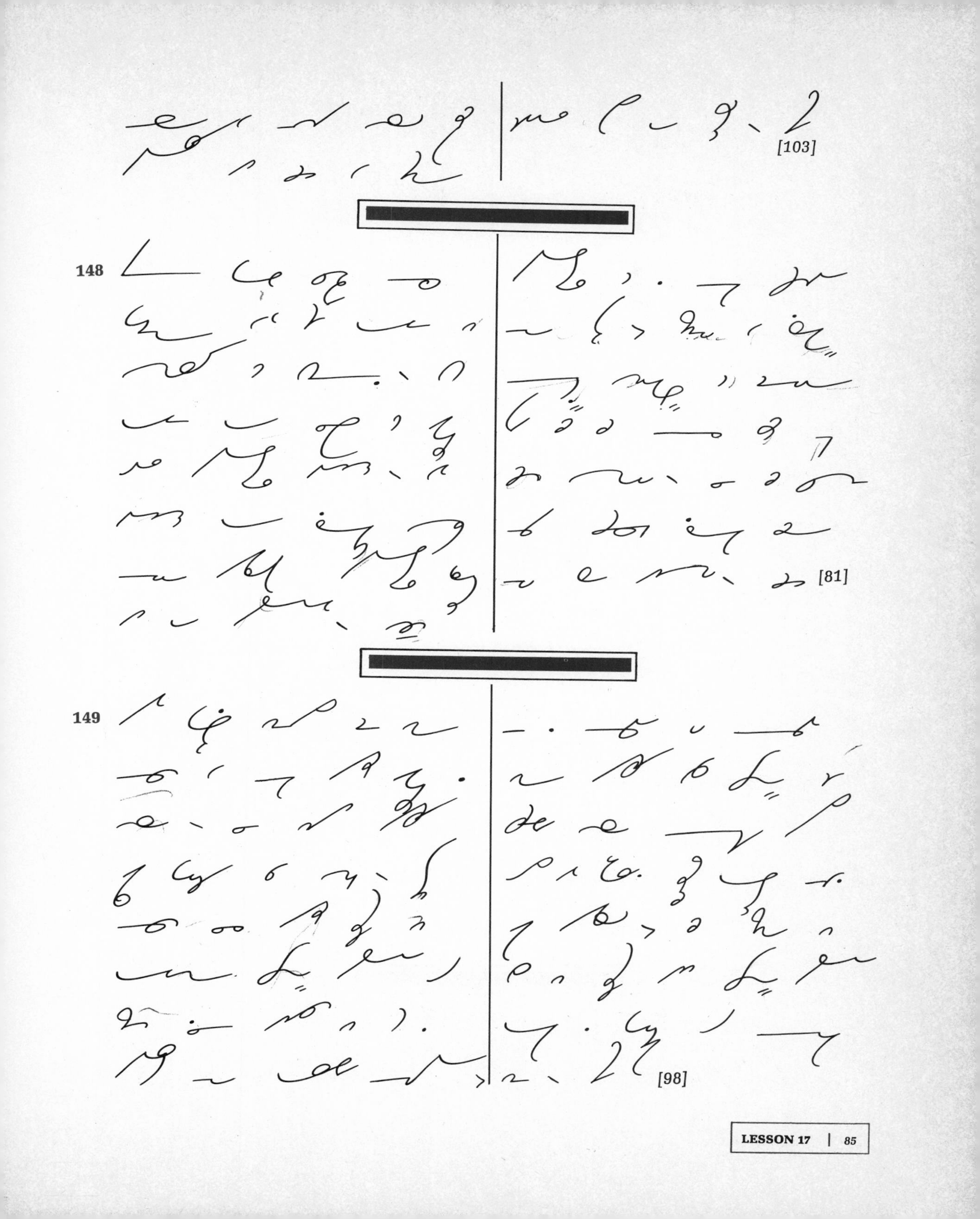

[103]

148

[81]

149

[98]

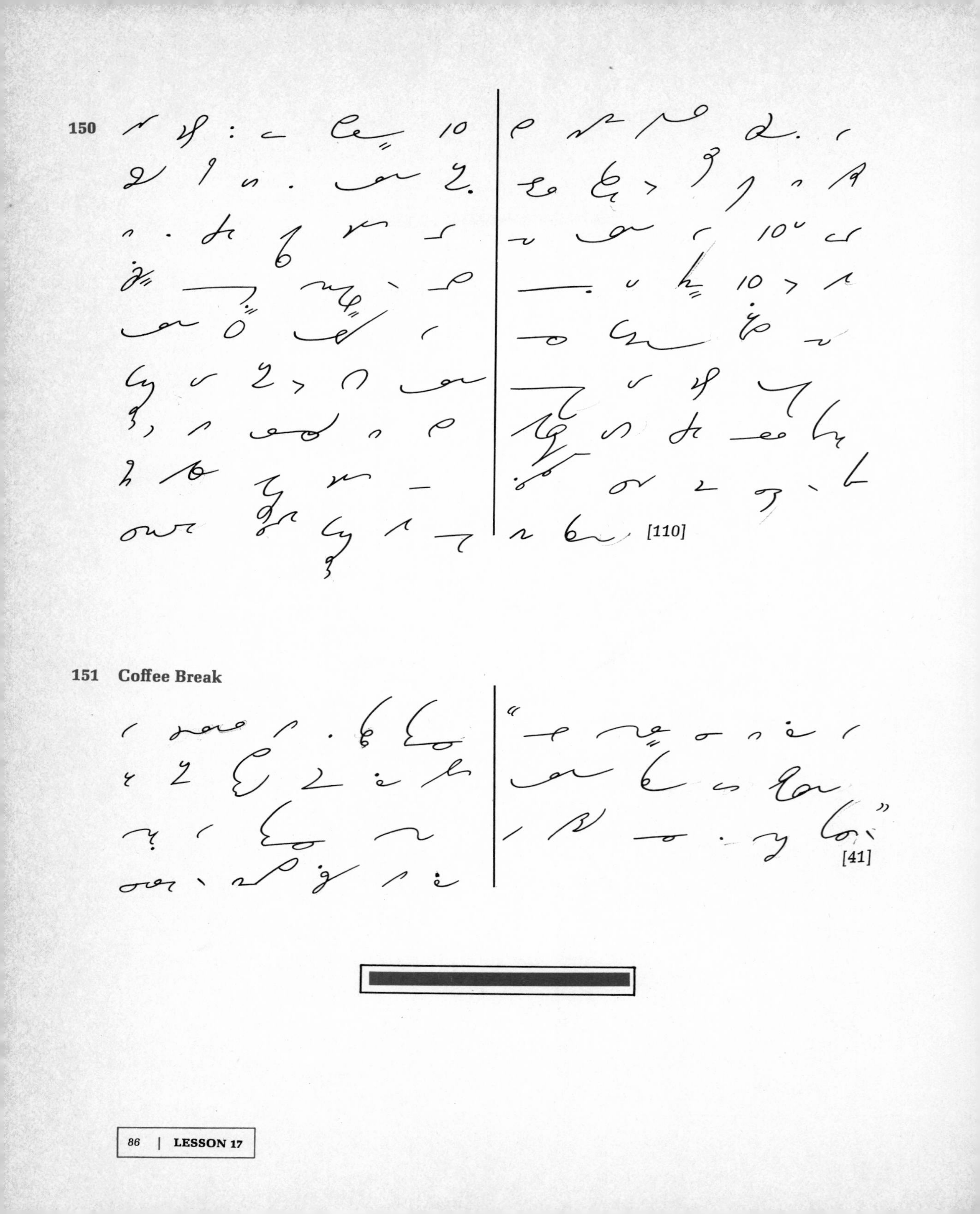

150

[110]

151 Coffee Break

[41]

Recall

Lesson 18 is another "breather" for you; it contains no new shorthand devices for you to learn. In this lesson you will find: (1) a number of additional principles of joining, (2) a Recall Chart, and (3) a Reading and Writing Practice that you will find not only interesting but informative as well.

Principles of joining

152 At the beginning of a word and after *k, g,* or a downstroke, the combination *oo-s* is written without an angle.

husky *gust* *just*

but

does *loose* *rust*

153 The word beginning *re-* is represented by *r* before a downstroke or a vowel.

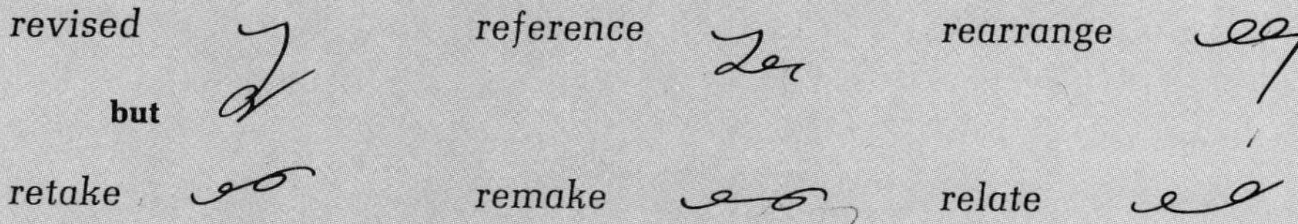

154 The word beginnings *de-, di-* are represented by *d* except before *k* or *g.*

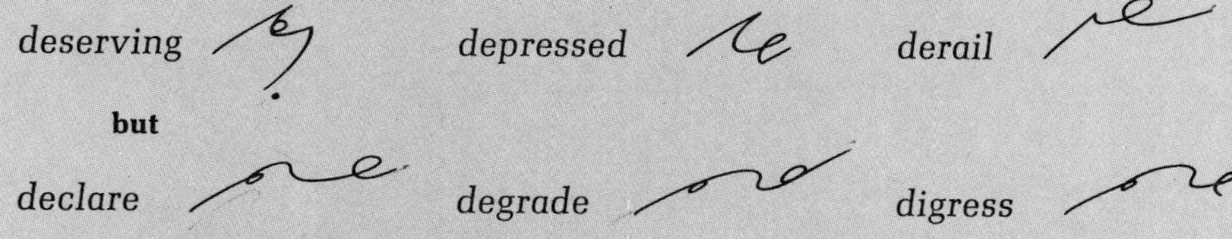

155 As you have perhaps already noticed from your study of Lessons 1 through 17, the past tense of a verb is formed by adding the stroke for the sound that is heard in the past tense. In some words, the past tense will have the sound of *t,* as in *baked;* in others, it will have the sound of *d,* as in *saved.*

baked | missed | faced
saved | changed | showed

156 **Recall Chart** This chart reviews all the brief forms in Chapter 3 as well as the shorthand devices you studied in Chapters 1, 2, and 3.

The chart contains 90 words and phrases. Can you read the entire chart in 8 minutes or less?

BRIEF FORMS AND DERIVATIVES

1
2
3
4

WORDS

5
6
7
8
9
10
11
12
13

PHRASES AND QUANTITIES

14
15

157

Business vocabulary builder	
	traits Qualities of mind and character.
	poised (*adjective*) Able to meet embarrassing situations calmly.
	cooperate Work with.

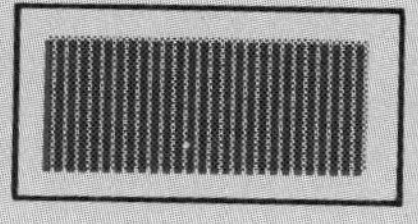

Reading and writing practice

Reading Scoreboard One of the factors in measuring your progress in shorthand is the rate at which you read shorthand. Wouldn't you like to determine your reading rate on the *first reading* of the articles in Lesson 18? The following table will help you.

Lesson 18 contains 350 words

If you read Lesson 18 in **14 minutes** *your reading rate is* **25 words a minute**
If you read Lesson 18 in **16 minutes** *your reading rate is* **22 words a minute**
If you read Lesson 18 in **18 minutes** *your reading rate is* **20 words a minute**
If you read Lesson 18 in **20 minutes** *your reading rate is* **17 words a minute**
If you read Lesson 18 in **22 minutes** *your reading rate is* **16 words a minute**
If you read Lesson 18 in **24 minutes** *your reading rate is* **15 words a minute**

If you can read Lesson 18 through the first time in less than 14 minutes, you are doing well indeed. If you take considerably longer than 24 minutes, here are some questions you should ask yourself:

1 *Am I spelling each outline I cannot read immediately?*

2 *Should I perhaps reread the directions for reading shorthand on page 10?*

After you have determined your reading rate, make a record of it in some convenient place. You can then watch your reading rate grow as you time yourself on the Reading Scoreboards in later lessons.

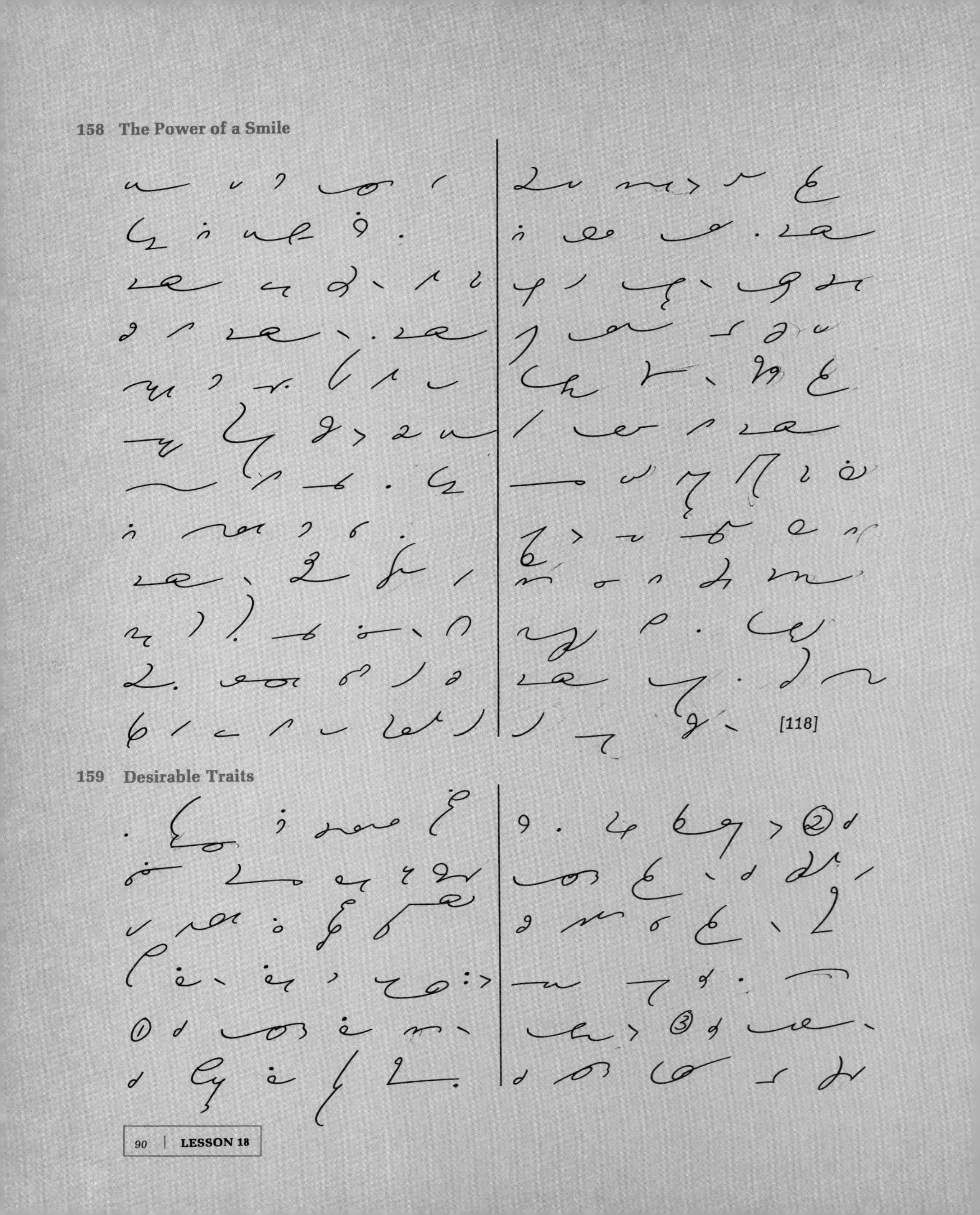

158 The Power of a Smile

[118]

159 Desirable Traits

[163]

160 Life or Death

[69]

Chapter 4

The secretary's day

Some people think that all a secretary does is take and transcribe dictation. Nothing could be farther from the truth. While taking and transcribing dictation is an important part of a secretary's job, it is only one of the many duties she performs.

What is a typical day in the life of a secretary? Let's suppose you are secretary to Mr. C. G. Marsden, sales manager of a successful publishing company. Here is what your day might be like.

8:45 Arrive at the office. Straighten and dust Mr. Marsden's desk. Check appointment calendar to be sure that his agrees with yours. You notice that he has made a 9:15 appointment with Mrs. Fuller. Get the correspondence you think he might need in talking with her.

8:55 Mr. Marsden arrives. Remind him of his 9:15 appointment and a luncheon date at 12:30 with Mr. Symond at the Belle Meade Restaurant. Ask him about arrangements for a 2:30 meeting of the advertising committee.

9:05 The mail arrives. Open all mail (except letters marked "Personal"). Read it and place it on Mr. Marsden's desk, along with any background correspondence he may need.

9:15 The receptionist calls you to say that Mrs. Fuller has arrived. You inform Mr. Marsden and then go out to the reception office to escort Mrs. Fuller in to see Mr. Marsden.

9:35 Mr. Marsden "buzzes" you on the intercom and tells you that Mrs. Fuller is leaving and asks you to get some papers that she is to take with her. You do so, bidding Mrs. Fuller good-bye at the elevator.

9:40-10:15 1. The telephone rings several times—company executives and outsiders asking for appointments and information.
2. A messenger brings you a package of books c.o.d., and you take the money from petty cash to pay him.
3. Other executives call in person to speak to Mr. Marsden.

10:15 Mr. Marsden calls you for dictation.

11:00 You return to your desk and begin transcribing.

11:15 Mr. Marsden asks for several papers that must be obtained from the files.

11:30 You call the receptionist

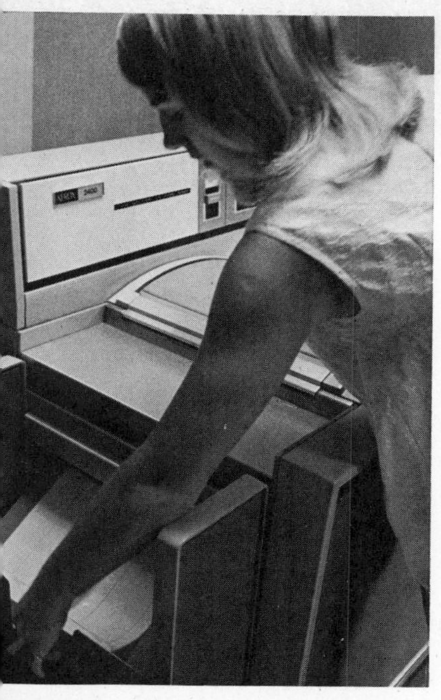

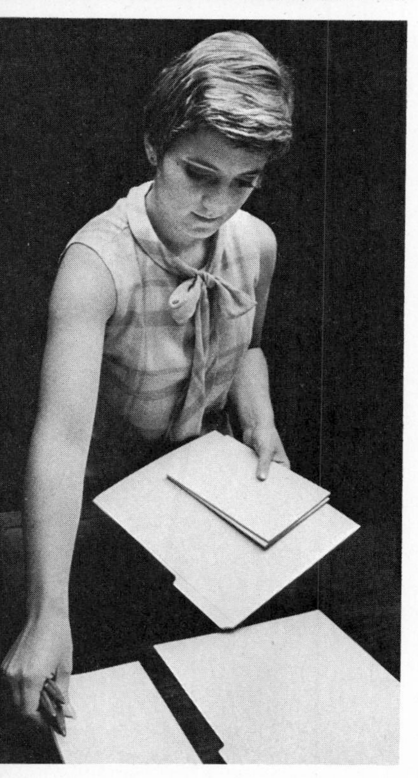

on the third floor to be sure that the conference room has been reserved for Mr. Marsden's 2:30 meeting.

12:00 You get ready to go to lunch with another secretary who works a few blocks away. Before leaving, you again remind Mr. Marsden about his luncheon date. You tell the relief receptionist that you are leaving for lunch.

12:55 Back from lunch, you return to your transcribing.

1:15-1:40 1. You answer several telephone calls.

2. You greet two callers who have come to see Mr. Marsden (neither has an appointment), and you persuade them to make an appointment for later in the week.

3. You duplicate the agenda for the advertising meeting and make photocopies of an advertising brochure to be discussed there.

4. You visit the conference room to see that there are enough chairs and that the room is in order. You distribute the materials for the meeting.

2:00 Mr. Marsden calls you in to dictate a short memo. He asks you to arrange to have a film and an operator in the conference room at three o'clock. You call the library for the film and office services to arrange for an operator.

2:25 You make sure that Mr. Marsden has all the necessary materials for the 2:30 meeting; then you return to your transcribing.

2:30-4:00 You get out two telegrams and finish transcribing Mr. Marsden's dictation. You telephone various people for information he needs for a report he is writing.

4:30 You prepare for Mr. Marsden's signature the letters that you have just typed and take them to him. After he has signed them, you get them ready for mailing.

5:00 You clear your desk, tell Mr. Marsden you are leaving (he is working late tonight), and then catch the first bus home.

As you think about the day's work, you are certain of only two things: (1) you did a good day's work, and (2) tomorrow's work schedule will be entirely different!

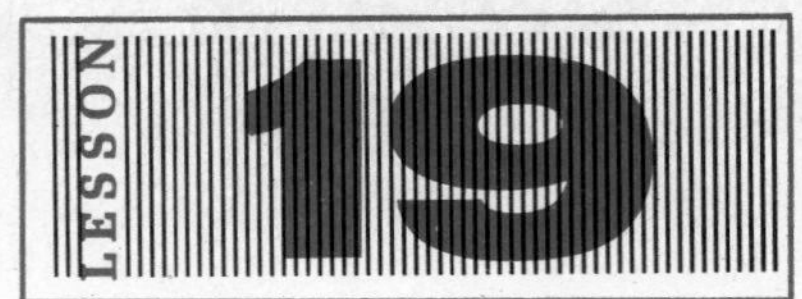

Principles

161 **Brief Forms** Here is another group of nine brief forms for common words.

present		advertise		immediate	
part		company		must	
after		wish		opportunity	

▶ Notice that there is no angle between the *k* and the *p* in the brief form *company.*

162 **U** The sound of u, as in *few,* is represented by .

Spell: *f-u, few*

few		unit		cute	
refuse		united		acutely	
reviewed		unique		usual	

163 **Word Ending -ment** The word ending -ment is represented by *m.*

Spell: *a-r-a-n-j-ment, arrangement*

arrangement		advertisement		replacements	
settlement		garments		shipments	
payment		assignment		elementary	

▶ Notice that in *assignment* the *m* for *-ment* is joined to the *n* with a jog.

164 SPELLING

The first impression you get of the letter on page 96 is a good one. It is positioned nicely; the margins are even; the date, inside address, and closing are all in their proper places. If you read the letter casually, you find that it makes good sense and apparently represents what the dictator said.

But if you read it carefully, you will quickly realize that the letter will never be signed; in fact, the dictator will no doubt have something to say to the stenographer who transcribed the letter. Why? It contains several misspelled words.

If you are to succeed as a stenographer or secretary, your letters must not only be an accurate transcript of what the dictator said, but they must also be free of spelling errors. A stenographer or secretary who constantly turns in transcripts with errors in spelling will not be welcome long in a business office!

To make sure that you will be able to spell correctly when you have completed your shorthand course, you will from this point on give special attention to spelling in each Reading and Writing Practice.

As you read the Reading and Writing Practice, you will occasionally find shorthand outlines printed in color. These outlines represent words that stenographers and secretaries often misspell. When you encounter an outline printed in color, finish reading the sentence in which it occurs; then glance at the margin, where you will find the word in type, properly syllabicated.

Spell the word aloud if possible, pausing slightly after each word division. (The word divisions indicated are those given in *Webster's Seventh New Collegiate Dictionary*.)

165 *Business vocabulary builder*

presentation A talk; a speech.

taped Recorded on tape.

tracer A follow-up investigation to locate a missing shipment of merchandise.

Reading and writing practice

166 Brief-Form Letter

LUNN

LUNN INCORPORATED

245 PARK AVENUE

NEW YORK, NY 10035

CHARLOTTE
COLUMBUS
DENVER
DUBUQUE
ELGIN
FLINT
FT. WAYNE
FT. WORTH
HUNTINGTON
LEXINGTON
MADISON
MEMPHIS
NASHVILLE
NORFOLK
PORTLAND
ST. LOUIS
ST. PAUL
SANTA FE
SAVANNAH
SEATTLE
TEXARKANA
TUCSON
TULSA
WICHITA

September 22, 19--

Mr. John Case
2001 Huron Street
Seattle, Washington 98117

Dear Mr. Case:

It is a comfortible feeling to know that the heating system in your home does not have to depend on the elements. Snow and ice cannot leave you shiverring when you heat with gas. It travels under ground.

The dependability of gas is only one of its many virtues. A gas heat system costs less to instal and less to operate. It needs lots less serviceing, and it lasts longer. It has no odor and makes no filmy deposits that cause extra work.

No wonder more than 400,000 users of other feuls changed to gas last year.

Why not let us show you how easy it is to instal gas heat in your home.

Yours truely,

Thomas A. Frost
Sales Manager

TAF:re

Can you find all the errors in this letter?

fac·ing

mov·ing

sim·ply

re·view

[128]

167

taped

Bu·reau

[107]

168

jew·el·ry

neph·ew

cat·a·log

[71]

169

30

trac·er

re·ceipt

[88]

170

18

ca·pa·ble

quick·ly

[107]

Principles

171 **Ow** The sound of *ow*, as in *now*, is written ○.

Spell: n-ow, now

now		proud		ounce	
allow		found		house	
doubt		account		amount	

172 **Word Ending -ther** The word ending *-ther* is represented by *th.*

Spell: oo-ith, other

other		together		rather	
whether		mother		leather	
neither		either		bothered	

173 **Word Beginnings Con-, Com-** The word beginnings *con-, com-* are represented by *k.*

Con-

Spell: con-s-e-r-n, concern

concern		consisted		contract	
confused		controlled		considerable	

Com-

Spell: com-p-o-s, compose

compose		completely		complaint	

compare *complain* *combine*

174 **Con-, Com- Followed by a Vowel** When *con-*, *com-* are followed by a vowel, these word beginnings are represented by *kn* or *km.*

connect *connote* *committee*

connection *commerce* *commercial*

Building transcription skills

175

Business vocabulary builder	**script** The written text matter of a play or movie or broadcast. **bid** (*noun*) Offer of a price to do something or provide something. **comment** (*verb*) Make a statement about.

Reading and writing practice

176 **Brief-Form Review Letter**

re·ceive

scripts

wheth·er

pro·ceed

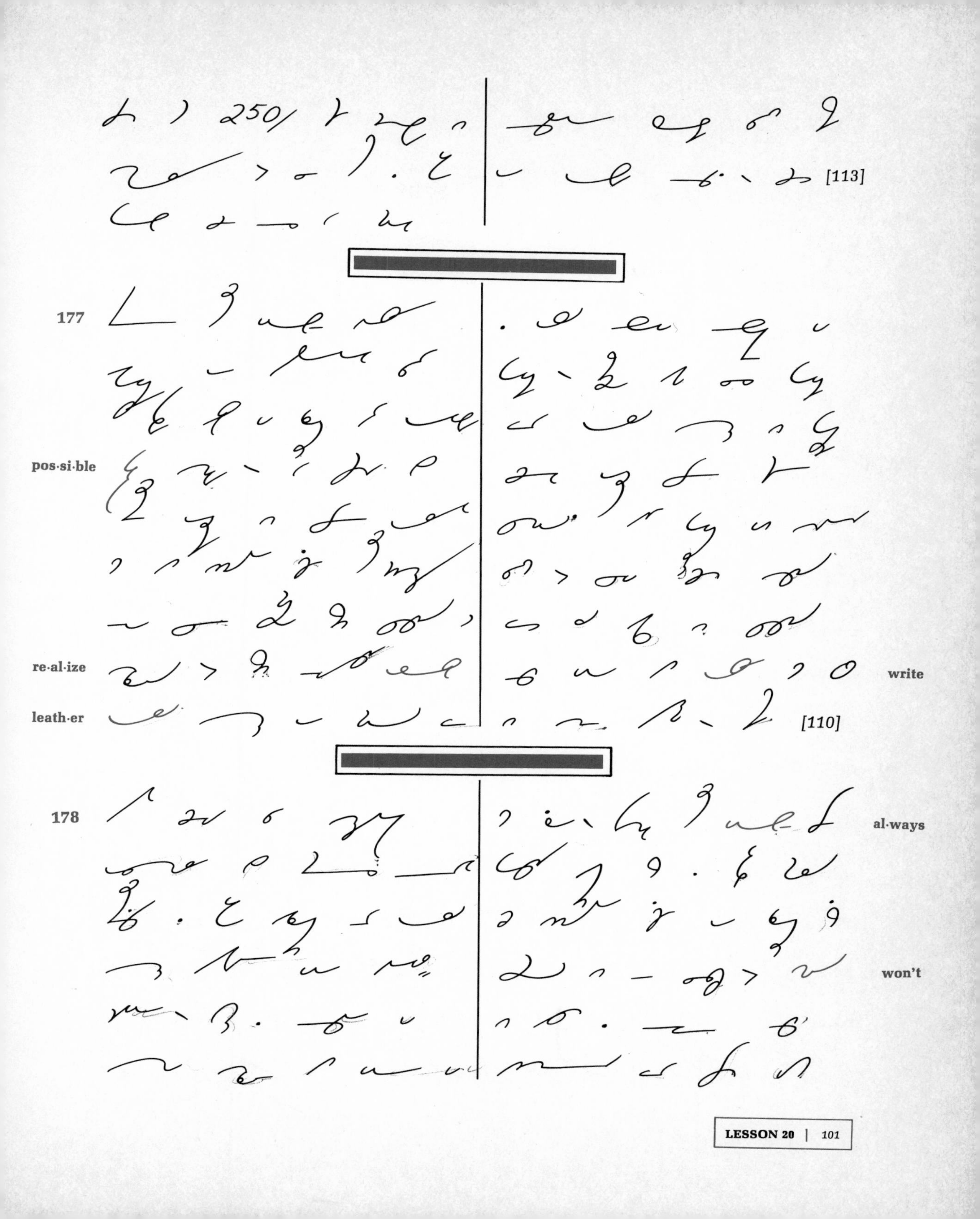

[113]

177

pos·si·ble

re·al·ize

write

leath·er

[110]

178

al·ways

won't

rea·sons

[108]

179

fair

de·ci·sion

[65]

180

ah

flow·er

enough

de·cade

[117]

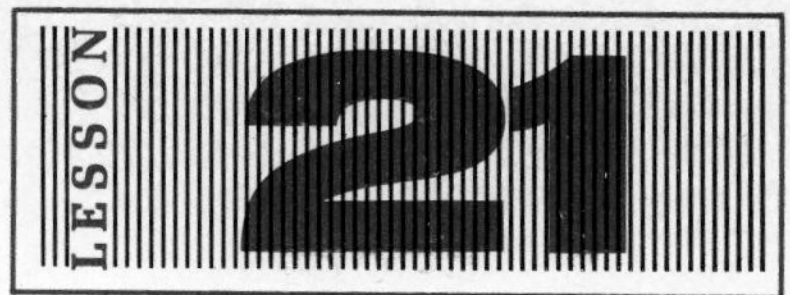

Principles

181 **Brief Forms**

advantage	suggest	correspond, correspondence
use	such	how, out
big	several	ever, every

182 **Den** By rounding off the angle between *d-n*, we obtain the fluent *den* blend.

Den

Spell: s-oo-den, sudden; den-r, dinner

sudden	confidently	dentist
wooden	president	danger
deny	evidently	dinner

183 **Ten** The stroke that represents *den* also represents *t-n*.

Spell: a-ten-d, attend; k-o-ten, cotton

attend	gotten	tonight
attention	competent	stands
written	bulletins	remittances
sentences	cotton	assistance

184 **Tain** The stroke that represents *d-n, t-n* also represents *tain.*

Spell: *o-b-tain, obtain*

obtain	*certain*	*obtainable*
contain	*attain*	*container*
maintain	*detain*	*certainly*

Building transcription skills

185

Business vocabulary builder

accommodate Take care of.

correspondents Those who write or answer letters.

competence Ability.

unique Being the only one of its kind. (It is, therefore, incorrect to say "more unique" or "most unique.")

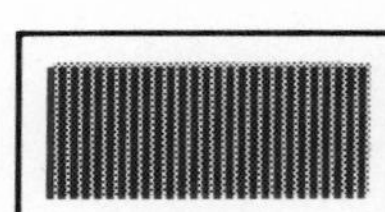

Reading and writing practice

186 **Brief-Form Letter**

enough

wor·ry

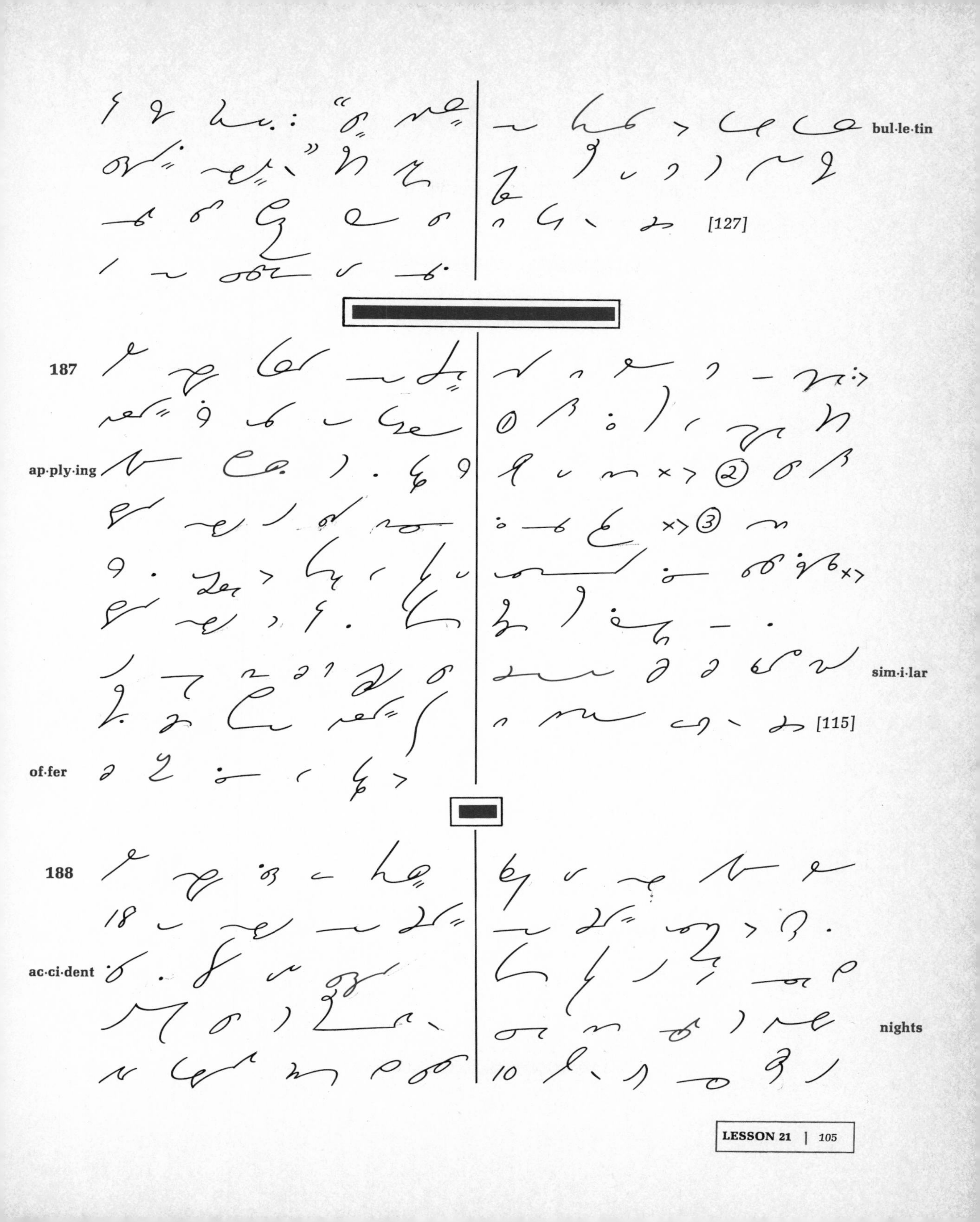

bul·le·tin

[127]

187

ap·ply·ing

sim·i·lar

[115]

of·fer

188

ac·ci·dent

nights

aban·don

[93]

189

unique

sam·ples

[93]

190

rea·son

cot·ton

es·caped

[93]

Principles

191 **Dem** By rounding off the angle between *d-m*, we obtain the fluent *dem* blend.

Dem

Compare: den dem

Spell: dem-a-end, demand; m-e-dem, medium

demand	random	domestic
demonstrate	freedom	damage
condemn	seldom	medium

192 **Tem** The stroke that represents *dem* also represents *t-m*.

Spell: tem-p-r; temper

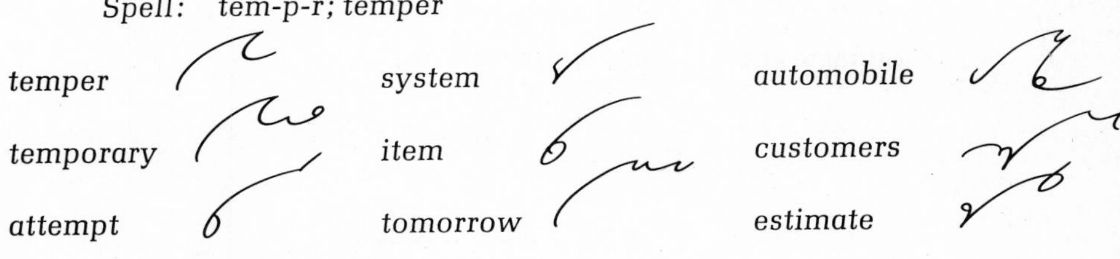

193 **Business Abbreviations** Here are additional salutations and closings frequently used in business.

Dear Mr.	Dear Miss	Cordially yours
Dear Mrs.	Yours sincerely	Very cordially yours

194 **Useful Phrases** With the *tem* and *ten* blends, we form these useful phrases.

to me	to know	to make

195 **Days of the Week**

Sunday		Wednesday		Friday	
Monday		Thursday		Saturday	
Tuesday					

196 **Months of the Year** You are already familiar with the outlines for several of the months, as they are written in full.

January		May		September	
February		June		October	
March		July		November	
April		August		December	

Building transcription skills

197

Business vocabulary builder

contemplate Intend to; consider doing.

snuffs out Puts out; extinguishes.

estimate *(noun)* An approximate calculation.

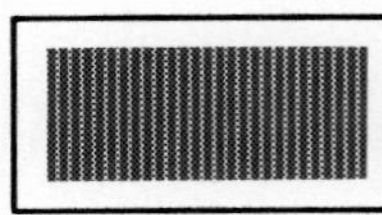

Reading and writing practice

198 **Brief-Form Review Letter**

growth

re·lief

sug·gest

[126]

199

dan·ger

put·ting

like·ly

to·mor·row

re·leas·es
stream

[137]

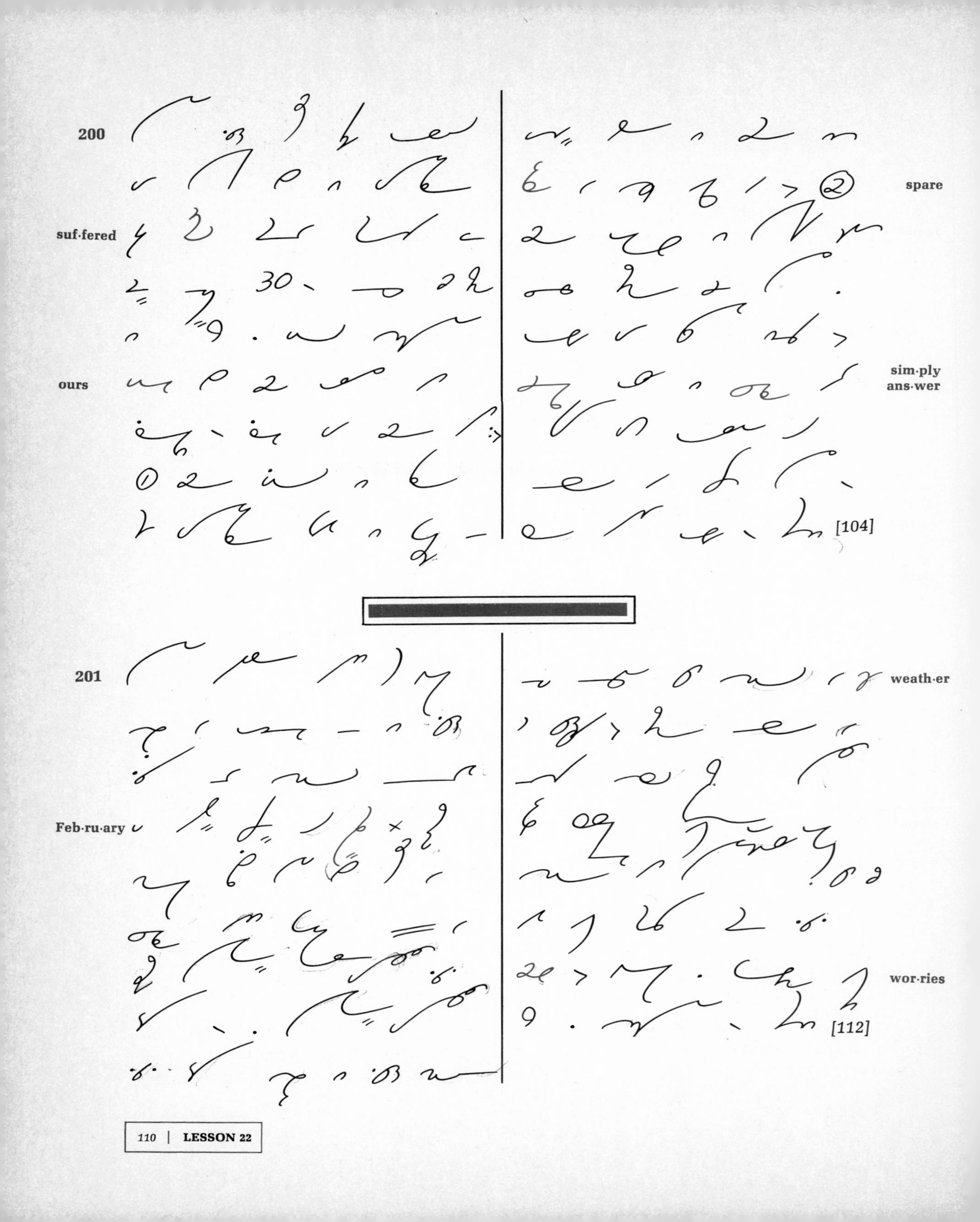

200

spare

suf·fered

ours

sim·ply
ans·wer

[104]

201

weath·er

Feb·ru·ary

wor·ries

[112]

Principles

202 Brief Forms After this group, you have only five more groups to learn.

time	*gone*	*question*
acknowledge	*during*	*yet*
general	**over*	*worth*

*The outline for *over* is written above the following character. It is also used as a prefix form, as in:

overdo	overcame	oversee

203 Def, Dif By rounding off the angle between *d-f*, we obtain the fluent *def, dif* blend.

Def, Dif

Spell: def-n-e-t, *definite*

definite	*defeat*	*different*
defied	*defined*	*differences*

204 Div, Dev The stroke that represents *def, dif* also represents *div* and *dev.*

Spell: div-ī-d, *divide*

divide	dividend	devised
division	devoted	developed

205 U represented by OO. The *oo* hook is often used to represent the sound of *u,* as in *new.*

Spell: *n-oo, new*

new	continue	induce
due	issue	duty
avenue	suits	volume

Building transcription skills

206 SIMILAR-WORDS DRILL | to, too, two

to (*preposition*) In the direction of. (*To* is also used as the sign of the infinitive.)

I should like to talk to you about this matter.

too Also; more than enough.

I, too, was in the Navy.

She receives too many personal telephone calls in the office.

two One plus one.

He spent two years in France.

The word in this group on which stenographers often stumble is *too*—they carelessly transcribe *to*. Don't *you* make that mistake.

207

Business vocabulary builder

overhead Business expenses such as rent, heat, and taxes.

tentative Not final.

defer Put off; delay.

sales volume The amount of sales made to customers.

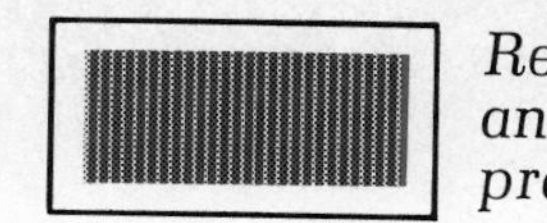

Reading and writing practice

208 Brief-Form Letter

raised

over·head

pol·i·cies

cat·a·log

[107]

209

re·ceipt

de·vised

vol·ume

[110]

210

week

Re·duc·ing

[114]

211

over·due

lose

de·fer

[113]

le·gal

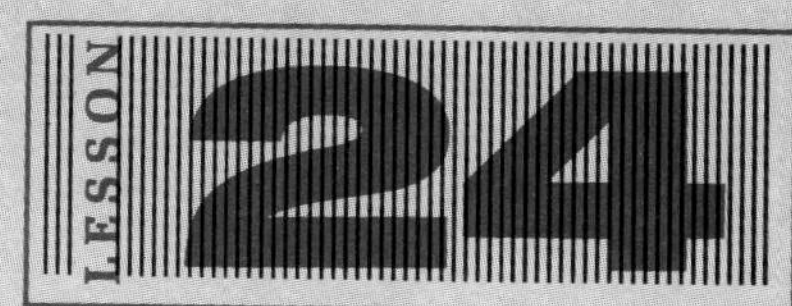

Recall

In Lesson 24 you will have no new shorthand devices to learn; you will have a little time to "digest" the devices that you have studied in previous lessons. In Lesson 24 you will find a new feature – Accuracy Practice – that will help you improve your shorthand writing style.

Accuracy practice

The speed and accuracy with which you will be able to transcribe your shorthand notes will depend on how well you write them. If you follow the suggestions given in this lesson when you work with each Accuracy Practice, you will soon find that you can read your own notes with greater ease and facility.

So that you may have a clear picture of the proper shapes of the shorthand strokes that you are studying, enlarged models of the alphabetic characters and of the typical joinings are given, together with a short explanation of the things that you should keep in mind as you practice.

To get the most out of each Accuracy Practice, follow this simple procedure:

a *Read the explanations carefully.*

b *Study the model to see the application of each explanation.*

c *Write the first outline in the Practice Drill.*

d *Compare what you have written with the enlarged model.*

e *Write three or four more copies of the outline, trying to improve your outline with each writing.*

f *Repeat this procedure with the remaining outlines in the Practice Drill.*

212 **R** **L** **K** **G**

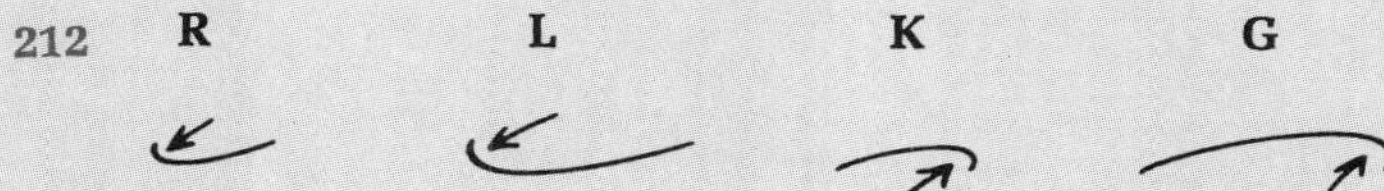

To write these strokes accurately:

a *Start and finish each one on the same level of writing.*

b *Make the* **beginning** *of the curve in* **r** *and* **l** *deep. Make the* **end** *of the curve in* **k** *and* **g** *deep.*

c *Make the* **l** *and* **g** *considerably longer than* **r** *and* **k**.

practice drill

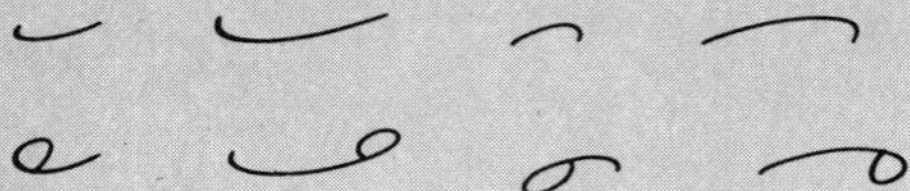

Are-our-hour; will-well; can, good.
Air, lay, ache, gay.

213 **Kr** **Rk** **Gl**

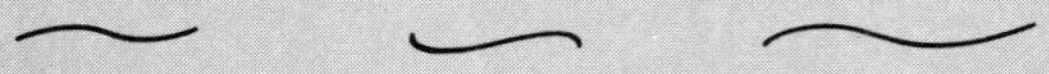

To write these combinations accurately:

a *Make the curves rather flat.*

b *Make the combinations* **kr** *and* **rk** *somewhat shorter than the combined length of* **r** *and* **k** *when written by themselves.*

c *Make the combination* **gl** *somewhat shorter than the combined length of* **g** *and* **l** *when written by themselves.*

practice drill

Cream, crate, maker, mark, dark.
Gleam, glean, glare, eagle.

214 **Recall Chart** This chart contains all the brief forms in Chapter 4 and one or more illustrations of all the shorthand devices you have studied in Chapters 1 through 4.

The chart contains 84 words. Can you read the entire chart in 7 minutes or less?

WORDS

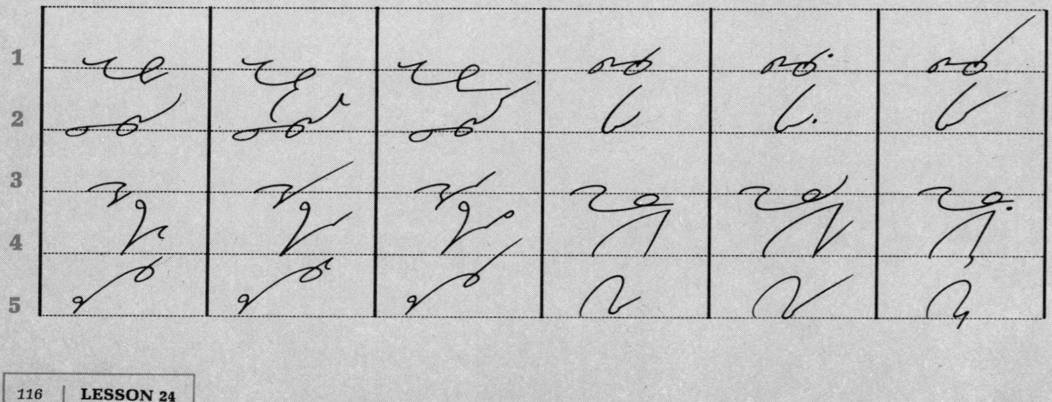

6

7

8

9

BRIEF FORMS AND PHRASES

10

11

12

13

14

Building transcription skills

215

Business vocabulary builder

prominent Readily noticeable; important.

participation Act of taking an active part in anything.

comprehend Understand.

skim Read quickly without concern for details.

Reading and writing practice

216 **A Race With the Clock**

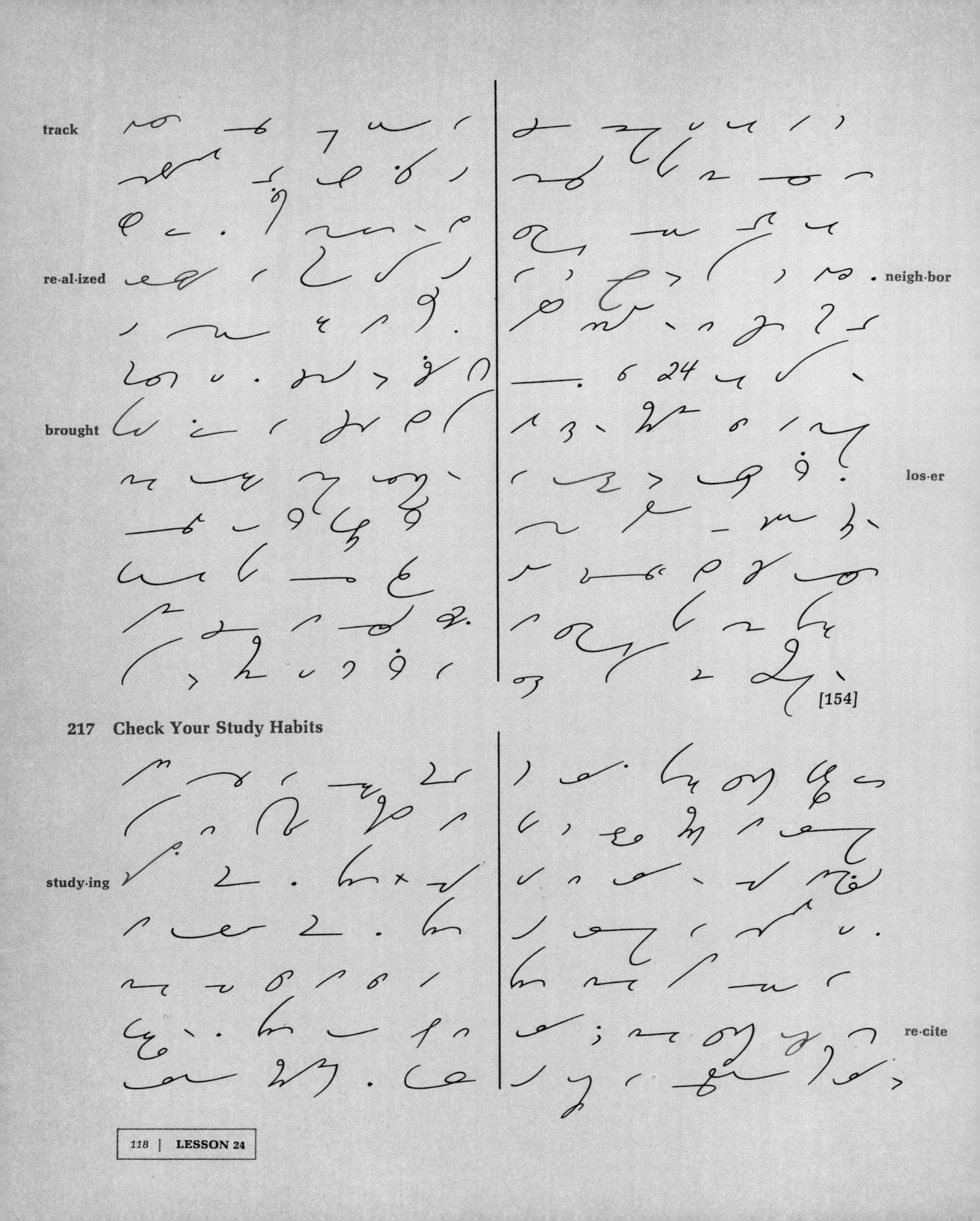

track

re·al·ized

neigh·bor

brought

los·er

[154]

217 Check Your Study Habits

study·ing

re·cite

through

graphs

brief

ses·sions

[282]

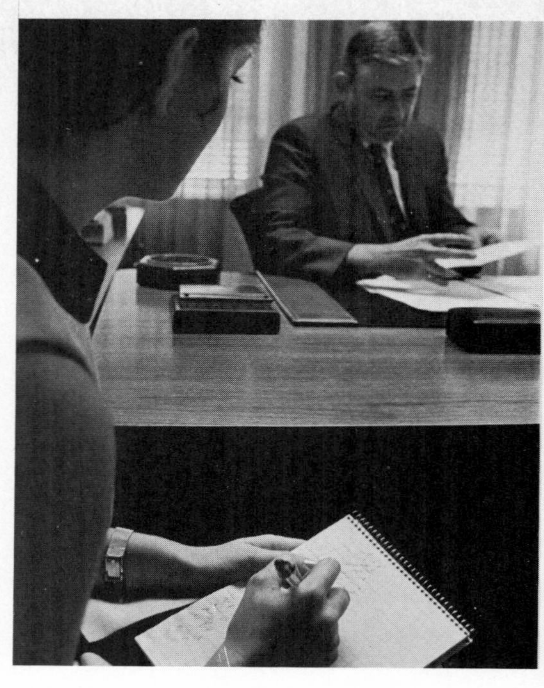

Chapter 5

The secretary takes dictation

A very important part of every executive's job is communications. Each day he must dictate letters to customers, memorandums to salesmen or other executives, and reports to the board of directors. The secretary who can take his dictation comfortably, without constantly interrupting him because he is dictating too fast, and who can transcribe rapidly and accurately is worth her weight in gold!

An efficient secretary quickly learns her boss's dictating habits so that executive and secretary can work together as a team. Some dictators know exactly what they want to say, and their secretaries must constantly use every ounce of skill to keep pace with them. Others think in spurts, that is,

there will often be long pauses between thoughts. Then when an idea has been framed in their minds, they are off at a fast clip for a minute or more. Then for a moment or so—nothing. Still other dictators are more deliberate. They think slowly, especially on difficult letters, and may change their minds many times during the dictation of a letter. Even so, their secretaries must be prepared for sudden bursts of speed when the dictators' ideas jell and they know what they want to say. No two executives dictate alike, and the secretary must be prepared for all types.

The good secretary has a reserve speed for any emergency. This reserve speed enables her to write for long periods of time without fatigue. It enables her to write legible notes that are easy to transcribe. It enables her to cope with the occasional spurts in her employer's dictation.

The more rapidly you can write, the easier will be your task of taking and transcribing dictation. It will pay you, therefore, to build up your speed to the highest point possible.

Principles

218 Brief Forms

difficult	*satisfy, satisfactory*	*state*
envelope	*success*	**under*
progress	*next*	*request*

*The outline for *under* is written above the following shorthand character. It is also used as a prefix form, as in:

underneath	*understudy*	*undertake*
undergo	*underpay*	*underground*

219 Cities and States In your work as a stenographer and secretary, you will frequently have occasion to write geographical expressions. Here are a few important cities and states.

Cities

New York	*Boston*	*Los Angeles*
Chicago	*Philadelphia*	*St. Louis*

States

Michigan	*Massachusetts*	*Missouri*
Illinois	*Pennsylvania*	*California*

220 Useful Business Phrases The following phrases are used so frequently in business that special forms have been provided for them. Study these phrases as you would study brief forms.

of course	to do	let us
as soon as	I hope	to us
as soon as possible	we hope	your order

Building transcription skills

221

Business vocabulary builder	
	statement Summary of a financial account showing the balance due.
	preserve Keep or save.
	manila envelope Envelope made of a strong brown paper.

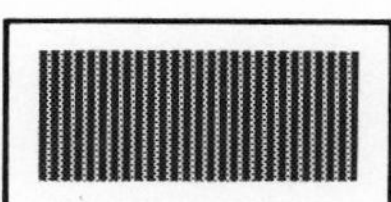

Reading and writing practice

222 Brief-Form Letter

re·ceive

re·quest

good·will

suc·cess

ours

[137]

223

ma·nila

al·ways

won't

[103]

224

guest

ques·tion

[116]

225

source

Chi·ca·go

sug·gest

[86]

226

con·fess

[114]

Principles

227 **Long I and a Following Vowel** Any vowel following long *i* is represented by a small circle within a large circle.

Compare: *quite* *quiet*

Spell: *s-īah-n-s, science*

science	prior	reliance
trial	drier	compliance
dial	client	reliant

228 **Ia, Ea** The sounds of *ia,* as in *piano,* and *ea,* as in *create,* are represented by a large circle with a dot placed within it.

Spell: *a-r-eah, area*

area	appropriate	initiate
created	appreciate	brilliantly
creating	piano	variation

229 **Word Beginnings In-, Un-, En-** The word beginnings *in-, un-, en-* are represented by *n* before a consonant.

Spell: *in-k-r-e-s, increase; un-f-a-r, unfair; en-j-oi, enjoy*

In-

increase	invest	insist
insure	injured	instant

Un-

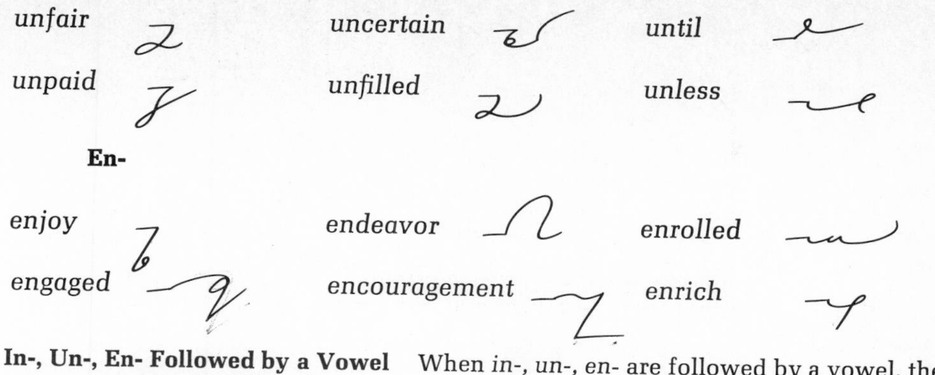

230 **In-, Un-, En- Followed by a Vowel** When *in-, un-, en-* are followed by a vowel, they are written in full.

innovation *unable* *enact*

Building transcription skills

231

Business vocabulary builder	**home appliances** Items for the home, such as refrigerators, stoves, dryers, and washing machines. **prior** Earlier in time; coming ahead. **associates** (*noun*) Fellow workers; partners. **appropriate** (*adjective*) Proper; fitting.

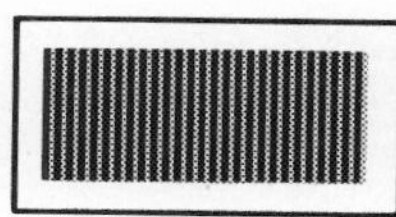

Reading and writing practice

232 **Brief-Form Review Letter**

ac·cept

nor·mal·ly

pri·or

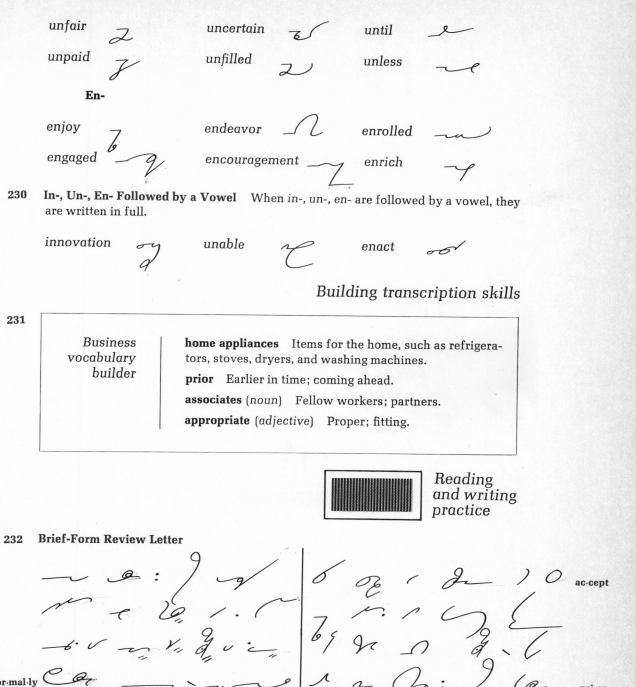

[118]

233

oc·cur

cre·at·ing

[117]

234

in·voice

pa·tient

266

[125]

past

235

un·veiled

[77]

un·du·ly

236

un·til

be·lieve

ma·chine

won't

[110]

Principles

237 **Brief Forms** After you have learned the following brief forms, you have only three more groups to go!

particular	speak	upon
probable	idea	street
regular	subject	newspaper

238 **Ng** The sound of *ng* is written .

Compare: seen sing

Spell: s-e-ing, sing; s-a-ing, sang

sing	wrong	lengthy
sang	long	strength
song	strong	angle
ring	bring	single

239 **Ngk** The sound of *ngk* (spelled *nk*) is written .

Compare: seem sink

Spell: r-a-ink, rank; oo-ink-l, uncle

rank	blank	drinking
frankly	banker	anxious

tanks | banquet | uncle
ink | link | shrink

240 Omission of Vowel Preceding -tion When *t, d, n,* or *m* is followed by *-ition, -ation,* the circle is omitted.

admission | commission | quotations
conditions | donation | permission
reputation | addition | stationed

Building transcription skills

241

Business vocabulary builder	
	stationery Such items as paper, pens, ink, clips.
	estimation Opinion; judgment.
	major Of great importance.

Reading and writing practice

242 Brief-Form Letter

sta·tio·nery

length

suf·fered
se·vere

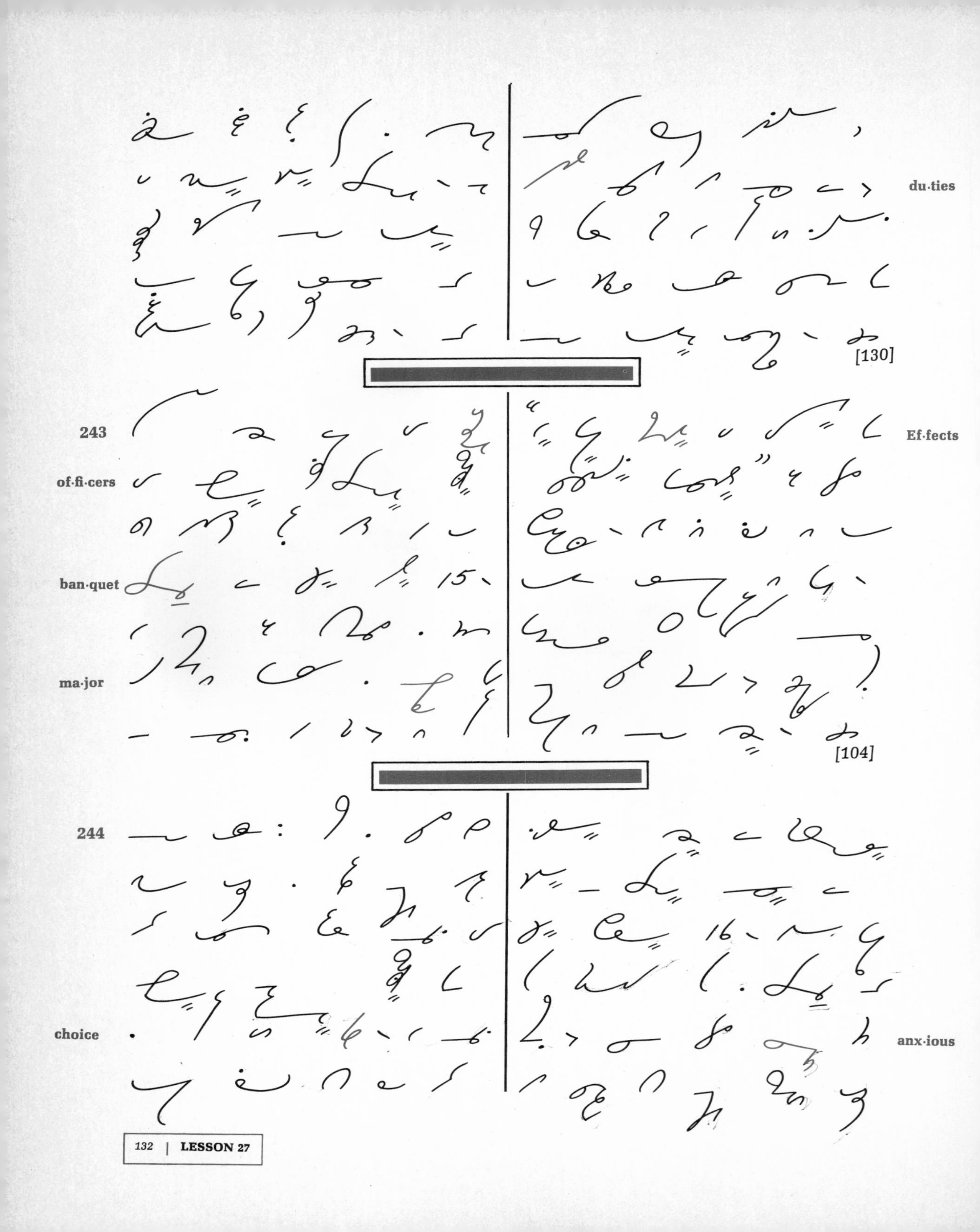

du·ties

[130]

243

Ef·fects

of·fi·cers

ban·quet

15

ma·jor

[104]

244

16

choice

anx·ious

[113]

245

sub·ject

ad·di·tion

ac·cept

ba

[100]

246

vi·cin·ity

edi·tion

ga

op·po·site

[116]

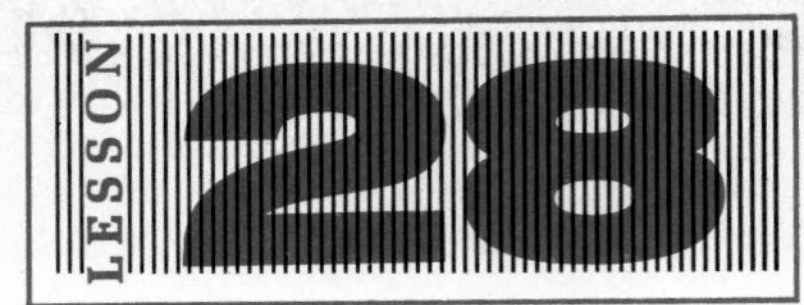

Principles

247 Ah, Aw A dot is used for *a* in words that begin with *ah* and *aw*.

Spell: *a-h-e-d, ahead; a-oo-a, away*

ahead	*awaited*	*awoke*
away	*awake*	*aware*
await	*awaken*	*award*

248 Y Before *o* and *oo*, *y* is represented by the small circle, as *y* is pronounced *e*. *Ye* is expressed by a small loop; *ya*, by a large loop.

Spell: *wē-l-o, yellow; wē-ard, yard*

yawn	*yellow*	*yard*
youth	*yielded*	*yarn*
yell	*yes*	*yoke*

249 X The letter *x* is usually represented by an *s* written with a slight backward slant.

Compare: *miss* *mix*

fees *fix*

Spell: *b-o-ex, box; b-o-exes, boxes*

box	*relax*	*tax*
boxes	*relaxes*	*taxes*

250 Omission of Short U In the body of a word, short *u* is omitted before *n, m,* or a straight downstroke.

Before N

son	ton	gun
fun	done	begun

Before M

some, sum	come	lumber
summer	become	column

Before a Straight Downstroke

rush	touch	budget
brushed	much	judged

Building transcription skills

251

Business vocabulary builder

budget The amount of money that is available for a particular purpose, as an advertising budget.

agenda List of things to be done.

perplexing Puzzling.

blunt Having an edge that is not sharp.

Reading and writing practice

252 Brief-Form Review Letter

aware

wel·come

bud·get

[111]

253

[94]

over·due

254

judg·ing

shipped

touch

wheth·er

[107]

255

nice·ly

plan·ning

fu·el

[103]

256 Confidential

[58]

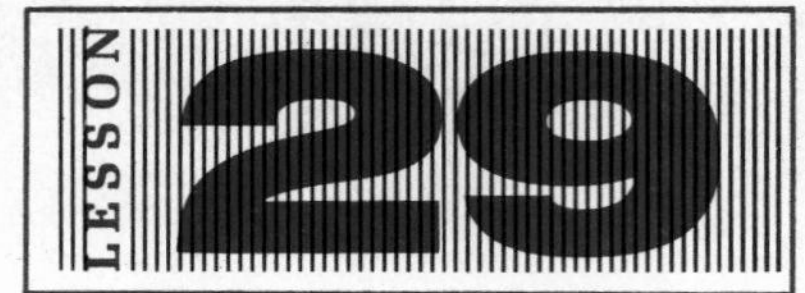

Principles

257 **Brief Forms**

purpose		circular		public	
regard		responsible		publish, publication	
opinion		organize		ordinary	

258 **Word Beginning Ex-** The word beginning ex- is represented by e-s.

Spell: *ex-p-n-s, expense*

expense		expert		extra	
expected		explained		executive	
expresses		extend		excuse	
expire		example		examine	

259 **Md, Mt** By rounding off the angle between *m-d,* we obtain the fluent *md* blend. The same stroke also represents *mt.*

Md, Mt

Compare: *seem* *seemed*

Spell: *f-r-a-emd, framed; emt-e, empty*

framed		named		prompt	
claimed		confirmed		promptly	

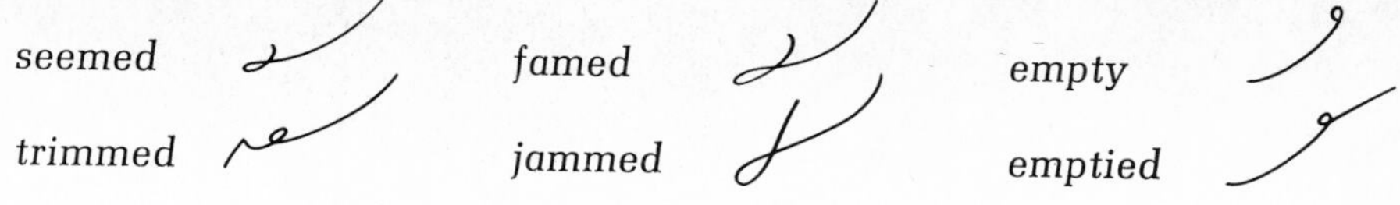

seemed trimmed famed jammed empty emptied

260 **Word Ending -ful** The word ending *-ful* is represented by *f*.

Spell: *k-a-r-ful, careful*

careful *thoughtful* *doubtful* *hopeful* *beautiful* *useful* *helpful* *helpfully* *helpfulness*

Building transcription skills

261 **SIMILAR-WORDS DRILL** | **addition, edition**

addition Anything added.

She will be a fine addition to your staff.

edition All the copies of a book printed at one time.

The second edition of the book is beautifully illustrated.

262

Business vocabulary builder

public relations department The people in an organization whose purpose is to develop goodwill between the organization and the public.

commended Praised.

overwhelmed Overpowered; crushed.

ailing Sick.

Reading and writing practice

263 **Brief-Form Letter**

cir·cu·lar

use·ful

[130]

prompt·ly

264

pa·tients

edi·tion

[147]

265

past

ail·ing

ad·di·tion

[118]

266

ini·tial

touch

[69]

Recall

After studying the new shorthand devices in Lessons 25 through 29, you have earned another breathing spell! Therefore, you will find no new shorthand strokes or principles in Lesson 30.

In this lesson you will find an Accuracy Practice devoted to the curved strokes of Gregg Shorthand, a Recall Chart, and a Reading and Writing Practice that offers you some interesting suggestions on how to be a good conversationalist.

Accuracy practice

To get the most benefit from this Accuracy Practice, be sure to follow the procedures suggested on page 115.

267 **B** **V** **P** **F** **S**

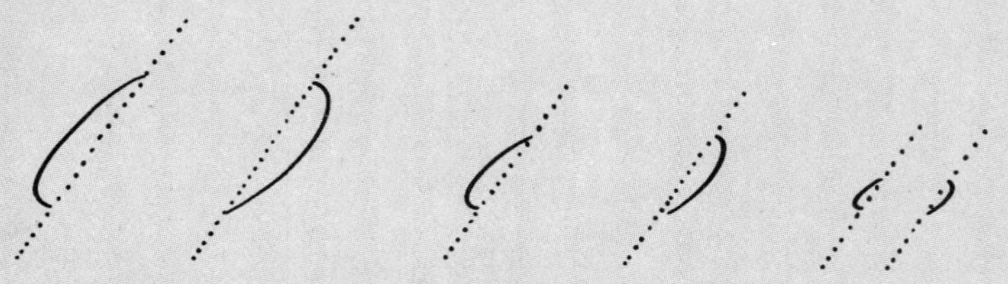

To write these strokes accurately:

a *Give them approximately the slant indicated by the dotted lines.*

b *Make the curve deep at the* **beginning** *of* **v, f,** *comma* **s;** *make the curve deep at the* **end** *of* **b, p,** *left* **s.**

practice drill

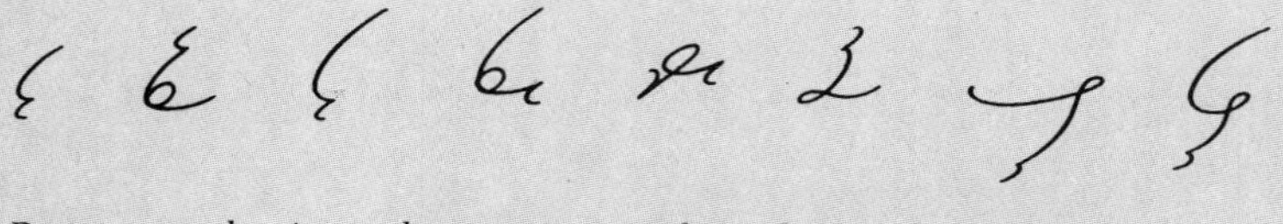

Puts, spare, business, bears, stairs, sphere, leaves, briefs.

268 **Pr** **Pl** **Br** **Bl**

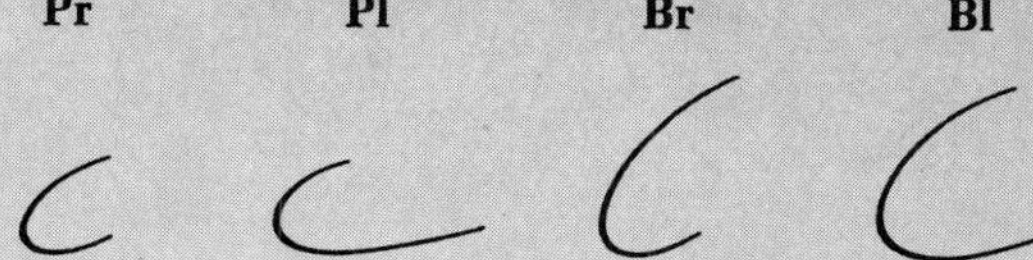

To write these combinations accurately:

a *Write each without a pause between the first and second letter of each combination.*

b *Watch your proportions carefully.*

practice drill

Press, pray, prim, plan, plate, place.
Brim, brief, bread, blame, blast.

269 **Fr** **Fl**

To write these combinations accurately:

a *Write them with one sweep of the pen, with no stop between the* **f** *and the* **r** *or* **l**.

practice drill

Free, freeze, frame, flee, flame, flap.

270 **Recall Chart** This chart contains all the brief forms in Chapter 5 and one or more illustrations of the word-building principles you studied in Chapters 1 through 5.

As you read through the words in this chart, be sure to spell each word that you cannot read immediately.

Can you read the 84 words in the chart in 6 minutes or less?

BRIEF FORMS AND DERIVATIVES

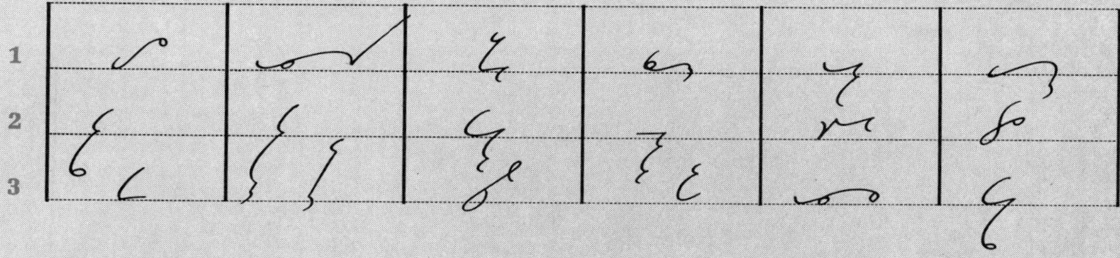

4

5

WORDS

6

7

8

9

10

11

12

13

14

Building transcription skills

271

Business vocabulary builder	**friction** Disagreement between two persons having different views. **digresses** Gets off the main subject. **minute** Very small; of little importance. **trite** Worn out; old.

Reading and writing practice

Reading Scoreboard The previous Reading Scoreboard appeared in Lesson 18. If you have been studying each Reading and Writing Practice faithfully, no doubt there has been an increase in your reading speed. Let us measure that increase on the *first reading* of the material in Lesson 30. The following table will help you:

Lesson 30 contains 504 words
If you read Lesson 30 in **14 minutes** *your reading rate is* **36 words a minute**
If you read Lesson 30 in **16 minutes** *your reading rate is* **31 words a minute**
If you read Lesson 30 in **18 minutes** *your reading rate is* **28 words a minute**
If you read Lesson 30 in **20 minutes** *your reading rate is* **25 words a minute**
If you read Lesson 30 in **22 minutes** *your reading rate is* **23 words a minute**
If you read Lesson 30 in **24 minutes** *your reading rate is* **21 words a minute**
If you read Lesson 30 in **26 minutes** *your reading rate is* **19 words a minute**

If you can read Lesson 30 in 14 minutes or less, you are doing well. If you take considerably longer than 26 minutes, perhaps you should review your homework procedures. For example, are you:

1 *Practicing in a quiet place at home?*

2 *Practicing without the radio or television set on?*

3 *Spelling aloud any words that you cannot read immediately?*

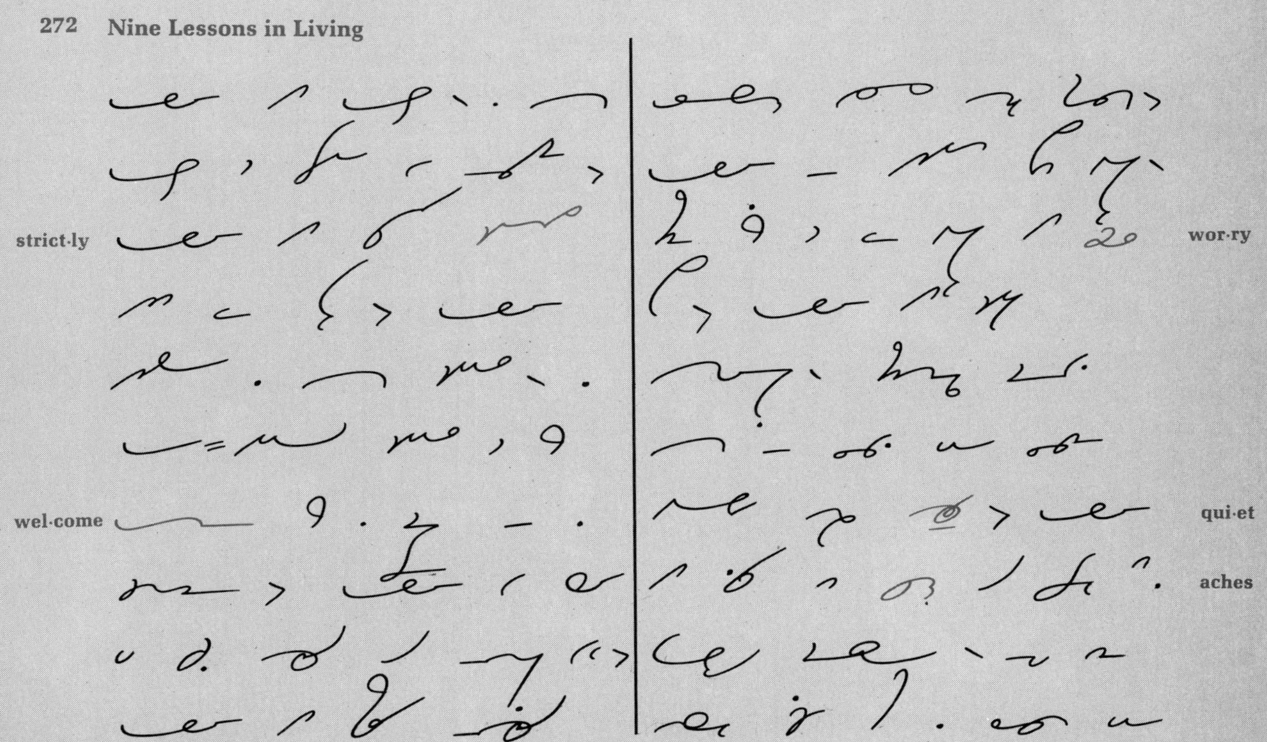

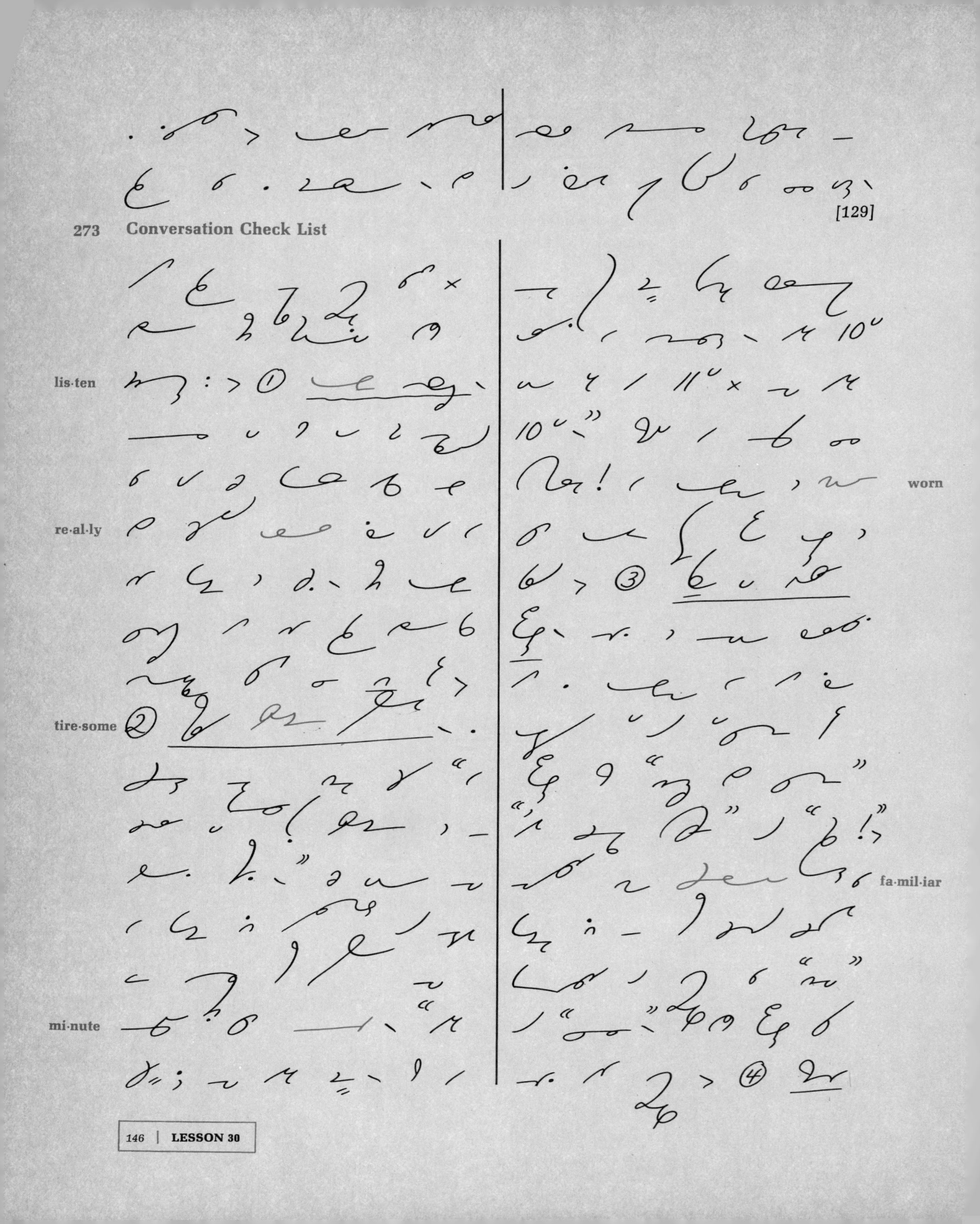

[129]

273 Conversation Check List

lis·ten

re·al·ly

tire·some

mi·nute

worn

fa·mil·iar

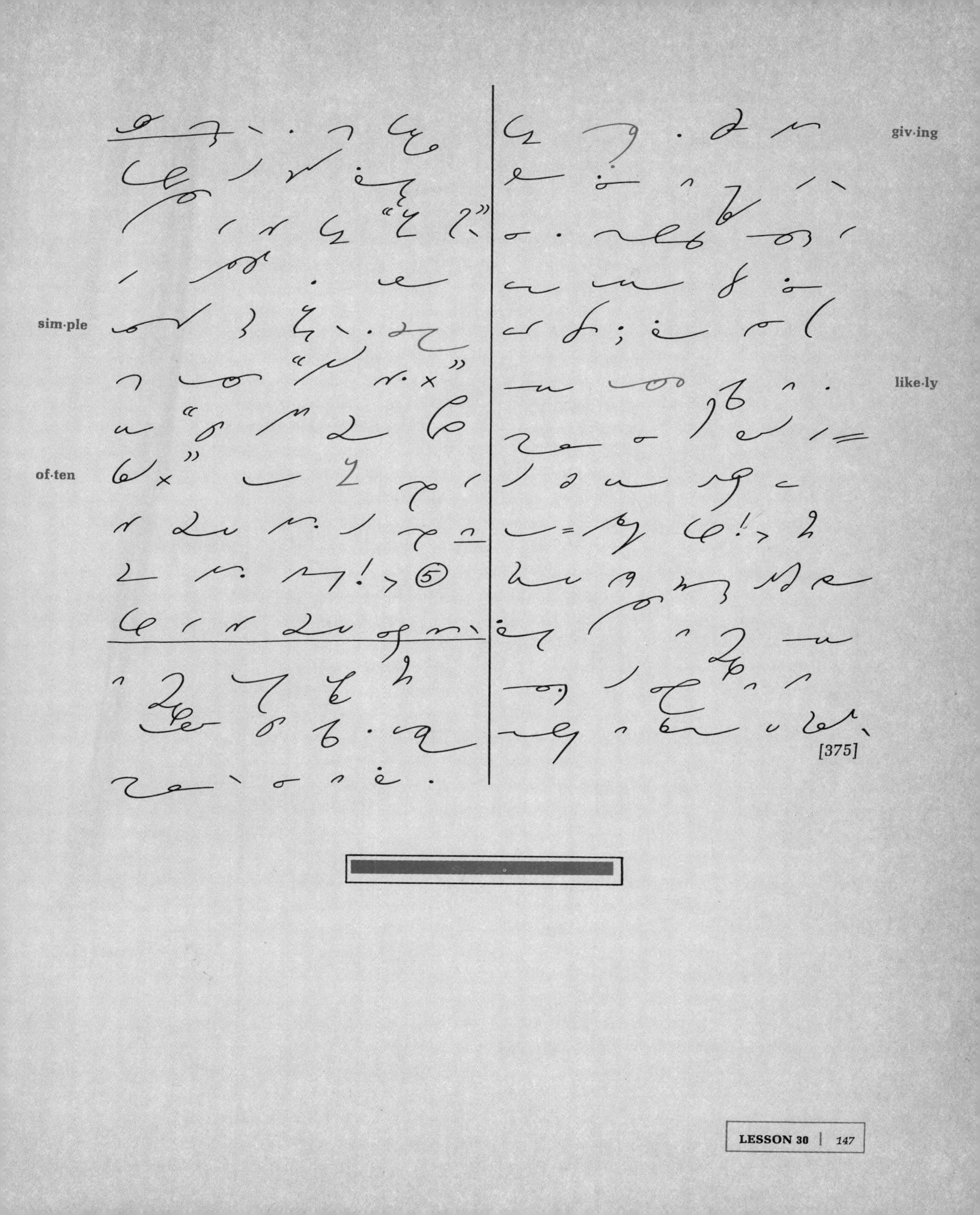

sim·ple

of·ten

giv·ing

like·ly

[375]

Chapter 6

The secretary— master of English

The successful secretary is a master of the English language. She has a large vocabulary to which she is constantly adding new words. She has a firm grasp of such mechanics of English as grammar, punctuation, and spelling. If you are to be a successful secretary, you, too, must become a master of the English language.

The executive for whom you will work will doubtless know what he wants to say, but he may not know the correct spelling, punctuation, and grammatical construction—that is, how to say it. He may have a college degree in engineering, accounting, history, or chemistry, but somewhere along the line he missed the opportunity to learn the finer points of grammar. This is where you come in. The executive's re-

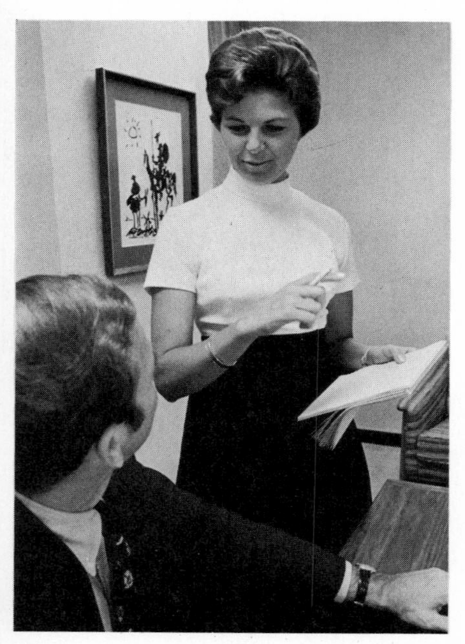

quest of the secretary, "Fix the letter so that it 'reads' right," is not rare. And he really means it.

Many employers are highly expert in the English language. They may dictate every punctuation mark and spell every unusual word. If you get one of these for a boss, your job of transcribing will be greatly simplified.

Then there is the dictator who thinks he knows grammar, but doesn't, and will expect you to transcribe everything just as he dictated it, whether it is really right or not. Of course, in this case there is nothing for you to do but to follow his wishes—he takes the responsibility.

But if your boss says, "You know English and I don't, so you fix this letter," then you must know. It is your responsibility. Badly constructed letters can cost your company a sale or can result in the loss of goodwill.

No matter how rapidly you can type or can write shorthand, these skills are greatly weakened if you cannot produce a finished transcript that is grammatically perfect. The top-notch secretary must be a real expert in business English. The surer she is of the accepted rules of English, the more secure her job and the better her chances for advancement.

Any time you spend improving your mastery of the English language and building your vocabulary will be well spent!

Principles

274 Brief Forms Only one more group to learn after this one!

merchant	*never*	*short*
merchandise	*experience*	*quantity*
recognize	*between*	*situation*

275 Word Ending -ure The word ending *-ure* is represented by *r*.

Spell: f-a-l-r, failure

failure	*procedure*	*nature*
figure	*picture*	*naturally*

276 Word Ending -ual The word ending *-ual* is represented by *l*.

Spell: g-r-a-d-l, gradual

gradual	*actually*	*annual*
equal	*eventual*	*annually*

Building transcription skills

277 PUNCTUATION PRACTICE

Another "must" for the successful stenographer or secretary is the ability to punctuate correctly. Most businessmen rely on their stenographers or secretaries to supply the proper punctuation when they transcribe. Because the inclusion or omission of a punctuation mark may completely alter the meaning of a sentence, it is important that you know when to use each punctuation mark.

To sharpen your punctuation skill, you will hereafter give special attention to punctuation in each Reading and Writing Practice.

In the lessons ahead you will review nine of the most common uses of the comma. Each time one of these uses of the comma occurs in the Reading and Writing Practice, it will be squared in the shorthand, thus calling it forcefully to your attention.

PRACTICE SUGGESTIONS

If you follow these simple suggestions in your homework practice hereafter, your ability to punctuate should improve noticeably.

1 Read carefully the explanation of each comma usage (for example, the explanation of the parenthetical comma given below) to be sure that you understand it. You will encounter many illustrations of each comma usage in the Reading and Writing Practice exercises, so that eventually you will acquire the knack of applying it correctly.

2 Continue to read and copy each Reading and Writing Practice, as you have done before. However, add these two important steps:

a *Each time you see a squared comma in the Reading and Writing Practice, note the reason for its use, which is indicated directly above the squared comma.*

b *As you copy the Reading and Writing Practice in your shorthand notebook, insert the commas in your shorthand notes, squaring them as in the textbook.*

PUNCTUATION PRACTICE | , parenthetical

A word or a phrase or a clause that is used parenthetically (that is, one not necessary to the grammatical completeness of the sentence) should be set off by commas.

If the parenthetical expression occurs at the end of the sentence, only one comma is used.

There is, of course, no charge for this service.

Never hesitate to let us know, Mr. Strong, when our organization can help you.

We actually print your picture on the card, Mr. Short.

Each time a parenthetical expression occurs in the Reading and Writing Practice, it will be indicated thus in the shorthand: par [,]

278

Business vocabulary builder	**reputable** Favorably known; respected.
	manual Handbook.
	revealing Bringing to light something that was not evident before.

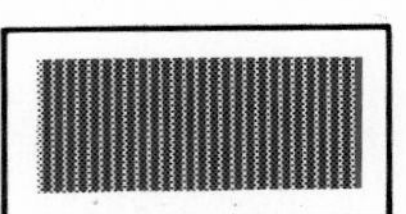

Reading and writing practice

279 **Brief-Form Letter**

quite

lose

their

hon·ored

rep·u·ta·ble

ex·pe·ri·ence

mer·chan·dise
sim·ply

par

par

par

[121]

280

par

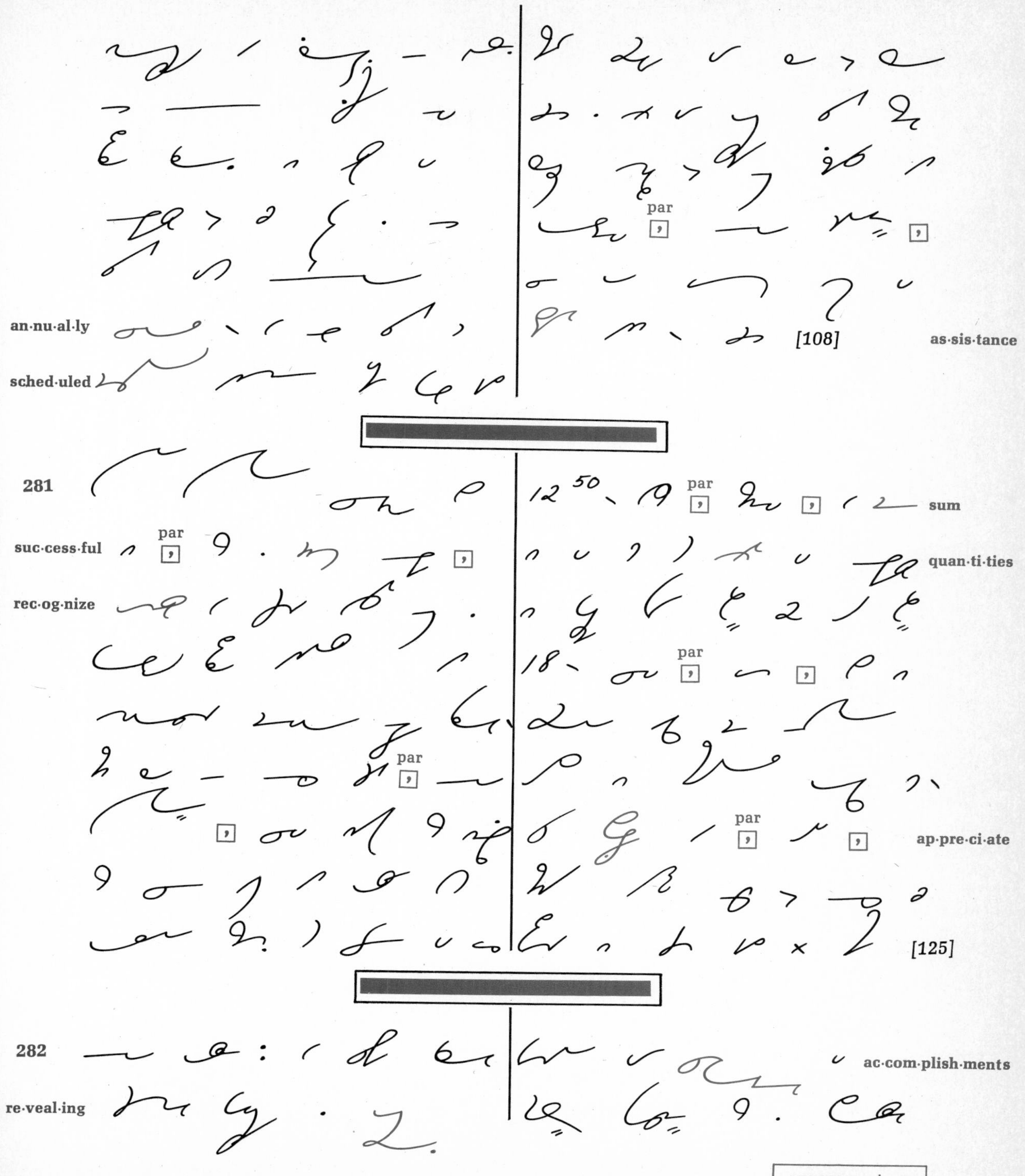
an·nu·al·ly
sched·uled
[108]
as·sis·tance
281
par
suc·cess·ful
rec·og·nize
sum
quan·ti·ties
12 50
18
ap·pre·ci·ate
[125]
282
re·veal·ing
ac·com·plish·ments

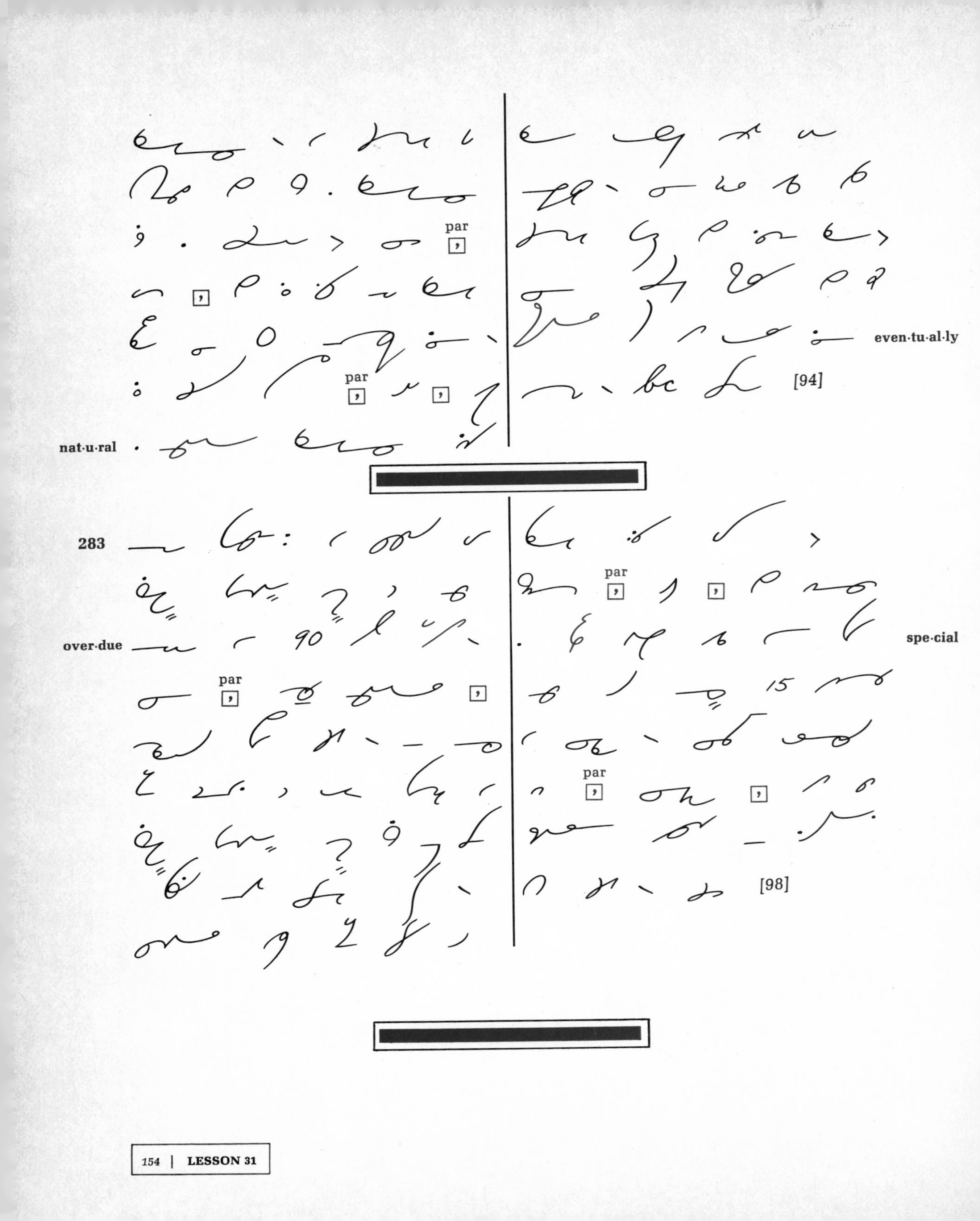

par

par

nat·u·ral

even·tu·al·ly

[94]

283

over·due

par

par

spe·cial

par

[98]

LESSON 32

Principles

284 **Word Ending -ily** The word ending *-ily* is expressed by a narrow loop.

Compare: steady   *steadily*

Spell: e-s-ily, easily

easily	*temporarily*	*heavily*
readily	*family*	*hastily*
heartily	*families*	*speedily*

285 **Word Beginning Al-** The word beginning *al-* is expressed by *o*.

Spell: all-s-o, also

also	*already*	*altered*
almost	*although*	*alteration*
altogether	*alter*	*alters*

286 **Word Beginning Mis-** The word beginning *mis-* is represented by *m-s*.

Spell: mis-t-a-k, mistake

mistake	*mislead*	*miscarry*
mistaken	*misplaced*	*mislaid*
misprint	*misery*	*misunderstood*

287 Word Beginnings Dis-, Des- The word beginnings *dis-, des-* are expressed by *d-s*.

Spell: dis-k-oo-shun, discussion; dis-k-r-ī-b, describe

Dis-

discussion	*discouragement*	*distances*
disposed	*discount*	*discover*

Des-

describe	*description*	*despite*

Building transcription skills

288 PUNCTUATION PRACTICE | , apposition

Sometimes a writer mentions a person or thing, and in order to make his meaning perfectly clear to the reader, he says the same thing in different words. The clarifying word or phrase or clause is known as an "expression in apposition." Each expression in apposition should be set off by commas. When the expression occurs at the end of a sentence, only one comma is necessary.

Our latest booklet, Gracious Living, *is enclosed.*
The meeting will be held on Friday, June 16, at the Hotel Brown.
Please have him get in touch with Mr. Roy, our personnel manager.
He lives in Chicago, Illinois.

▶ Note: When the clarifying term is very closely connected with the principal noun so that the sense would not be complete without the added term, no commas are required.

My sister Jane will be home soon.
The word embarrass *is often misspelled.*

Each time an expression in apposition occurs in the Reading and Writing Practice, it will be indicated thus in the shorthand: ap [,]

289

Business vocabulary builder	
	merchandising Building sales by presenting goods to the public attractively.
	disturbing Troubling.
	in the red Losing money.

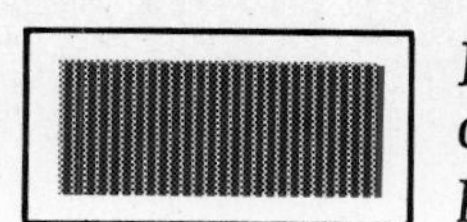

Reading and writing practice

290 Brief-Form Review Letter

ap

rec·og·nized

leath·er

vol·ume

al·ready

par

mer·chan·dis·ing

par

quan·ti·ties

22

28

ap

[142]

291

5

de·scrib·ing

par

mis·spelled

13

par

de·scrip·tive
con·ven·tion

ap 19

ap

[121]

292

ap ar·ea

dis·cuss

ap

par

ap

Gra·cious

[118]

293

ap dis·con·tin·ue

dis·ap·point·ing

ap

31

mis·con·cep·tion

par

heav·i·ly

debt

[124]

294 Quick Service

[69]

STUDY-HABIT CHECK LIST

No doubt as a conscientious student you do your home assignments faithfully. Do you, however, derive the greatest benefit from the time you devote to practice?

☐ You *do* if you practice in a quiet place that enables you to concentrate.

☐ You *don't* if you practice with one eye on the television and the other on your practice work!

☐ You *do* if once you have started your assignment, you do not leave your desk or table until you have completed it.

☐ You *don't* if you interrupt your practice from time to time to call a friend or raid the refrigerator!

Principles

295 **Brief Forms** This is the last set of brief forms you will have to learn.

railroad	*throughout*	*character*
world	*object*	*govern*

296 **Word Beginnings For-, Fore-** The word beginnings *for-*, *fore-* are represented by *f*. The *f* is joined with an angle to *r* or *l* to indicate that it represents a word beginning. The *f* is disjoined if the following character is a vowel.

Spell: *for-gay-e-v, forgive*

forgive	*force*	*forerunner*
forget	*effort*	*forlorn*
form	*forth*	*forever*
informed	*foreclose*	*forearm*

297 **Word Beginning Fur-** The word beginning *fur-* is also represented by *f*.

Spell: *fur-n-a-s, furnace*

furnace	*furnish*	*furniture*
further	*furnished*	*furlough*

298 **Ago in Phrases** In expressions of time, *ago* is represented by g.

days ago	*weeks ago*	*long ago*
years ago	*minutes ago*	*months ago*

299 PUNCTUATION PRACTICE | , series

When the last member of a series of three or more items is preceded by *and, or,* or *nor,* place a comma before the conjunction as well as between the other items.

The railroads are recognized to be a major problem confronting the cities, towns, and villages throughout the country.

The meetings will be held on June 5, July 8, and July 16.

Her duties consisted of receiving calls, answering the telephone, and opening the mail.

▶ Note: Some authorities prefer to omit the comma before the conjunction. In your shorthand textbook, however, the comma will always be inserted before the conjunction.

Each time a series occurs in the Reading and Writing Practice, it will be indicated thus in the shorthand: ser [,]

300 *Business vocabulary builder*

confronting Facing.

character reference One who vouches for the qualities, habits, and behavior of another.

foreman The man in charge of a gang or crew of workers.

succeeded Followed; took the place of.

Reading and writing practice

301 Brief-Form Letter

ma·jor

ser [,] [,]

ap [,]

Gov·ern·ment

par

[114]

302 de·sign·ers

ser

ex·hib·it
fif·ty

par

fore·most

[119]

303

ref·er·ence

ap

as·sis·tant

ser

ser

re·spon·si·ble

ser

[119]

304

par

al·ready
por·ing

ser

par

owe
due

60/

[130]

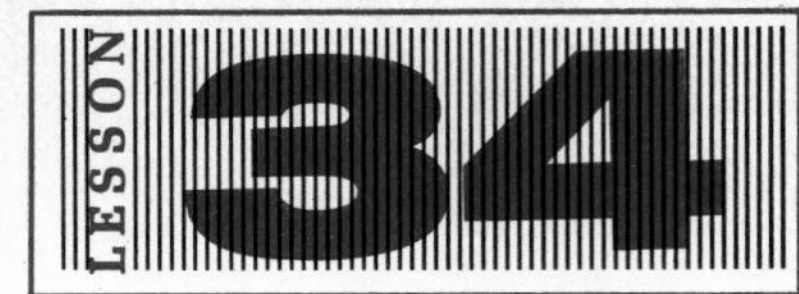

Principles

305 **Want in Phrases** In phrases, *want* is represented by *nt.*

I want · *he wants* · *if you want*

you want · *I wanted* · *do you want*

306 **Ort** The *r* is omitted in the combination *ort.*

Spell: re-p-o-t, report

report · *quart* · *sort*

exported · *quarterly* · *mortally*

307 **R Omitted in -ern, -erm** The *r* is omitted in the combinations *tern, term, thern, therm, dern, derm.*

Spell: t-e-n, turn

turn · *term* · *southern*

returned · *termed* · *thermometer*

eastern · *determine* · *modern*

308 **Word Endings -cal, -cle** The word endings *-cal, -cle* are represented by a disjoined *k.*

Spell: k-e-m-ical, chemical; a-r-t-ical, article

chemical · *technical* · *article*

critical · *practical* · *physically*

medical · *logical* · *politically*

309

Business vocabulary builder	
	decorators Those who design the inside of a home or office and select the furniture.
	clerical help Stenographers, clerks, bookkeepers, typists, etc.
	routine Commonplace; ordinary.

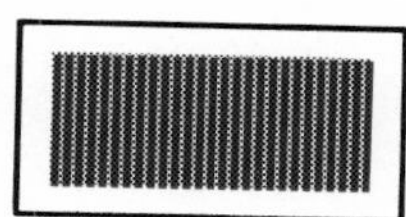

Reading and writing practice

310 Brief-Form Review Letter

par ser par ser [124]

agen·cies
hun·dreds
prac·ti·cal
ad·vice
wheth·er

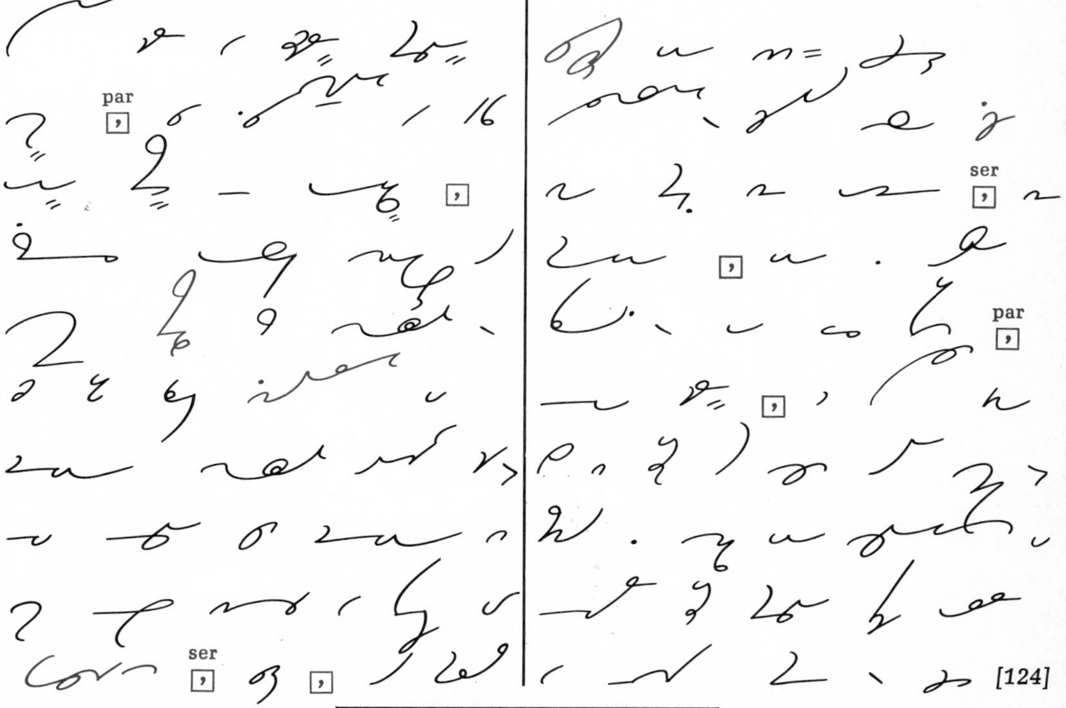

311

ser par

chem·i·cal
med·i·cal
pour·ing

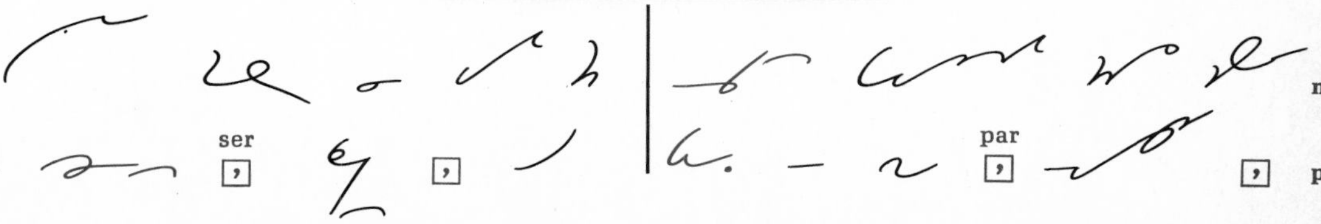

par

ser

ap

Tem·po·rary

[109]

312

par

ap

men's

par

log·i·cal

choose

[110]

313

sight

of·fi·cials

ser ser ser par

mod·ern

re·turn

[131]

BRIEF-FORM CHECK LIST

Are you making good use of the brief-form chart that appears on the inside back cover of your textbook? Remember, the brief forms represent many of the commonest words in the language; and the better you know them, the more rapid progress you will make in developing your shorthand speed.

Are you—

☐ **1** Spending a few minutes reading from the chart each day?

☐ **2** Timing yourself and trying to cut a few seconds off your reading time with each reading?

☐ **3** Reading the brief forms in a different order each time—from left to right, from right to left, from top to bottom, from bottom to top?

Principles

314 **Word Beginnings Inter-, Intr-, Enter-, Entr-** The word beginnings *inter-, intr-, enter-, entr-* are represented by a disjoined *n.* This disjoined word beginning, as well as other disjoined word beginnings that you will study in later lessons, is placed above the line of writing, close to the remainder of the word.

Inter-

Spell: *inter-s-t, interest*

interest	*international*	*interrupt*
interfere	*interview*	*interval*

Intr-

Spell: *intro-d-oo-s, introduce*

introduce	*introduces*	*intricate*

Enter-, Entr-

Spell: *enter-d, entered; enter-n-s, entrance*

entered	*enterprise*	*entrance*
entertained	*enterprises*	*entrances*

315 **Word Ending -ings** The word ending *-ings* is represented by a disjoined left *s.*

Spell: *o-p-n-ings, openings*

openings	*meetings*	*hearings*
savings	*evenings*	*holdings*

earnings proceedings clippings

316 **Omission of Words in Phrases** It is often possible to omit one or more unimportant words in a shorthand phrase. In the phrase *one of the*, for example, the word *of* is omitted; we write *one the*. When transcribing, the stenographer will insert *of*, as the phrase would make no sense without that word.

one of the *up to date* *will you please*

one of them *able to say* *many of these*

some of our *in the world* *in the future*

Building transcription skills

317 **SIMILAR-WORDS DRILL | quite, quiet**

quite Completely; entirely.

You will be quite pleased with our books.

quiet Free of noise; not excited.

Notice how quiet the room is.

He is a quiet person who seldom has anything to say.

318

Business vocabulary builder	
	absorb Soak up.
	interior Inside.
	instantly Without the least delay.
	expire Die; come to an end.

Reading and writing practice

319 Phrase Letter This letter contains several illustrations of the omission of words in phrases.

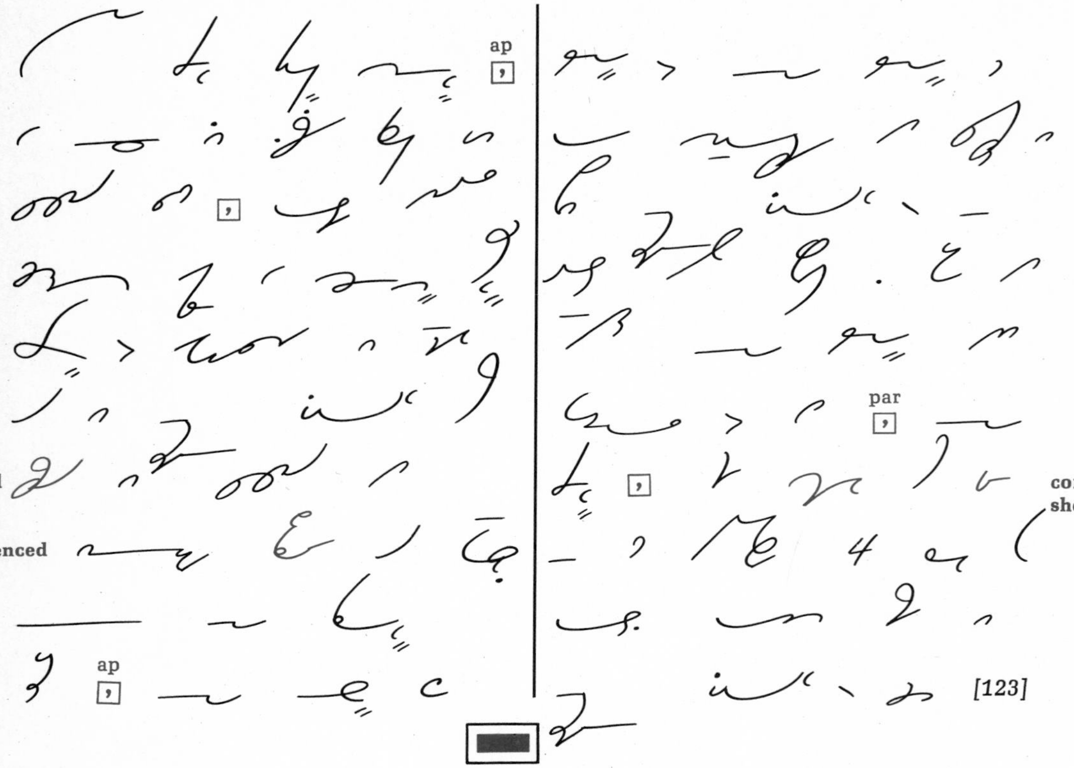

ap

par

as·signed

con·fi·dence shown

ex·pe·ri·enced

ap

[123]

320

ser

in·for·ma·tive

par

ap

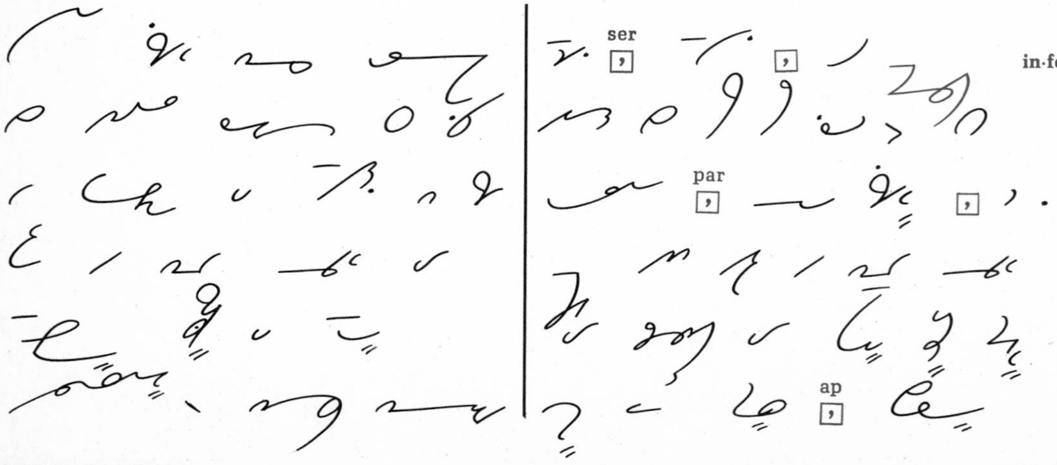

par par

par po·si·tion

ex·pens·es [130]

321

par

qui·et

par

ceil·ings

par

ab·sorb [133]

322 ap

in·tro·duc·to·ry [58]

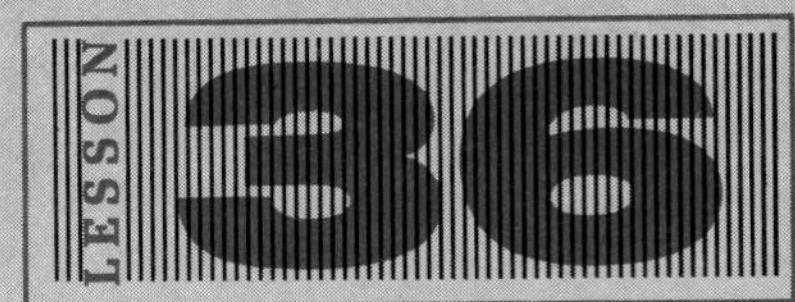

Recall

Lesson 36 is another breather. In Lesson 36 you will find the last principle of joining, a chart that contains a review of the shorthand devices you studied in Lessons 1 through 35, and a Reading and Writing Practice that tells what businessmen think about their secretaries. It should give you food for thought!

Principles of joining

323 The word endings *-ure* and *-ual* are represented by *r* and *l* except when those endings are preceded by a downstroke.

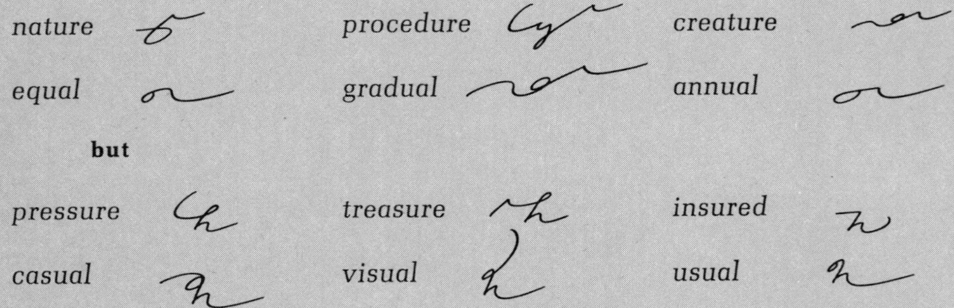

Accuracy practice

324 **O** **On** **Sho** **Non**

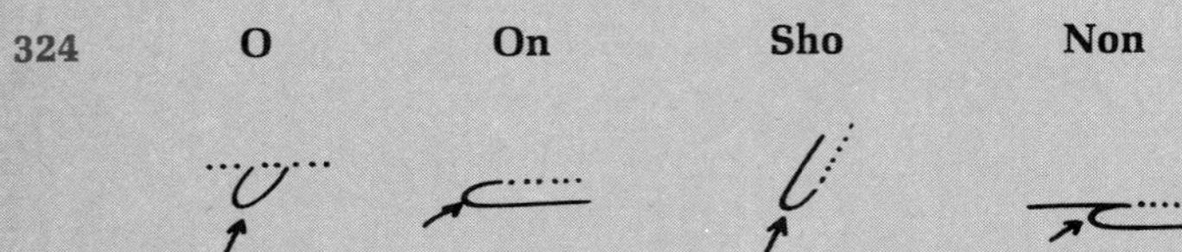

To write these combinations accurately:

a *Keep the* **o** *hook narrow, being sure that the* **beginning** *and* **end** *are on the same level of writing, as indicated by the dotted line.*

b *Keep the* **o** *in* **on** *and* **sho** *parallel with the consonant, as indicated by the dotted line.*

c *Make the* **beginning** *of the* **o** *in* **non** *retrace the* **end** *of the first* **n.**

d *Avoid a point at the* **curved** *part indicated by the arrows.*

practice drill

Of, know, low, own, home, hot, known, moan, shown.

325 **OO** **Noo** **Noom**

To write these combinations accurately:

a *Keep the* **oo** *hook narrow and deep.*

b *Keep the* **beginning** *and* **end** *of the hook on the same level of writing.*

c *In* **noo** *and* **noom,** *keep the hook parallel with the straight line that precedes it.*

d *In* **noom,** *retrace the* **beginning** *of the* **m** *on the* **bottom** *of the* **oo** *hook.*

e *Avoid a point at the places indicated by arrows.*

practice drill

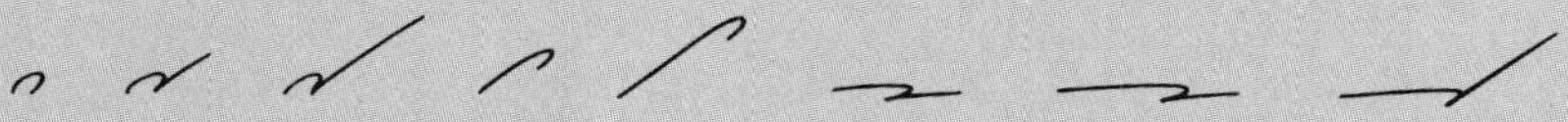

You-your, yours truly, you would, to-too-two, do, noon, moon, mood.

326 **Hard** **Hailed**

To write these combinations accurately:

a *Give the* **end** *of the* **r** *and of the* **l** *a lift upward.*

b *Do not lift the* **end** *too soon, or the strokes may resemble the* **nd, md** *combinations.*

practice drill

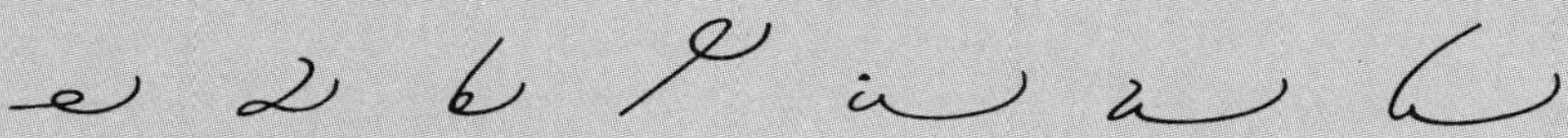

Neared, feared, cheered, dared, hold, sold, bold.

327 **Recall Chart** This chart contains a review of the shorthand devices you studied in previous lessons. It contains 78 brief forms, words, and phrases. Can you read the entire chart in 5 minutes?

BRIEF FORMS AND DERIVATIVES

WORDS

PHRASES

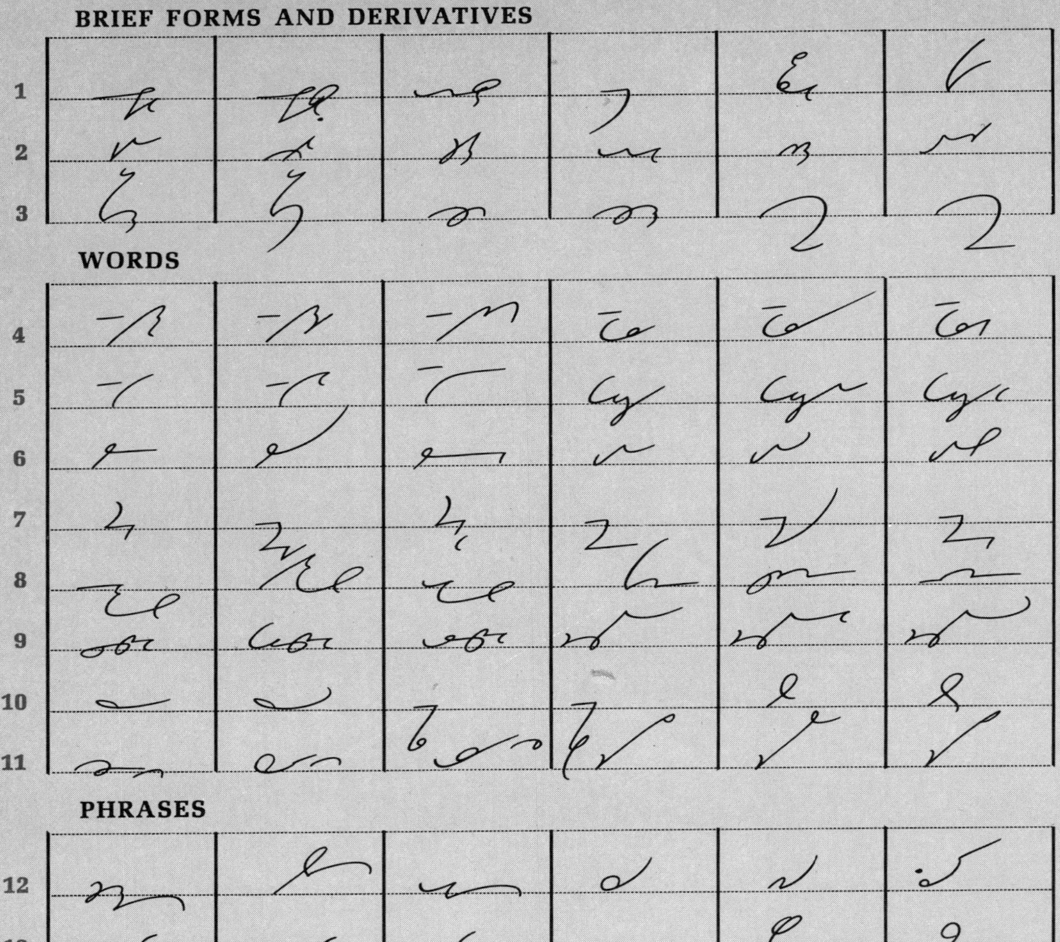

Building transcription skills

328

Business vocabulary builder	
	utmost Greatest.
	conservative Tending to maintain existing views or conditions.
	comprehensive Covering a wide range.
	indispensable Absolutely necessary; essential.

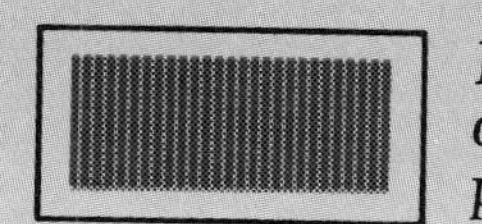

Reading and writing practice

329 Business Dress

par

clothes

oc·ca·sion

par

over·dressed

cheer·ful

ser

[159]

330 How Do You Look?

peeves

ap·pear·ance

par

jaws

ser

glam·our

night

ser

ap

cloth·ing

match col·ors

in·dis·pens·able

ser

[218]

331 Courtesy

cour·te·sy

par

ser

pleas·ant

pres·ence

ab·sence

[157]

greet

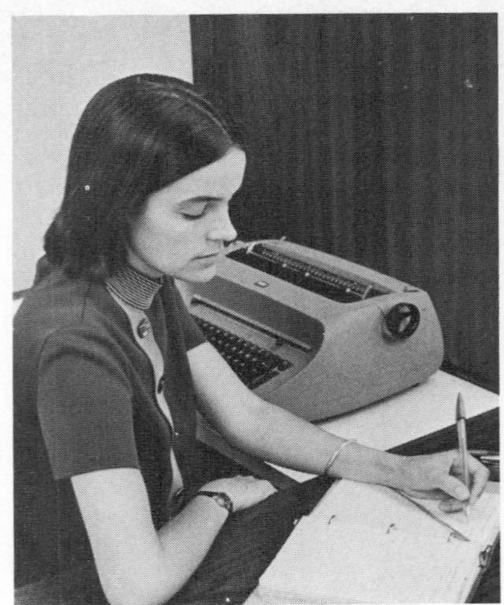

Chapter 7

What does a secretary do?

The answer to the question, "What does a secretary do?" will be different for almost every secretary. Most people think of a secretary as one who merely takes dictation and transcribes it. The fact is that taking dictation and transcribing it is a highly important— if not the most important—part of the secretary's job. But it is only one of many things that occupy her time.

The business executive thinks of the secretary as his "strong right arm." She frees him of the details of his job so that he will have time for managing people and procedures. Besides taking his dictation and transcribing it into good-looking letters, memoranda, and reports, she keeps his appointment calendar, answers his telephone, meets callers who wish to see him, files his important papers, writes letters and short reports, takes care of his mail, and arranges his business-travel accommodations. She may also do his banking and keep his income tax records—she may even shop for him and his family.

Each secretary has duties connected with her job that differ in some respects from those of another secretary, depending on the kind of work her boss is engaged in and his willingness to delegate details to her.

The secretary to an accountant, to a retail store owner, or to a company treasurer is likely to need to know bookkeeping. The secretary to a lawyer must know legal forms and terminology. The secretary to a doctor may be required to know something about medical laboratory procedures and

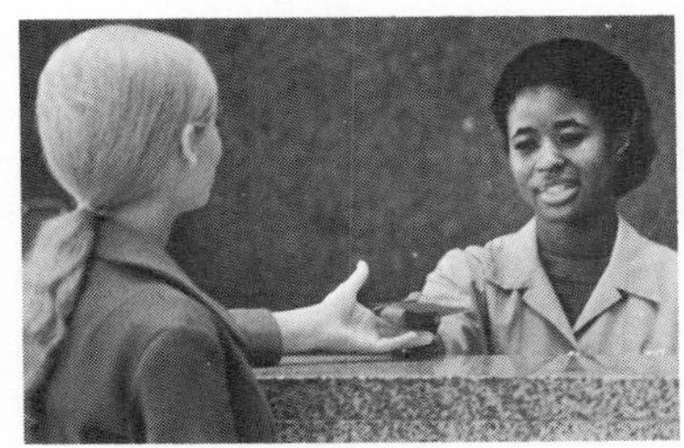

medical record keeping; she most certainly will have to know medical terminology. The secretary to a dentist may double as a technician—preparing the dental equipment for use, sterilizing instruments, assisting the dentist with X rays, keeping his records, and following up on appointments.

No two secretarial jobs are alike. Each is different, and each has its interesting facets. But there is a common thread that runs through all of them—taking dictation and transcribing it quickly and accurately.

Principles

332 Word Ending -ingly The word ending *-ingly* is represented by a disjoined *e* circle.

Spell: *a-k-o-ard-ingly, accordingly*

accordingly · *increasingly* · *surprisingly*
exceedingly · *willingly* · *knowingly*

333 Word Beginning Im- The word beginning *im-* is represented by *m*.

Spell: *im-p-o-t, import*

import · *impose* · *improve*
impressed · *impossible* · *improperly*

334 Word Beginning Em- The word beginning *em-* is also represented by *m*.

Spell: *em-p-l-oi, employ*

employ · *embrace* · *emphatically*
emphasis · *embarrassed* · *empire*

335 Im-, Em- Followed by a Vowel When *im-, em-* are followed by a vowel, they are written in full.

immodest · *immoral* · *emotionally*

336 Omission of Minor Vowel When two vowel sounds come together, the minor vowel may be omitted.

courteous · *genuine* · *period*
serious · *situated* · *theory*

previously union ideal

Building transcription skills

337 **PUNCTUATION PRACTICE | , if clause**

One of the most frequent errors made by the beginning transcriber is the failure to make a complete sentence. In most cases the incomplete sentence is a dependent or subordinate clause introduced by *if, as,* or *when.* The dependent or subordinate clause deceives the transcriber because it is a complete sentence except that it is introduced by a word such as *if;* therefore, it requires another clause to complete the thought.

The dependent or subordinate clause often signals the coming of the main clause by means of a subordinate conjunction. The commonest subordinating conjunctions are *if, as,* and *when.* Other subordinating conjunctions are *though, although, whether, unless, because, since, while, where, after, whenever, until, before,* and *now.* In this lesson you will consider clauses introduced by *if.*

A subordinate clause introduced by *if* and followed by the main clause is separated from the main clause by a comma.

If you can do this for us, we will be exceedingly grateful.

If I can help you obtain material for the bulletin, please let me know.

Each time a subordinate clause beginning with *if* occurs in the Reading and Writing Practice, it will be indicated thus in the shorthand: if ,

338

Business vocabulary builder	
	exceedingly Very much.
	previous Coming before.
	imperative Not to be avoided; urgent.

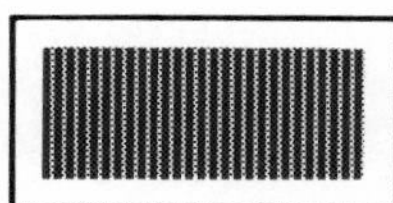

Reading and writing practice

339 **Brief-Form Review Letter**

ap , em·ploy·ee

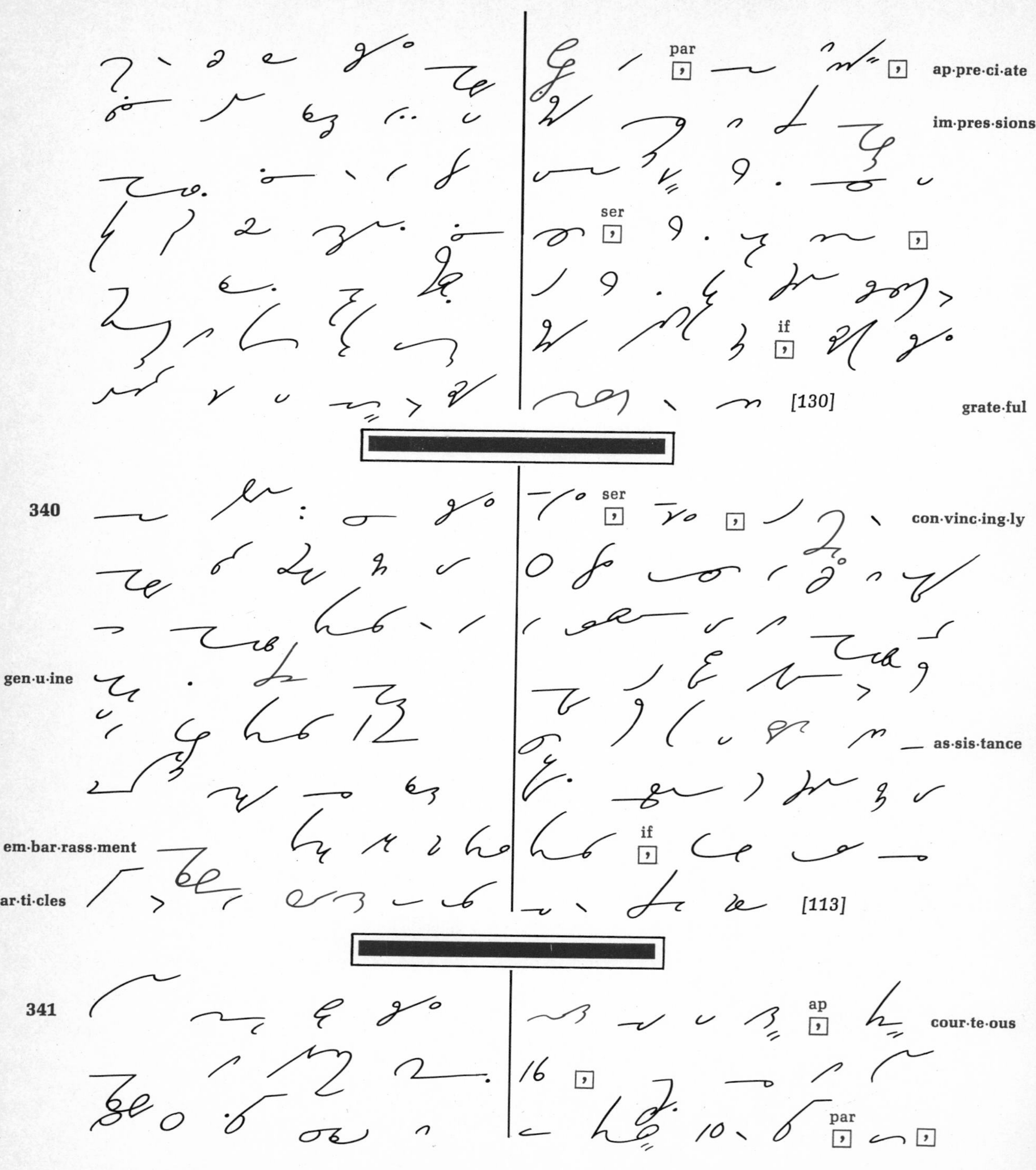
par
ap·pre·ci·ate
im·pres·sions
ser
if
[130]
grate·ful
340
ser
con·vinc·ing·ly
gen·u·ine
as·sis·tance
em·bar·rass·ment
if
ar·ti·cles
[113]
341
ap
cour·te·ous
16
10
par

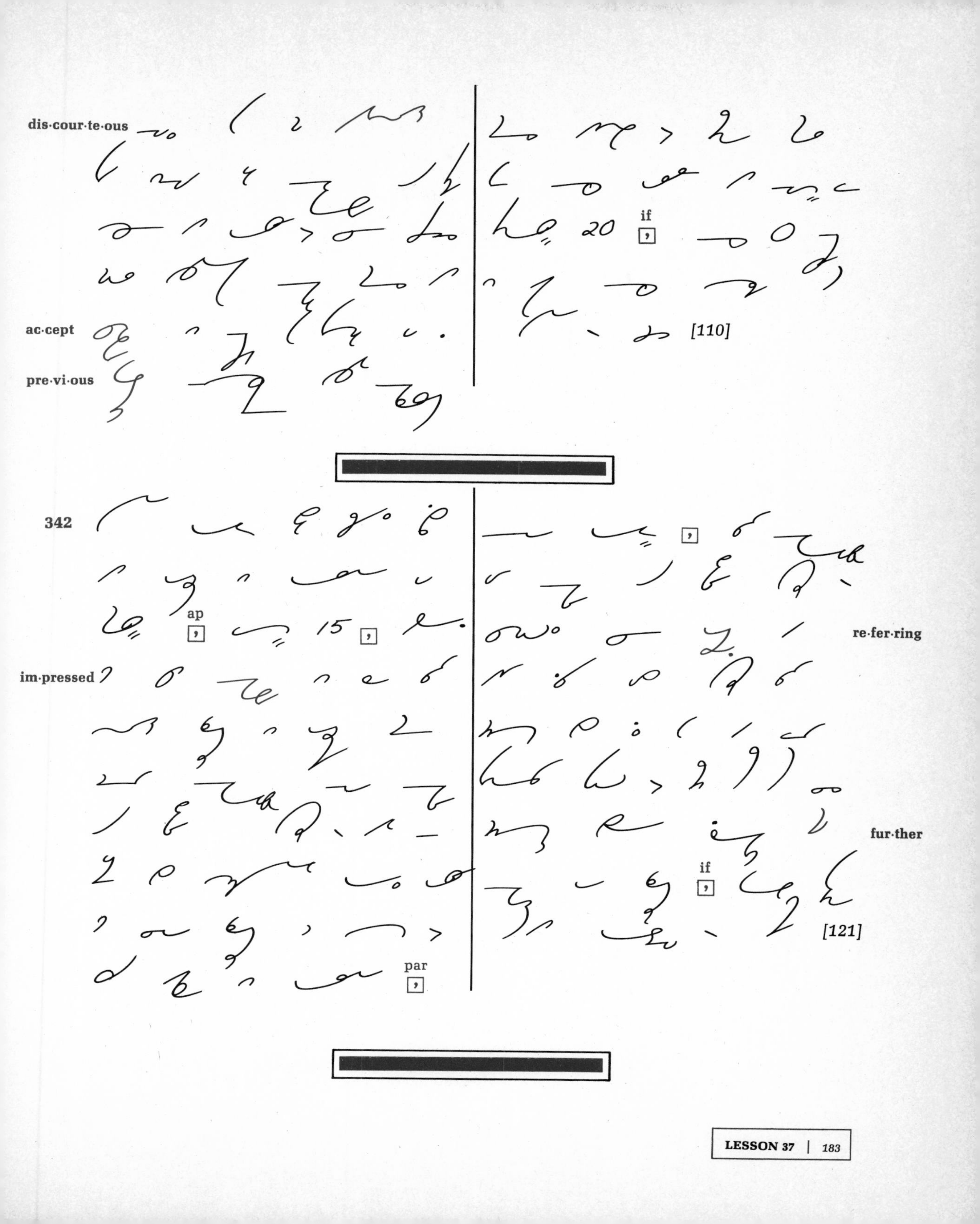

dis·cour·te·ous

if

[110]

ac·cept

pre·vi·ous

342

re·fer·ring

ap

15

im·pressed

fur·ther

if

[121]

par

Principles

343 Word Ending -ship The word ending *-ship* is represented by a disjoined *sh.*

Spell: *s-t-e-m-ship, steamship*

steamship membership townships

friendship relationship scholarships

344 Word Beginning Sub- The word beginning *sub-* is represented by s.

Spell: *sub-m-e-t, submit*

submit substantial sublet

subscribed subdivide suburbs

345 Joining of Hook and Circle Vowels When a hook and a circle vowel come together, they are written in the order in which they are pronounced.

poem poetry folio

poet radio snowy

Building transcription skills

346 PUNCTUATION PRACTICE | , as clause

A subordinate clause introduced by *as* and followed by a main clause is separated from the main clause by a comma.

As you know, there is a substantial sum due on your account.

As you will see by the enclosed report, our plans for the convention are almost complete.

Each time a subordinate clause beginning with *as* occurs in the Reading and Writing Practice, it will be indicated thus in the shorthand: as [,]

347

Business vocabulary builder	
	colleagues Fellow workers.
	substantially To a large extent.
	jeopardizing Risking the loss of.

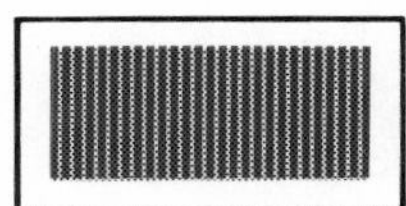

Reading and writing practice

348 Brief-Form Review Letter

ser [,] [,] if [,]

col·leagues

[126] sub·stan·tial·ly

349 as [,]

can·cel·ing

sub·scrip·tion

sum

par

as

[107]

350

ser

16 17

18

10/

if

par

au·to·mat·i·cal·ly

as

as·so·ci·a·tion

bul·le·tin

an·nu·al

[117]

351

16

as

50/

com·pe·ti·tion

if

sub·mit·ted

ap

as

par

prompt·ly

10

[113]

352

as

over·due

jeop·ar·diz·ing

par

dis·turb·ing

re·la·tion·ship

pre·serve

550

[110]

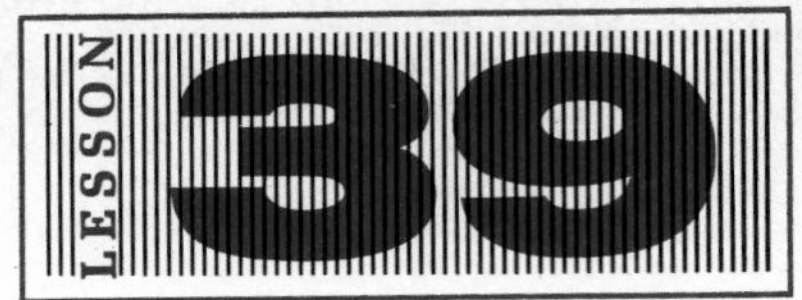

Principles

353 Word Ending -rity The word ending *-rity* is represented by a disjoined r.

Spell: s-e-k-rity, security

security | majority | sincerity
authorities | minority | prosperity
maturity | popularity | celebrity

354 Word Ending -lity The word ending *-lity* is represented by a disjoined *l*.

Spell: a-b-lity, ability

ability | possibility | locality
facilities | reliability | qualities
personality | utility | vitality

355 Word Ending -lty The word ending *-lty* is also represented by a disjoined *l*.

Spell: f-a-k-ulty, faculty

faculty | penalty | loyalty

356 Word Endings -self, -selves The word ending *-self* is represented by s; *-selves*, by ses.

Spell: h-e-r-self, herself; your-selves, yourselves

herself | himself | myself

itself	*yourself*	*yourselves*
oneself	*themselves*	*ourselves*

Building transcription skills

357 PUNCTUATION PRACTICE | , when clause

A subordinate clause introduced by *when* and followed by the main clause is separated from the main clause by a comma.

When I was in town last month, I discussed with you the possibility of holding our meetings in your hotel.

When you delay paying your bills, you are endangering your credit reputation.

Each time a subordinate clause beginning with *when* occurs in the Reading and Writing Practice, it will be indicated thus in the shorthand: when [,]

358

Business vocabulary builder	
	faculty Teachers in a school.
	reality Fact; a real event.
	security holdings Stocks and bonds that an investor owns.
	impressive Creating a feeling of admiration.

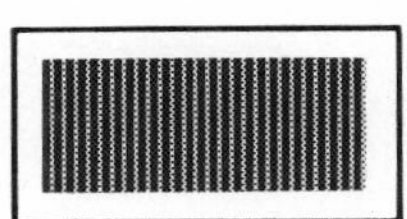

Reading and writing practice

359 Brief-Form Review Letter

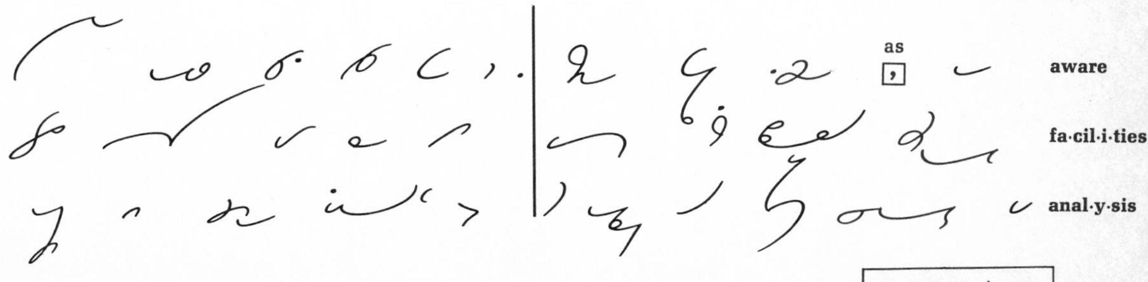

ap

par

[102]

360

when

dis·cussed

fac·ul·ty

ser

16 17

par

26 par

ac·knowl·edge

[107]

361

fa·mil·iar·i·ty

be·lieve

par

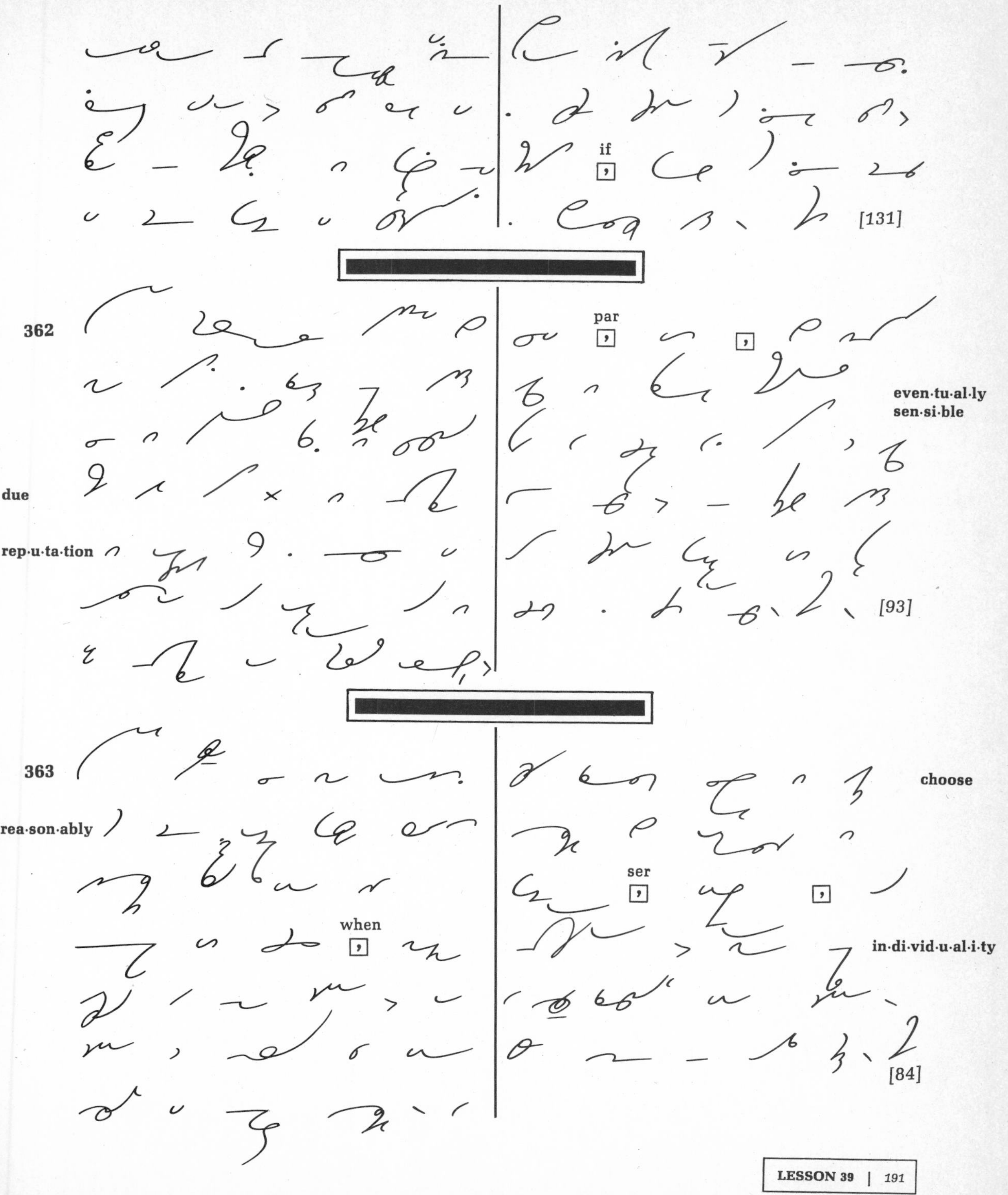
if
[131]
362
par
even·tu·al·ly
sen·si·ble
due
rep·u·ta·tion
[93]
363
choose
rea·son·ably
ser
when
in·di·vid·u·al·i·ty
[84]

Principles

364 **Abbreviated Words—in Families** Many long words may be abbreviated in shorthand by dropping the endings. This device is also used in longhand, as *Jan.* for *January.* The extent to which you use this device will depend on your familiarity with the words and with the subject matter of the dictation. When in doubt, write it out! The ending of a word is not dropped when a special shorthand word-ending form has been provided, such as *-lity.*

Notice how many of the words written with this abbreviating device fall naturally into families of similar endings.

-tribute

tribute	*contribute*	*distribute*
attribute	*contributed*	*distributor*

-quent

consequent, consequence	*subsequent*	*frequent*
consequently	*subsequently*	*eloquent*

-quire

require	*inquiries*	*inquiry*
requirement	*inquired*	*esquire*

-titute

substitute	*institute*	*constitution*

-titude

aptitude	*gratitude*	*latitude*

365 **PUNCTUATION PRACTICE | , introductory**

A comma is used to separate the subordinate clause from a following main clause. You have already studied the application of this rule to subordinate clauses introduced by *if, as,* and *when.* Here are additional examples:

While I understand the statement, I do not agree with it.

Although it was only 3 o'clock, he closed the office.

Before you award your next advertising contract, give us an opportunity to discuss it with you.

A comma is also used after introductory words or phrases such as *furthermore, on the contrary,* and *for instance.*

Furthermore, you made a mistake in grammar.

On the contrary, you are at fault.

For your convenience in sending me the information I need, I am enclosing a stamped envelope.

Each time a subordinate (or introductory) word, phrase, or clause other than one beginning with *if, as,* or *when* occurs in the Reading and Writing Practice, it will be indicated thus in the shorthand: intro [,]

▶ Note: If the subordinate clause or other introductory expression follows the main clause, the comma is usually not necessary.

I am enclosing a stamped envelope for your convenience in sending me the information I need.

366

Business vocabulary builder	
	counsel *(noun)* Advice.
	eloquent Marked by forceful expression.
	distributors Agents who market goods.
	attributes *(noun)* Characteristics; qualities.

Reading and writing practice

367 **Brief-Form Review Letter**

re·spon·si·ble

intro

ex·traor·di·nar·i·ly

ser

growth

ex·pe·ri·enced

par

[117]

368

ap

el·o·quent

intro

wheth·er

intro

prep·a·ra·tion

par

[124]

369

rec·om·mend·ing

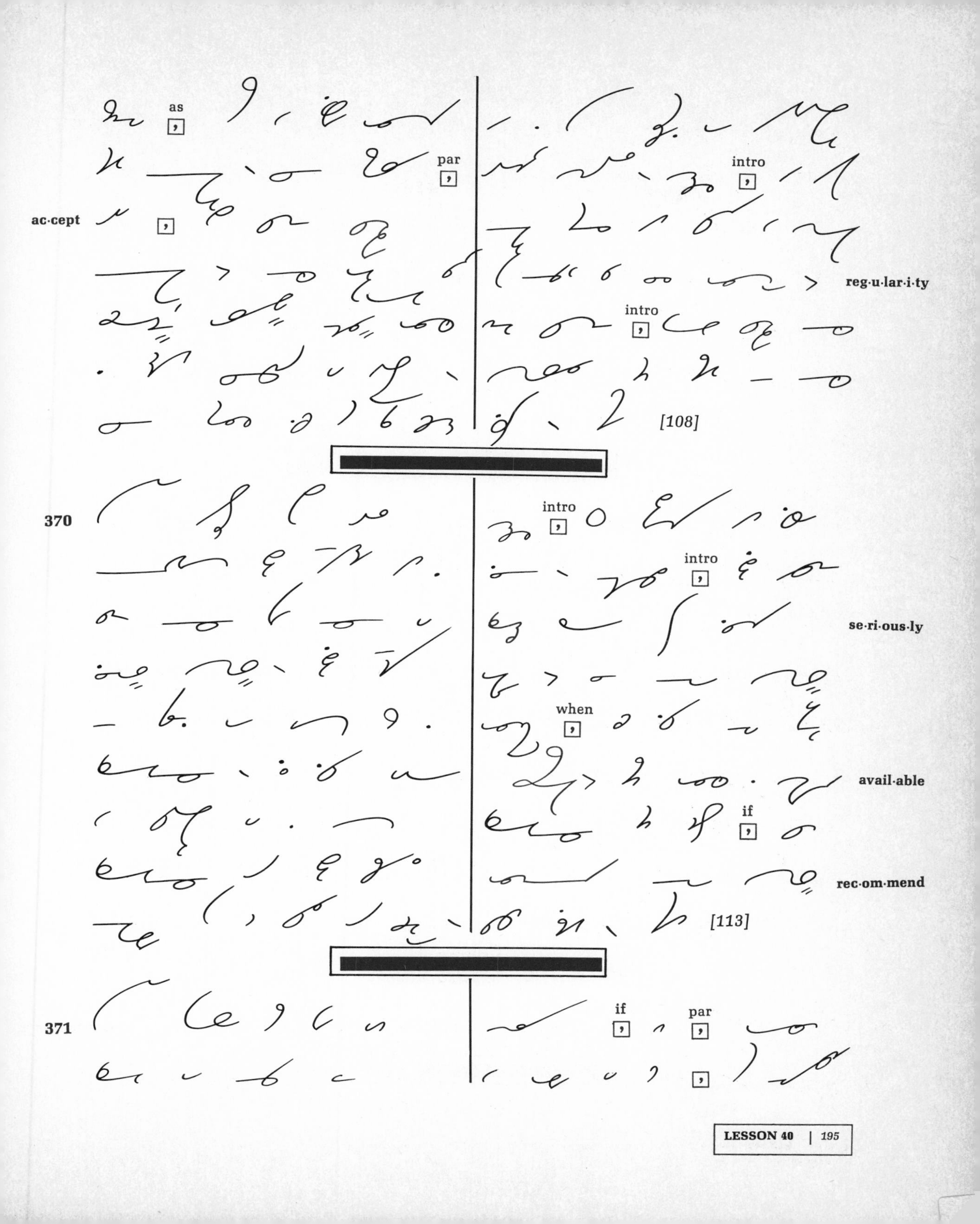

as

par

ac·cept

intro

reg·u·lar·i·ty

intro

[108]

370

intro

intro

se·ri·ous·ly

when

avail·able

if

rec·om·mend

[113]

371

if

par

de·lin·quent

when

intro

dis·trib·u·tor

par

intro

par

co·op·er·ate

[107]

372 Addition

[59]

Principles

373 Abbreviated Words—Not in Families The ending may be omitted from some long words even though they do not fall into a family.

anniversary	*equivalent*	*privilege*
convenient, convenience	*significant, significance*	*privileges*
memorandum	*reluctant, reluctance*	*privileged*

374 Word Beginning Trans- The word beginning *trans-* is represented by a disjoined *t*.

Spell: *trans-a-k-t, transact*

transact	*transported*	*transplant*
transacted	*transmission*	*transit*
translate	*transferred*	*transcriber*

375 Word Ending -ification The word ending *-ification* is represented by a disjoined *f*.

Spell: *k-l-a-s-ification, classification*

classification	*notification*	*specifications*
justification	*modification*	*qualifications*
verification	*ratification*	*identification*

Building transcription skills

376 SIMILAR-WORDS DRILL | their, there

their Belonging to them.

I cannot approve the plans in their present form.

there In or to that place.

I went there at his request.

(Also watch out for *they're*, the contraction of *they are*.)

377

Business vocabulary builder	
	significant Important.
	clarification Act of making something clear or understandable.
	gratification Satisfaction.
	reluctant Unwilling.

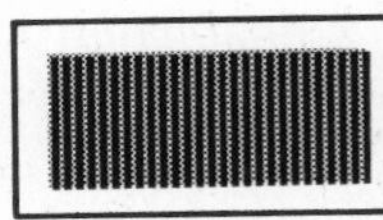

Reading and writing practice

378 Brief-Form Review Letter

ar·ea

em·ploy·ees

con·ve·nient

par

ac·cept

priv·i·lege

Gov·ern·ment's

ap

[124]

379

sig·nif·i·cant

en·gi·neers

par

par

proud

ser

re·vi·sion

[115]

as

380

ap

an·ni·ver·sa·ry

ap

16

10

ac·knowl·edge

suc·cess

[118]

381

intro

intro

if

their

knowl·edge

ap

per·mis·sion

there

[114]

382

as

past

if

[72]

Recall

There are no new shorthand devices for you to learn in Lesson 42. However, it does contain an Accuracy Practice and a review of the word beginnings and endings you have studied thus far. The Reading and Writing Practice contains some suggestions that you should heed carefully if you wish to get ahead in business.

Accuracy practice

383 **My** **Lie** **Fight**

To write these combinations accurately:

a *Join the circle in the same way that you would join an* **a** *circle, but turn the* **end** *inside the circle.*

b *Before turning the* **end** *of the circle inside, be sure that the stroke touches the stroke to which the* **i** *is joined.*

c *Avoid making a point at the places indicated by arrows.*

practice drill

My, night, sight, line, mile.

384 **Ow** **Oi**

To write these combinations accurately:

a *Keep the hooks deep and narrow.*

b *Place the circles* **outside** *the hooks as indicated by the dotted lines.*

practice drill

How-out, now, doubt, scout, toy, soil, annoy.

385 **Th** **Nt, Nd** **Mt, Md**

To write these combinations accurately:

a *Slant the strokes as indicated by the dotted lines.*

b *Start these strokes to the right and upward.*

practice drill

There are, and will, empty, health, lined, ashamed.

Compare:

Hint, heard; tamed, detailed.

386 **Recall Chart** There are 84 words in the following chart containing word beginnings and word endings. Can you read them in 5 minutes?

WORD BEGINNINGS AND ENDINGS

1

2

3

4

5

6

7

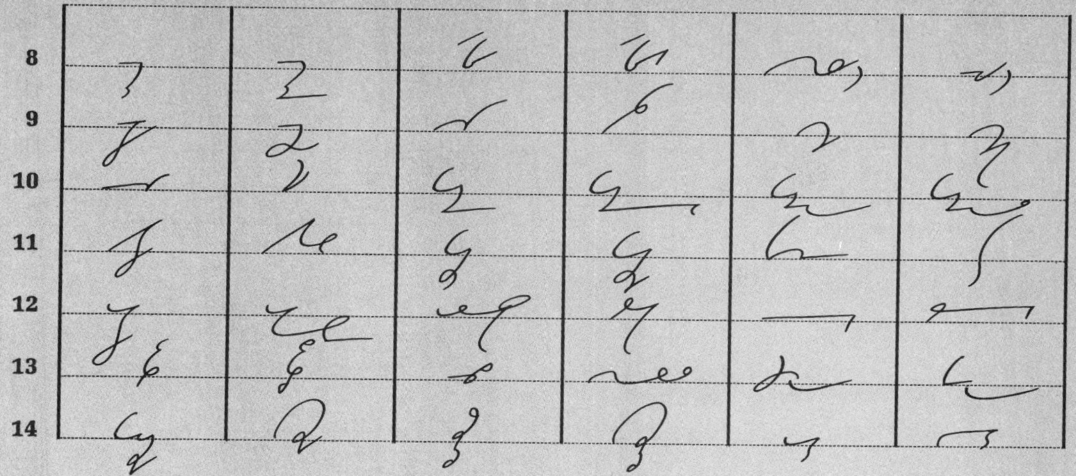

Building transcription skills

387

Business vocabulary builder	
glance (*noun*)	A quick look.
vaguely	In an unclear manner; uncertainly.
compile	Collect facts into a list or into a volume.

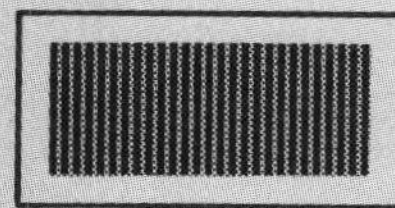

Reading and writing practice

Reading Scoreboard Twelve lessons have gone by since you last measured your reading speed. You have, of course, continued to do each Reading and Writing Practice faithfully, and consequently your reading speed will reflect this faithfulness! The following table will help you measure your reading speed on the *first reading* of Lesson 42.

Lesson 42 contains 350 words

If you read Lesson 42 in **10 minutes** *your reading rate is* **35 words a minute**
If you read Lesson 42 in **12 minutes** *your reading rate is* **29 words a minute**
If you read Lesson 42 in **14 minutes** *your reading rate is* **25 words a minute**
If you read Lesson 42 in **16 minutes** *your reading rate is* **22 words a minute**
If you read Lesson 42 in **18 minutes** *your reading rate is* **19 words a minute**
If you read Lesson 42 in **20 minutes** *your reading rate is* **17 words a minute**

If you can read Lesson 42 through the first time in less than 10 minutes, you are doing well. If you take considerably longer than 20 minutes, perhaps you should:

1 *Pay closer attention in class while the shorthand devices are being presented to you.*
2 *Spend less time trying to decipher outlines that you cannot read.*
3 *Review, occasionally, all the brief forms you have studied through the chart on the inside back cover.*

388 How Is Your Vocabulary?

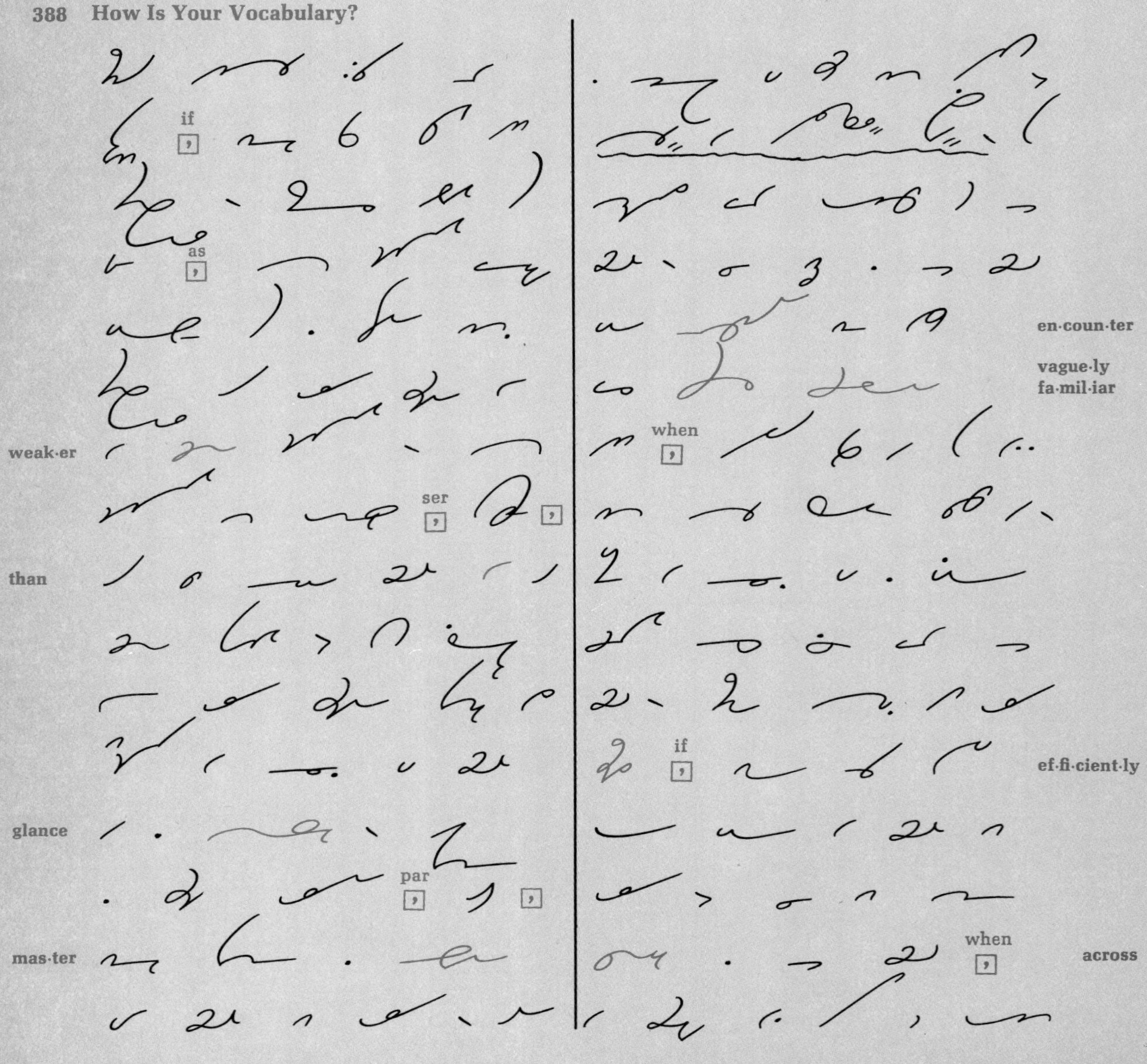

lan·guage

usu·al·ly

read·i·ly

intro

intro

when

lat·er

intro

am·bi·tion

if

con·stant·ly

[350]

Chapter 8

The secretary communicates

What is communication? In the office, communication refers to anything having to do with the written or spoken word. Most of what the secretary does in the office is concerned with communications in one form or another.

In the first place, she talks in person or by phone to many people outside the company for which she works — friends of her boss, customers, business executives, sales representatives, messengers, and various visitors. She talks with many people inside the company — her boss, other executives, secretaries, department heads, accountants, repairmen, receptionists, and janitors. She talks informally in groups and more formally in meetings. Oral communication goes on con-

stantly — much of it highly important, some of it trivial. All of it, however, requires skill. Skill in "handling" people by means of the spoken word is vital to harmonious relations both inside and outside the company. The secretary's boss depends on her to say the right thing at the right time, because what she says and how she says it reflects on him.

The secretary needs skill in written communications, too. She must know how to write letters — letters asking for information, letters answering requests for information, and thank-you letters for favors received. She needs to know how to write interoffice memos — memos about meetings, about changes in procedures, or about routine matters of

company business. She may write telegrams, minutes of meetings, and messages of various kinds.

The extent to which the secretary is given responsibility for written communications depends entirely on her own initiative and the willingness of her boss to delegate these details to her. In all cases, however, her shorthand comes in very handy. Shorthand is an ideal instrument for composing written communications of all kinds. It helps the writer to think through what he is going to say before he types it — he can revise to his heart's content without sacrificing too much time and energy. Form the habit now of using your shorthand for thinking through all your written work.

Principles

389 Word Ending -ulate The word ending *-ulate* is represented by a disjoined *oo* hook.

Spell: *a-k-u-m-ulate, accumulate*

accumulate *tabulate* *regulate*

circulate *stipulate* *regulator*

congratulate *stipulated* *regulates*

390 Word Ending -ulation The word ending *-ulation* is represented by *oo-tion.*

Spell: *s-e-r-k-ulation, circulation*

circulation *tabulation* *stimulation*

population *calculation* *congratulations*

391 Word Beginning Post- The word beginning *post-* is represented by a disjoined *p.*

Spell: *post-j, postage*

postage *post office* *postpone*

postman *postmark* *postponed*

392 Word Beginning Super- The word beginning *super-* is represented by a disjoined right *s.*

Spell: *super-v-ī-s, supervise*

supervise *superintendent* *superhuman*

supersede *superimpose* *superior*

393 PUNCTUATION PRACTICE ▌, conjunction

A comma is used to separate two independent clauses that are joined by one of the following conjunctions: *and, but, or, for, nor.*

An independent clause (sometimes called a main or a principal clause) is one that has a subject and a predicate and that could stand alone as a complete sentence.

Your speech was taped by one of our people, and I have had my secretary transcribe it.

The first independent clause is:

Your speech was taped by one of our people

and the second independent clause is:

I have had my secretary transcribe it

Both clauses could stand as separate sentences, with a period after each. Because the thoughts of the two clauses are closely related, however, the clauses were joined to form one sentence. Because the two independent clauses are connected by the coordinating conjunction *and*, a comma is used between them, before the conjunction.

Each time this use of the comma occurs in the Reading and Writing Practice, it will be indicated thus in the shorthand: conj [,]

394

Business vocabulary builder	**stimulating** Exciting to greater activity. **superb** Of great excellence. **circulation** The total number of copies of a publication distributed per issue.

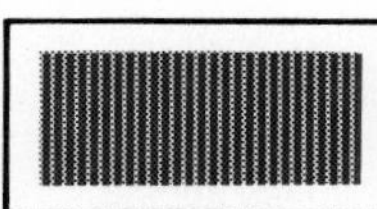

Reading and writing practice

395 Brief-Form Review Letter

par

cal·cu·la·tor

conj

par

par

be·gin·ning

[117]

396

tran·scribe

ap

ser

su·per·vi·sors

su·perb

ap

su·per·vi·so·ry

Ex·plo·sion

taped

conj

[111]

397

sup·plies

250

ser

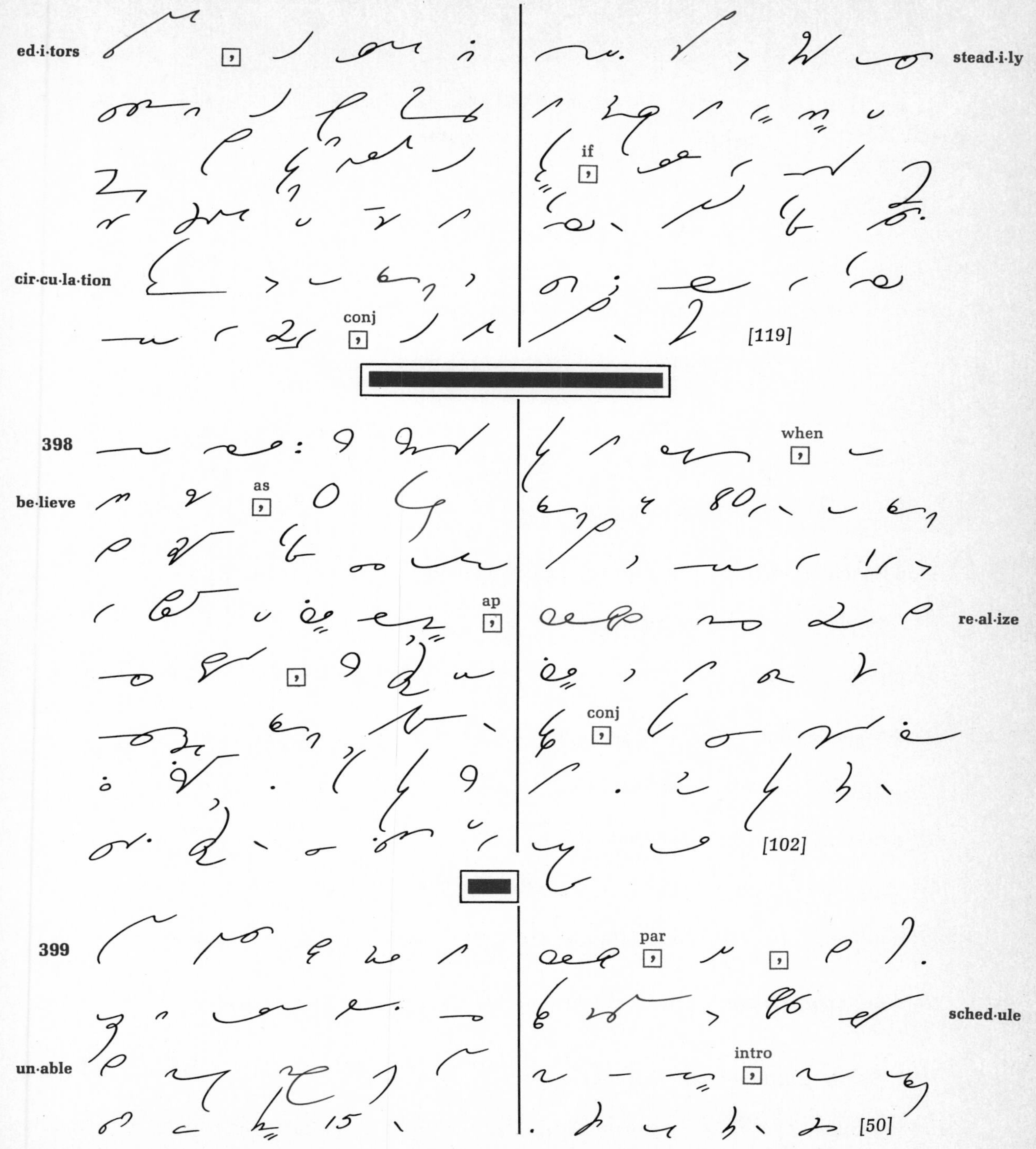

ed·i·tors
steadily
stead·i·ly
if
cir·cu·la·tion
conj
[119]
398
when
be·lieve
as
80
ap
re·al·ize
conj
[102]
399
par
sched·ule
un·able
intro
15
[50]

Principles

400 Word Ending -sume The word ending *-sume* is represented by *s-m*.

Spell: *re-s-m, resume*

resume	assumes	consume
resumes	presume	consumer
assume	presumably	consumed

401 Word Ending -sumption The word ending *-sumption* is represented by *s-m-shun*.

Spell: *re-s-m-shun, resumption*

resumption	consumption	presumption

402 Word Beginning Self- The word beginning *self-* is represented by a disjoined left *s*.

Spell: *self-m-a-d, self-made*

self-made	self-reliant	selfish
self-supporting	self-styled	selfishness
self-confident	self-defense	selfishly

403 Word Beginning Circum- The word beginning *circum-* is also represented by a disjoined left *s*.

Spell: *circum-s-ten-s, circumstance*

circumstance	circumstances	circumstantial

404 PUNCTUATION PRACTICE | , and omitted

When two or more adjectives modify the same noun, they are separated by commas.

He was a quiet, efficient worker.

However, the comma is not used if the first adjective modifies the combined idea of the second adjective plus the noun.

She wore a beautiful green dress.

▶ Note: You can quickly determine whether to insert a comma between two consecutive adjectives by mentally placing *and* between them. If the sentence makes good sense with *and* inserted between the adjectives, then the comma is used. For example, the first illustration would make good sense if it read:

He was a quiet and *efficient worker.*

Each time this use of the comma occurs in the Reading and Writing Practice, it will be indicated thus in the shorthand: and o [,]

405

Business vocabulary builder	
	clarity Clearness.
	dynamic Having lots of force or energy.
	consumer One who buys or uses merchandise or services.
	manuscript The written or typewritten copy prepared for publication.

Reading and writing practice

406 Brief-Form Review Letter

ap [,] [,] intro [,]

self-in·ter·est

conj

per·son·al·ly

and o

[121]

407

when

clar·i·ty

and o

self-as·sur·ance

ser

dy·nam·ic

self-re·li·ance

qual·i·ties

if

if

[105]

408

as

sub·scrip·tion

su·per·vi·sors

conj

be·gin·ning
cur·rent

[88]

409

when

mod·ern

and o

wheth·er

oc·curred

intro

trans·mit·ting

[111]

PERSONAL-USE CHECK LIST

Do you substitute shorthand for longhand wherever possible when you—

☐ **1** Take down your daily assignments?

☐ **2** Correspond with your friends who know shorthand?

☐ **3** Draft compositions and reports?

☐ **4** Make entries in your diary?

☐ **5** Make notes to yourself on things to do, people to see, appointments to keep, etc.?

Principles

410 Word Ending -hood The word ending *-hood* is represented by a disjoined *d*.

Spell: *n-a-b-r-hood, neighborhood*

neighborhood	*childhood*	*motherhood*
manhood	*brotherhood*	*boyhood*

411 Word Ending -ward The word ending *-ward* is also represented by a disjoined *d*.

Spell: *o-n-ward, onward*

onward	*backward*	*forward*
afterward	*awkwardly*	*forwarded*

412 Ul *Ul* is represented by *oo* when it precedes a forward or upward stroke.

Spell: *con-s-ul-t, consult*

consult	*ultimate*	*multiply*
result	*adults*	*culminate*

413 Quantities and Amounts Here are a few more helpful abbreviations for quantities and amounts.

$500	*5,000,000,000*	*several hundred*
5,000,000	*a dollar*	*4 pounds*
$5,000,000	*a million*	*8 feet*

▶ Notice that the *m* for *million* is written beside the figure, as a positive distinction from *hundred,* in which the *n* is written underneath the figure.

414 SPELLING FAMILIES | silent e dropped before -ing

An effective device to improve your ability to spell is to study words in related groups, or spelling families, in which all the words contain the same spelling problem, for example, words in which silent *e* is dropped before *ing*.

To get the most benefit from these spelling families, practice them in this way:

1 *Spell each word aloud, pausing slightly after each syllable.*

2 *Write the word once in longhand, spelling it aloud as you write it.*

You will find several of the words in the following spelling family used in the Reading and Writing Practice.

Words In Which Silent E Is Dropped Before -ing

de·sir·ing	**guid·ing**	**pro·duc·ing**
en·clos·ing	**hous·ing**	**re·ceiv·ing**
ex·am·in·ing	**in·creas·ing**	**typ·ing**
forc·ing	**mer·chan·dis·ing**	**us·ing**

415

Business vocabulary builder

consultation Act of asking for advice or opinion.

ultimately Finally.

awkward Causing embarrassment.

Reading and writing practice

416 Brief-Form Review Letter

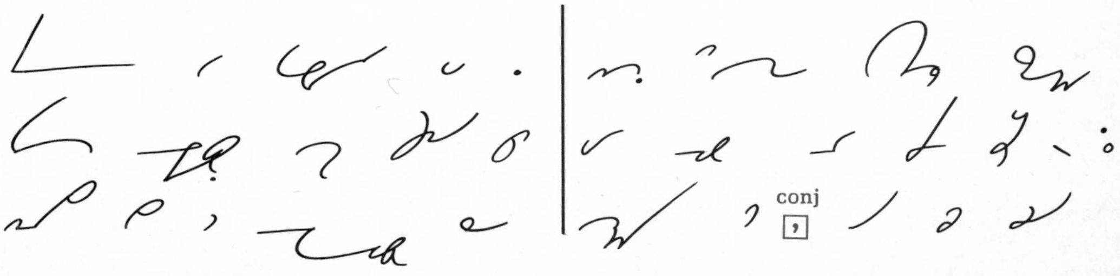

conj

ex·pe·ri·enced

sur·vey

ef·fi·cient

intro

if

neigh·bor·hood

conj

[125]

417

ap

en·gi·neers

when

and o

for·wards

intro

[94]

418

intro

awk·ward

and o

as

at·tor·neys

sit·u·a·tion

intro

ser

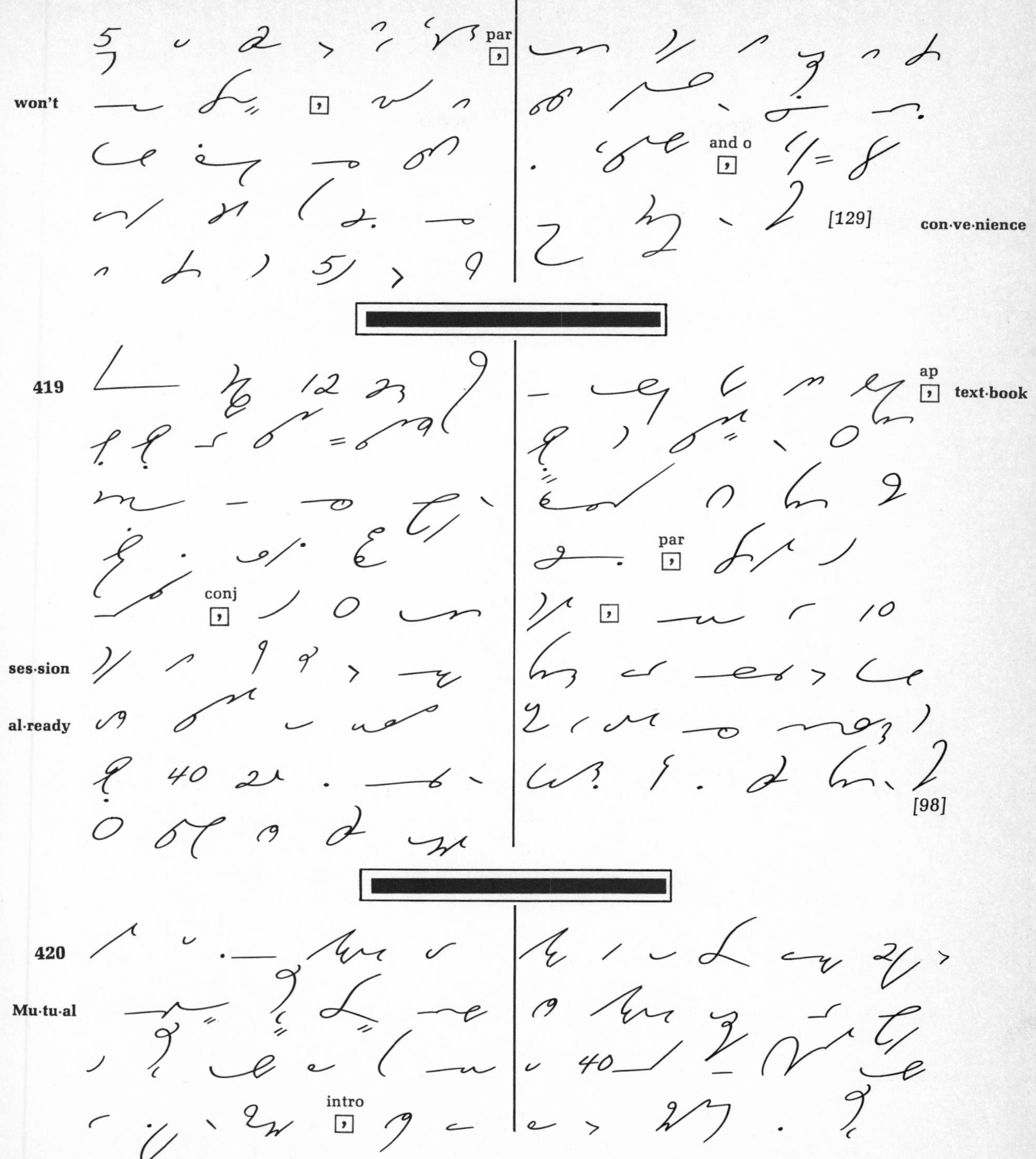
par
won't
and o
[129]
con·ve·nience
419
ap
text·book
par
conj
ses·sion
al·ready
[98]
420
Mu·tu·al
intro

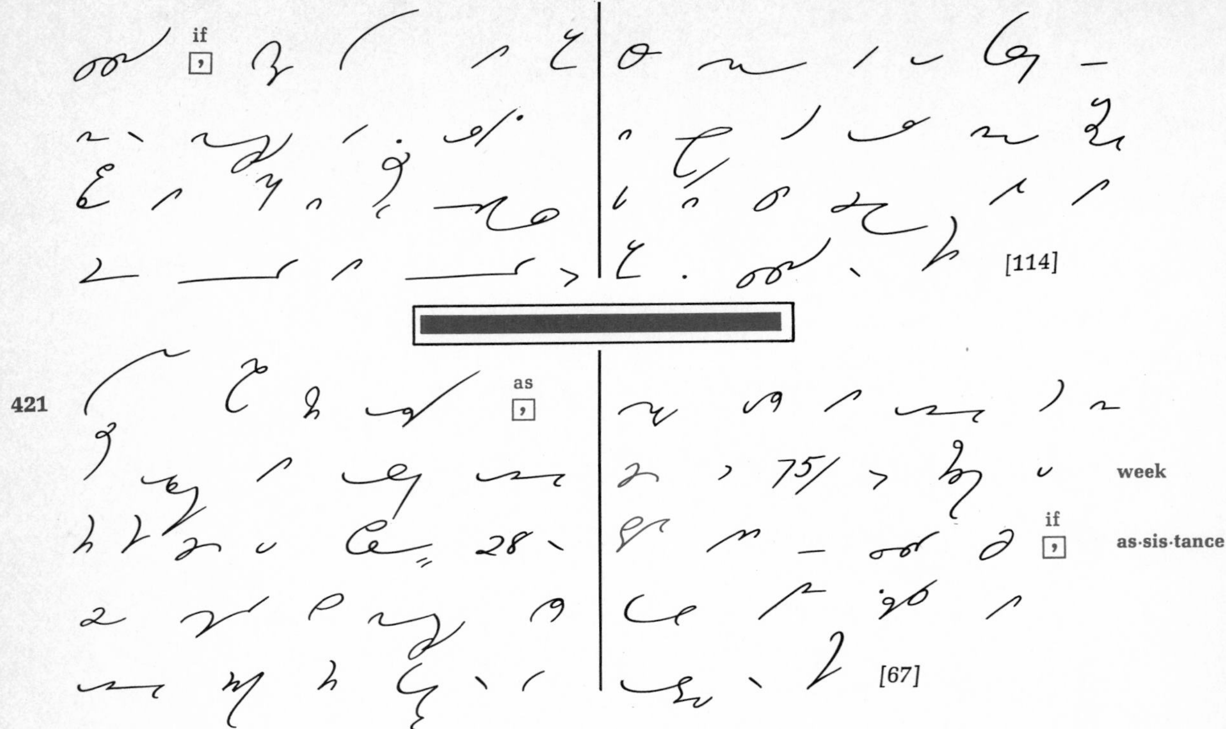

HOMEWORK CHECK LIST

When you do your homework assignment each day—

☐ **1** Do you study the Business Vocabulary Builder and the other transcription helps in the lesson before you start your work on the Reading and Writing Practice?

☐ **2** Do you read aloud each Reading and Writing Practice before copying it?

☐ **3** Do you spell each shorthand outline that you cannot immediately read? Remember, nothing builds shorthand speed more rapidly than the regular reading and writing of shorthand.

☐ **4** Do you note carefully the reason for the use of each comma that is boxed in the Reading and Writing Practice?

☐ **5** Do you spell aloud all the words given in the margins of the shorthand in the Reading and Writing Practice?

Principles

422 Word Ending -gram The word ending *-gram* is represented by a disjoined g.

Spell: t-e-l-gram, telegram

telegram	*programs*	*radiogram*
diagram	*cablegram*	*monogram*

423 Word Beginning Electric The word beginning *electric* is represented by a disjoined *el.*

Spell: electric-l, electrical

electric	*electrically*	*electric wire*
electrical	*electric fan*	*electric motor*

424 Word Beginning Electr- The word beginning *electr-* is also represented by a disjoined *el.*

Spell: electro-n-e-k, electronic

electronic	*electrotype*	*electroplate*

425 Compounds Most compound words are formed by simply joining the outlines for the words that make up the compound. In some words, however, it is desirable to modify the outline for one of the words in order to obtain a facile joining.

anyhow	*someone*	*within*
anywhere	*worthwhile*	*withstand*
anybody	*however*	*notwithstanding*

426 Intersection Intersection, or the writing of one character through another, is sometimes useful for special phrases. You should not, however, attempt to memorize lists of such phrases; you should devise such phrases only when the constant repetition of certain phrases in your dictation makes it clearly worthwhile to form special outlines.

a.m.		*vice versa*	
p.m.		*Chamber of Commerce*	

Building transcription skills

427 SIMILAR-WORDS DRILL | brought, bought

brought The past tense and past participle of *bring.*

John brought *the book back after having read it.*

bought Purchased.

We bought *some typewriters and electric calculators.*

428

Business vocabulary builder	**proof** In printing, the copy of typeset material on which corrections and changes are indicated. **alerted** Warned of possible danger. **transmission wires** The wires through which electricity is conducted.

Reading and writing practice

429 Brief-Form Review Letter

10 5

mis·spelled

par

conj

or·di·nar·i·ly

ser

cir·cu·lar

and o

suc·cess·ful

[119]

worth·while

430

dis·cuss

for·ward

in·stal·la·tion

ap

intro

[104]

431

intro

mir·a·cle

pi·ano

brought

intro

neigh·bor·hood

ap

wel·come

de·vel·ops

[116]

tones

432

sac·ri·fice

breaks
trans·mis·sion

10

24

par

5

elec·tri·cal

3

when

ser

intro

and o

grate·ful

su·per·vi·sors
not·with·stand·ing

intro

[126]

pa·tience

Principles

433 **Geographical Expressions** In geographical expressions, *-burg* is represented by *b;* *-ingham,* by a disjoined *m;* *-ington,* by a disjoined *ten* blend; *-ville,* by *v.*

-burg

Spell: *h-a-r-e-s-berg, Harrisburg*

Harrisburg *Pittsburgh* *Newburgh*

-ingham

Spell: *b-oo-k-ingham, Buckingham*

Buckingham *Cunningham* *Framingham*

-ington

Spell: *l-e-x-ington, Lexington*

Lexington *Washington* *Wilmington*

-ville

Spell: *n-a-ish-ville, Nashville*

Nashville *Jacksonville* *Evansville*

Building transcription skills

434 **GRAMMAR CHECKUP | subject and verb**

Most businessmen have a good command of the English language. Some rarely make an error in grammar. There are times, though, when even the best dictators will perhaps use a plural verb with a singular noun or use the objective case when they should have used the nominative. They usually know better. In concentrating intently on expressing a thought or idea, however, they occasionally suffer a grammatical lapse.

It will be your job as a stenographer or secretary to catch these occasional errors in grammar and to correct them when you transcribe.

From time to time in the lessons ahead you will be given an opportunity to brush up on some of the rules of grammar that are frequently violated.

subject and verb

A verb must agree with its subject in number.

Our representative is *looking forward to the pleasure of serving you.*
Your canceled checks are *mailed to you each month.*

The inclusion of a phrase such as *in addition to, as well as,* or *along with* after the subject does not affect the number of the verb. If the subject is singular, use a singular verb; if the subject is plural, use a plural verb.

Our representative, *as well as our managers,* is *looking forward to the pleasure of serving you.*
Your canceled checks, *along with your statement,* are *mailed to you each month.*

435

Business vocabulary builder

professional men Doctors, lawyers, engineers.
authorized (*verb*) Gave permission to.
duplicate (*verb*) Make copies of an original.
complicated Hard to solve.

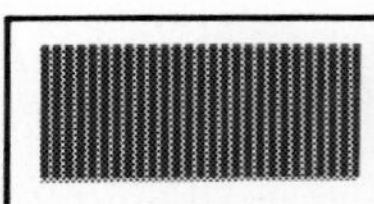

Reading and writing practice

436 Brief-Form Review Letter

sur·prise

par

as

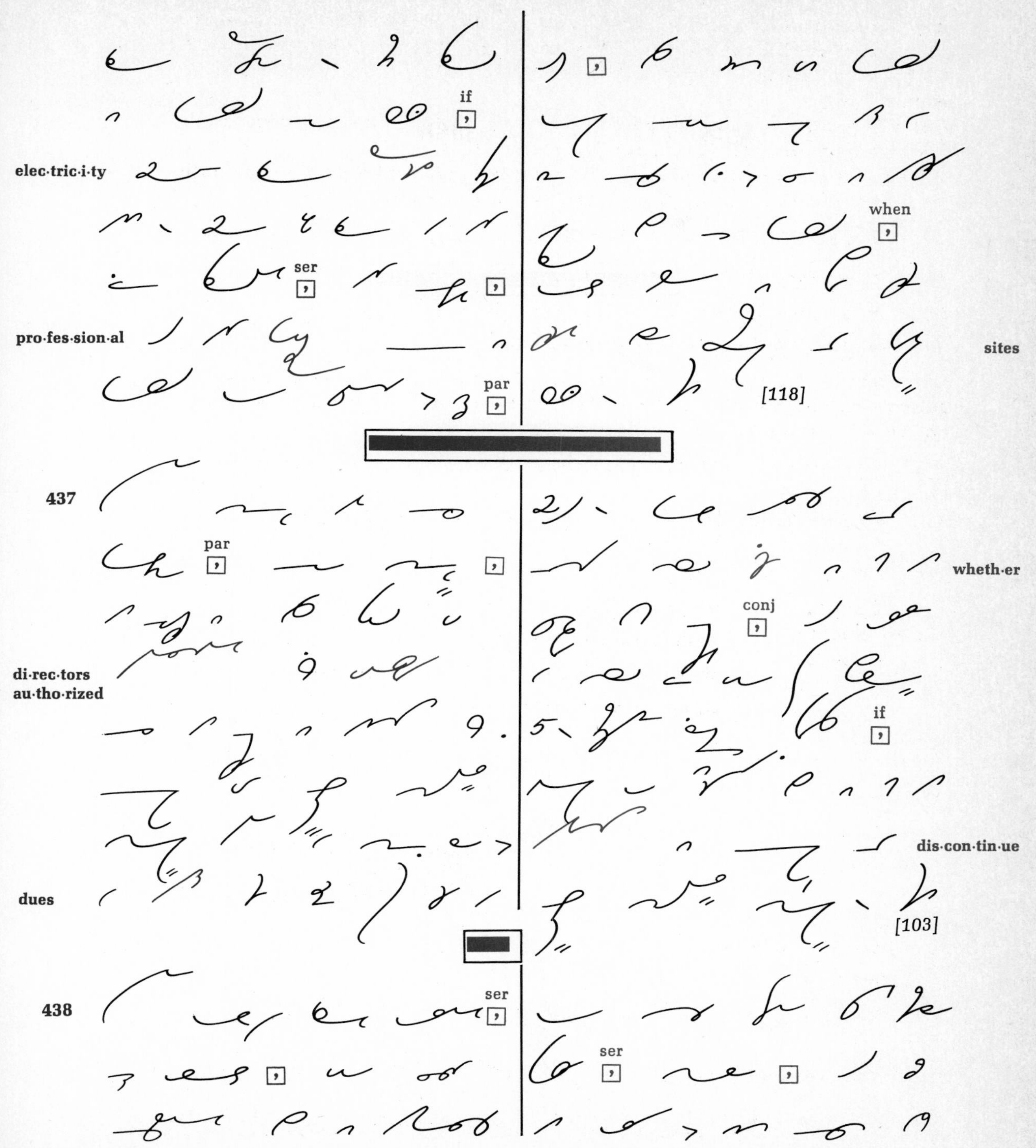
if
elec·tric·i·ty
ser
pro·fes·sion·al
par
when
sites
[118]
437
par
wheth·er
conj
di·rec·tors
au·tho·rized
if
dis·con·tin·ue
dues
[103]
438
ser
ser

intro

[85]

439

conj

ser

com·plete·ly

par

ap

ser·vice

[109]

440

and o

well-known

if

par

[70]

Recall

In Lesson 47 you studied the last of the new shorthand devices of Gregg Shorthand. In this lesson you will find an Accuracy Practice, a Recall Chart that reviews all the word-building principles of Gregg Shorthand, and a Reading and Writing Practice that contains some "food for thought."

Accuracy practice

441 **Def**

To write this stroke accurately:

a *Make it large, almost the full height of your notebook line.*

b *Make it narrow.*

c *Start and finish the strokes on the same level of writing, as indicated by the dotted lines.*

practice drill

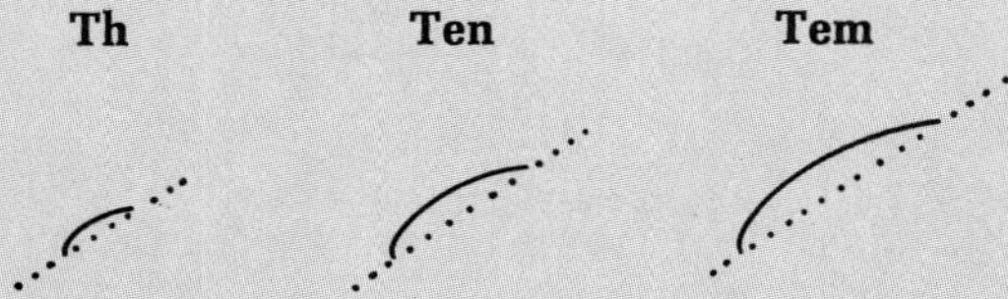

Divide, definite, defeat, devote, differ, endeavor.

442 **Th** **Ten** **Tem**

To write these strokes accurately:

a *Slant the strokes as indicated by the dotted lines.*

b *Make the* **beginning** *of the curves deep.*

c *Make the* **tem** *large, about the full height of the line; the* **th** *small; the* **ten** *about half the size of the* **tem.**

practice drill

In the, in time, tender, teeth, detain, medium.

443 **Recall Chart** This chart contains one or more illustrations of every word-building and phrasing principle of Gregg Shorthand.

WORDS

1
2
3
4
5
6
7
8
9
10
11
12
13
14
15

PHRASES

16
17

444

Business vocabulary builder	
	equivalent Equal in amount or value.
	snap decision Course of action decided upon without sufficient thought.
	contrary Against.

Reading and writing practice

445 Faithful Servant

par

if

intro

de·liv·ery

minds

dai·ly

conj

dis·tance

par

[161]

446 Self-Control

los·ing theirs

intro

ex·am·ine traits

if

ser

calm·ly

intro

per·son·al

intro

con·trary

conj

[150]

447 Good Sign

[45]

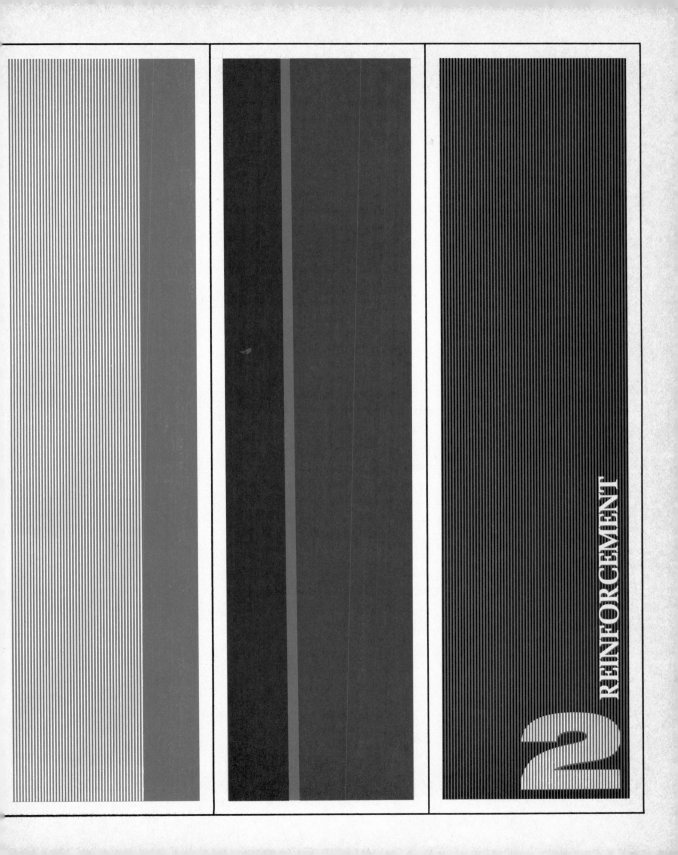

2
REINFORCEMENT

Chapter 9

The secretary "looks it up"

Suppose a strange word is given to you in dictation. It sounds like "ingenuous." Or was it "ingenious"? Both are perfectly good words. But which is correct? You read your notes carefully and you look up these two words in the dictionary; then you make your choice. You are right, because you make sure the word fits the meaning your notes show was intended. The smart secretary doesn't guess—she looks it up.

"I don't expect my secretary to be a 'walking encyclopedia,'" says the executive, "but I do expect her to know when she doesn't know—and to know where to look things up."

Do you know when and where to look things up? Now is the time to begin forming the habit of looking things up when you aren't sure. Even the experienced secretary turns to several reference sources during the course of a day to make absolutely sure she is right. She may use the dictionary, a grammar handbook, a company style manual for typists and stenographers, an encyclopedia, a book on filing, a letter-writing handbook, and a book on etiquette. Nothing is left to chance. To be right is important. It's the smart secretary who knows when she doesn't know.

Do you know how to address a member of the clergy? a senator? Do you know how to write an acceptance to a formal invitation? Do you know the correct salutation when writing to a company composed entirely of women? Which is correct: "Whom are you expecting?" or "Who are you expecting?" How do you address a package to someone in a foreign country? What is meant by the Latin expression sine qua non? *You may have to answer questions such as these every day. Of course, you aren't expected to know the answers to everything asked of you, but you are expected to know where to find the information you need. It's smart to be right.*

The practice material in this lesson concentrates on the shorthand principles you studied in Chapter 1.

448 BRIEF FORMS AND DERIVATIVES

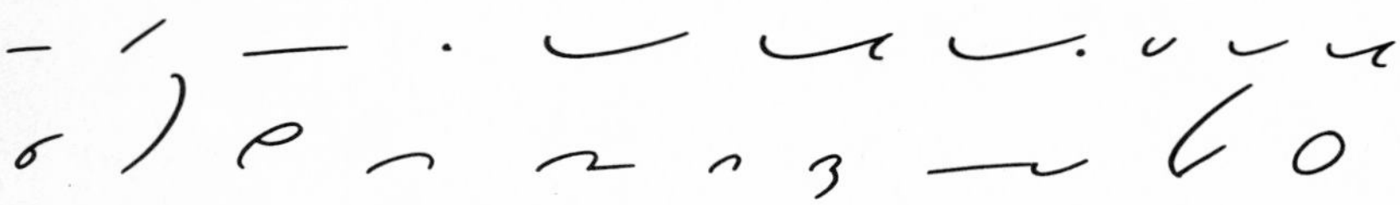

In-not, it-at, am, a-an, will-well, wills, willing, of, are-hour-our, ours.
With, have, that, can, cannot, you-your, yours, Mr., but, I.

Reading practice

449

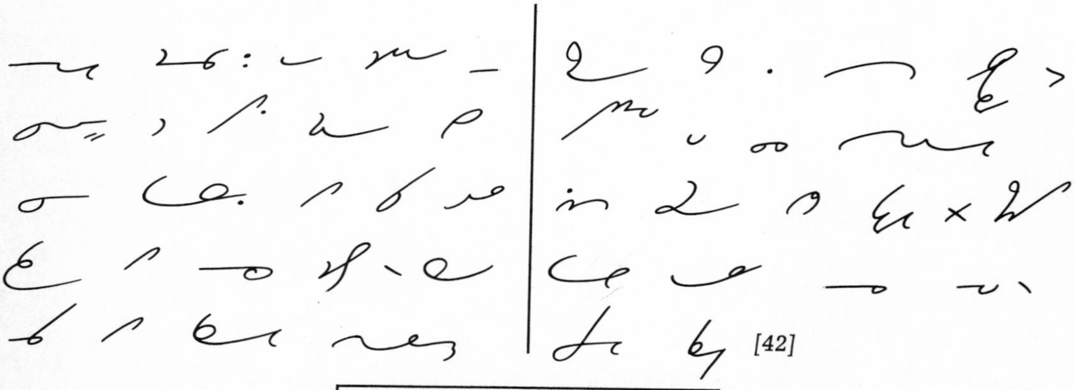

[42]

450

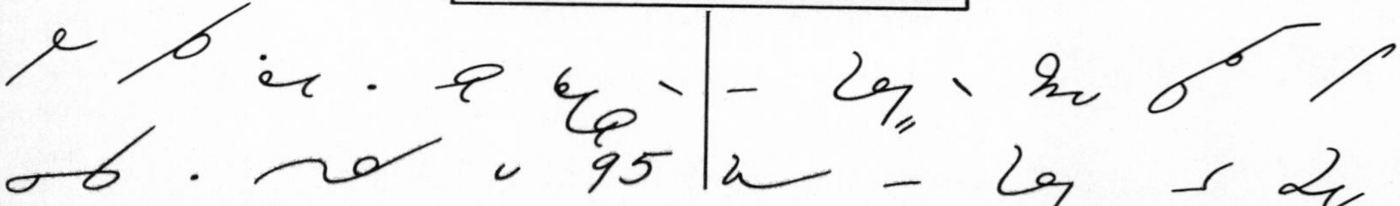

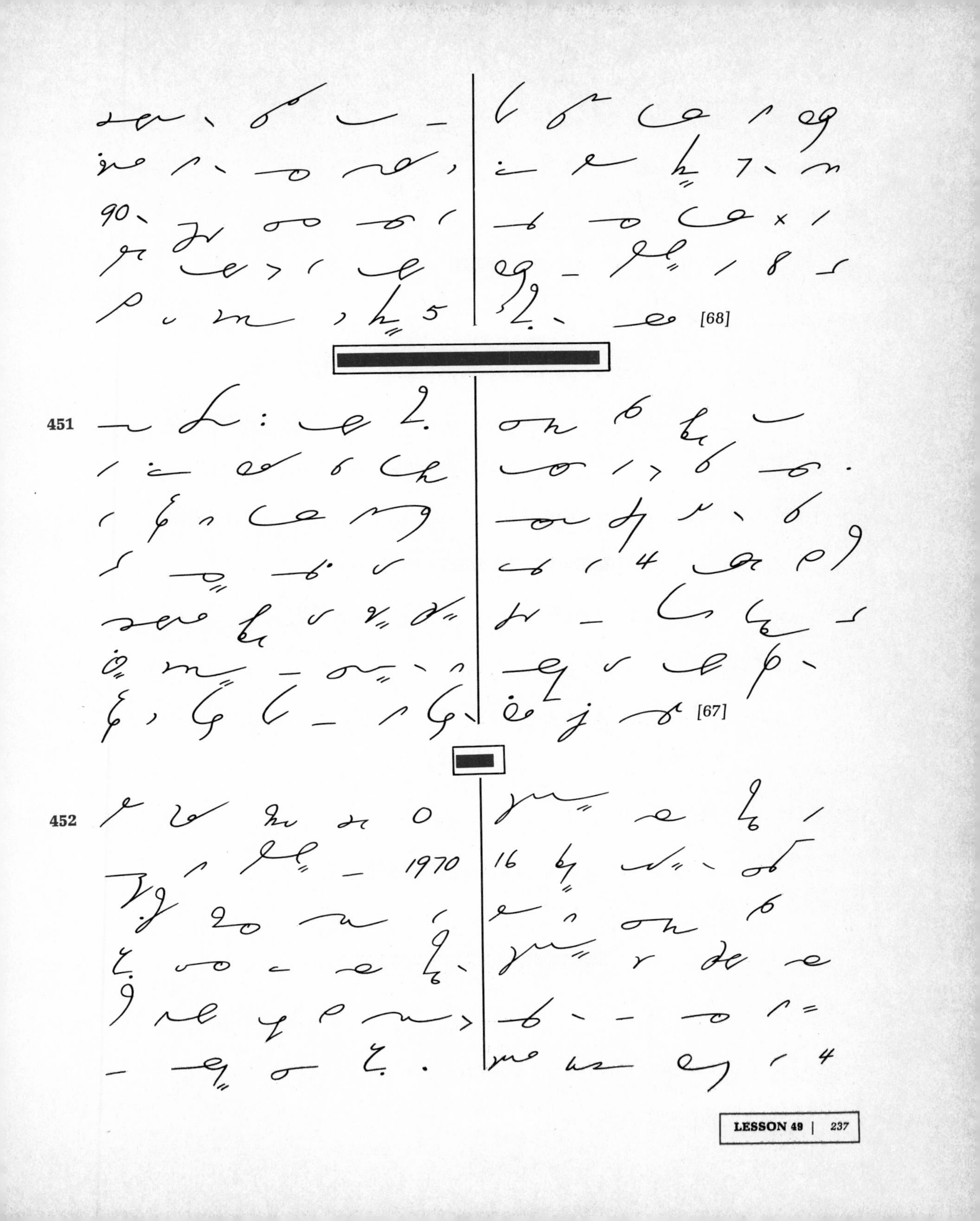

[68]

451

[67]

452

[94]

453

[46]

454

[65]

455

[79]

PHRASING AND SHORTHAND SPEED

Occasionally, students gain the impression that phrasing is the key to shorthand speed and that the more a writer phrases, the faster he will write. Consequently, they try to phrase as many combinations of words as possible and sometimes even devise phrases of their own.

This practice may seriously reduce a writer's speed rather than increase it. Why? A phrase is valuable only if it can be written without the slightest hesitation. If the writer must pause for even the smallest fraction of a second in composing or thinking of a phrase, that phrase becomes a speed handicap.

The phrase that can be written without hesitation is the one that has occurred again and again in the writer's practice work, so that it has impressed itself permanently on his mind. If you have been reading and copying each Reading and Writing Practice faithfully, you have encountered the common phrases of the English language many times. These phrases will come to you naturally when you take dictation.

If you have the feeling that you should be phrasing more, dismiss the matter from your mind. Simply continue to read and copy faithfully each Reading and Writing Practice, and your ability to phrase will take care of itself.

The practice material in this lesson concentrates on the shorthand principles you studied in Chapter 2.

456 **BRIEF FORMS AND DERIVATIVES**

Good, goods, this, their-there, would, putting, being, which, shall, for.
Them, they, was, when, from, should, could, send, sender.

Building transcription skills

457

Business vocabulary builder	
	rendered Gave.
	talents Abilities.
	released Set free.

Reading and writing practice

458

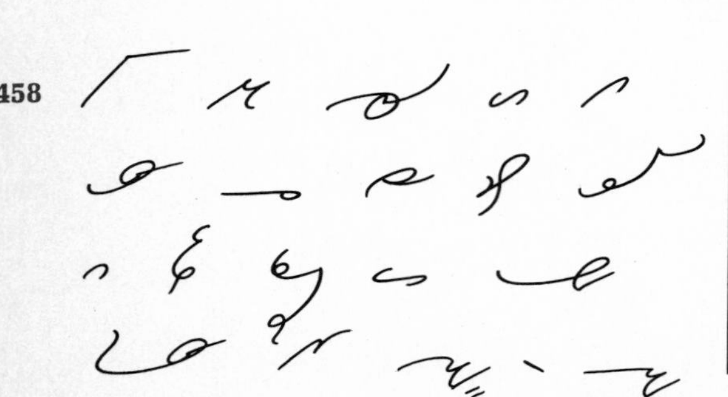

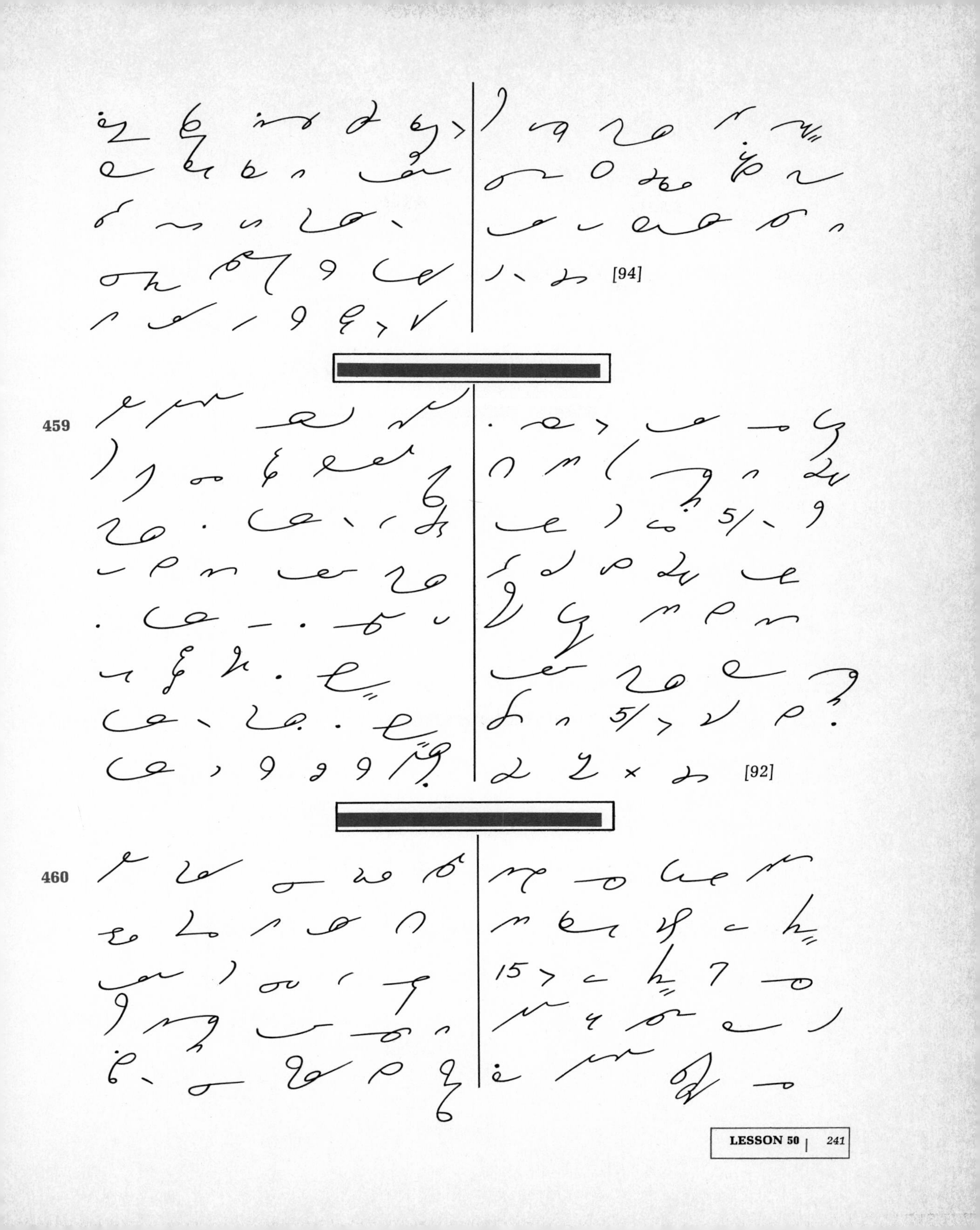

[94]

459

[92]

460

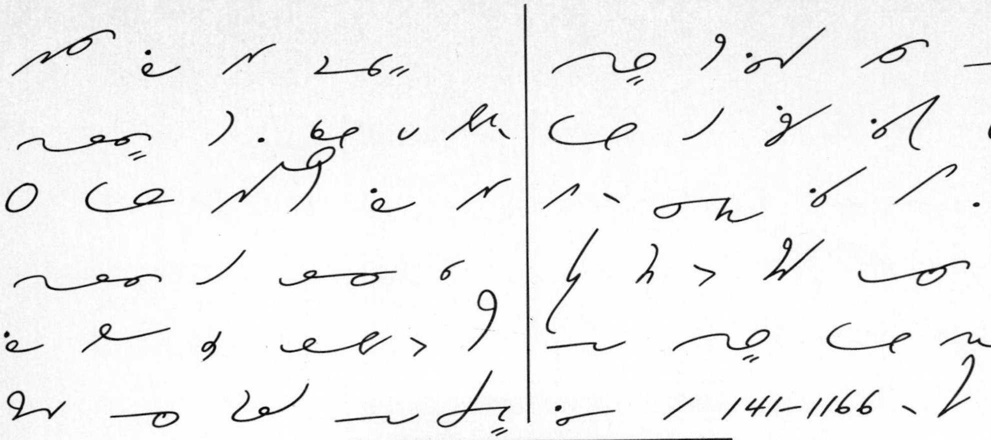

[124]

461

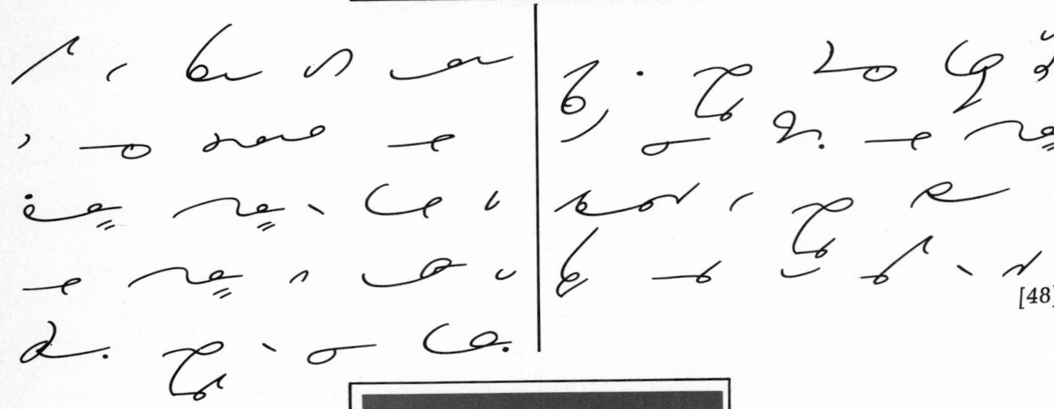

[48]

462

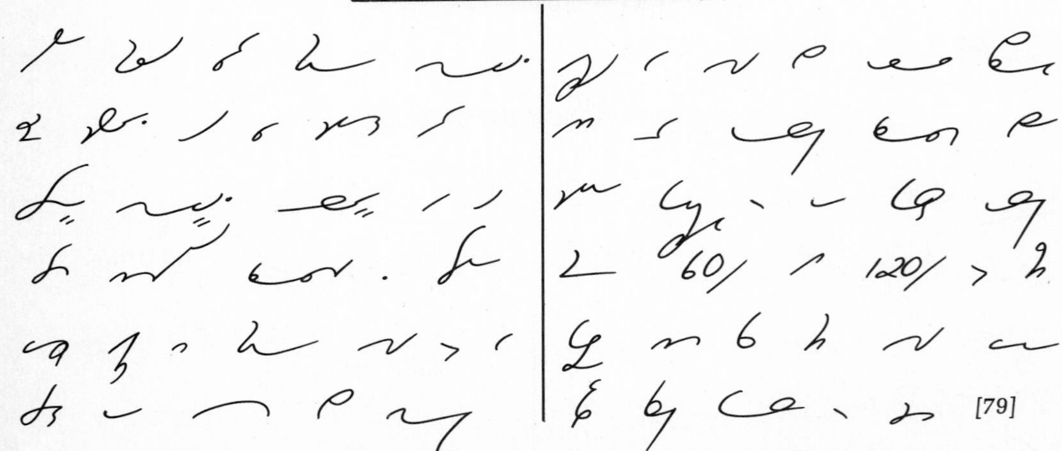

[79]

The practice material in this lesson concentrates on the shorthand principles you studied in Chapter 3.

463 BRIEF FORMS AND DERIVATIVES

Gladly, worker, yesterday, orders, thanks, very, soon, enclosed, years.
Values, than, once, what, about, greater, businesses, why, thinking.
Gentlemen, morning, important-importance, those, where, manufacturer.

Building transcription skills

464

Business vocabulary builder	
	register (*verb*) Enroll.
	brochure Pamphlet or booklet.
	offended Displeased; angered.

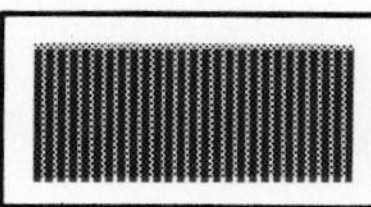

Reading and writing practice

465

15
10
[105]

466

[64]

467

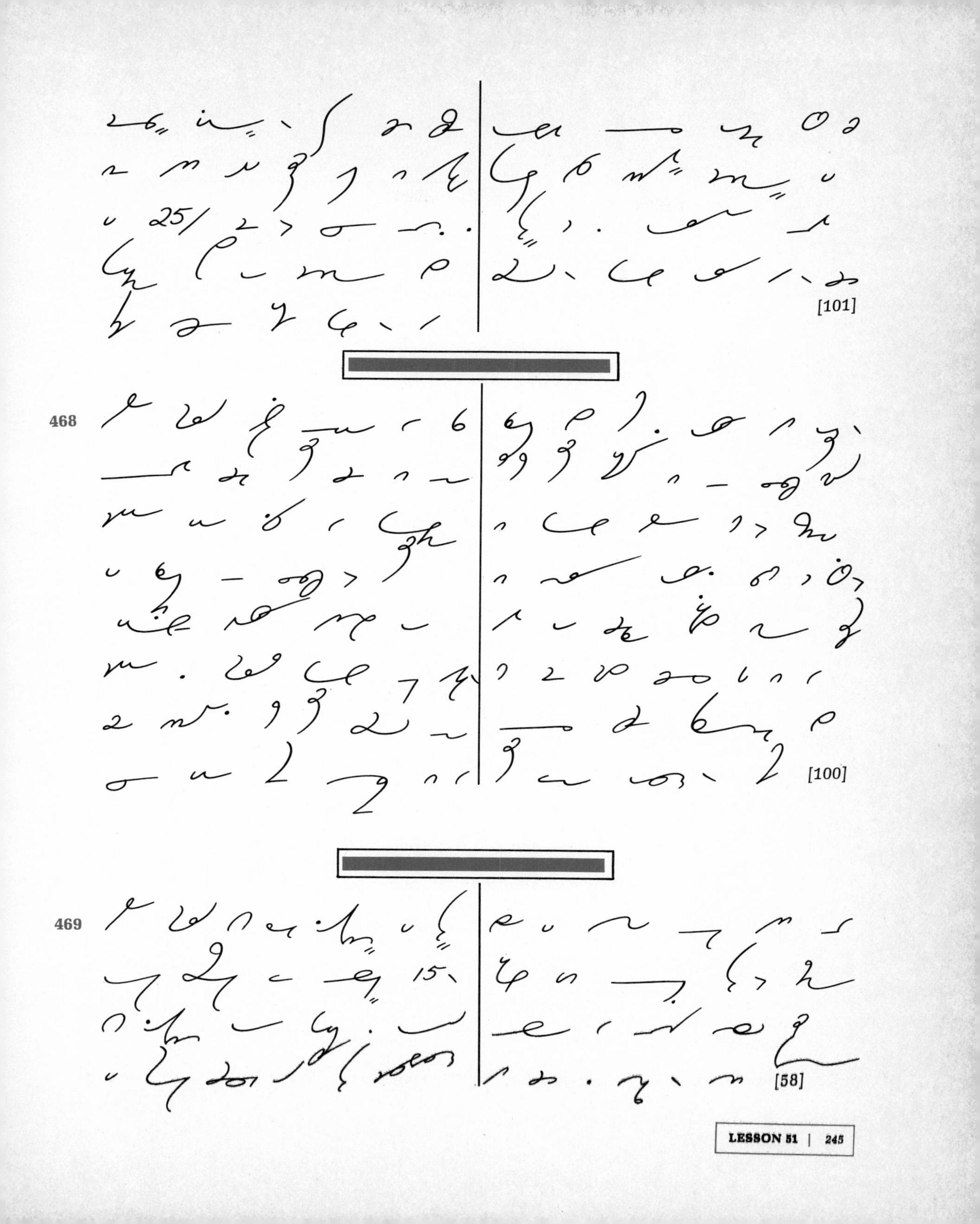

25 15

[101]

468

[100]

469

[58]

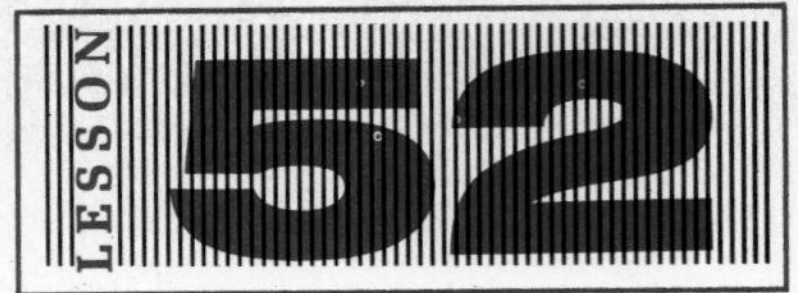

The practice material in this lesson concentrates on the shorthand principles you studied in Chapter 4.

470 **BRIEF FORMS AND DERIVATIVES**

Presently, parted, after, advertises, companies, wishes, immediately, must, opportunities.
Advantages, used, bigger, suggestion, such, several, corresponds, how-out, ever-every.
Times, acknowledged, generally, gone, during, overdue, questions, yet, worthy.

Building transcription skills

471 **SPELLING FAMILIES** ▎**-tion, -sion**

Words Ending in -tion

ac·tion	**con·nec·tion**	**lo·ca·tion**
ap·pli·ca·tion	**cor·rec·tion**	**po·si·tion**
col·lec·tion	**dem·on·stra·tion**	**ques·tion**
com·ple·tion	**il·lus·tra·tion**	**re·la·tion**

Words Ending in -sion

con·clu·sion	**di·vi·sion**	**pro·vi·sion**
de·ci·sion	**pen·sion**	**tele·vi·sion**
de·pres·sion	**per·sua·sion**	**ten·sion**

472

Business vocabulary builder	
	depart Leave.
	confidential Private; secret.
	gratifying Pleasing; satisfying.

Reading and writing practice

473

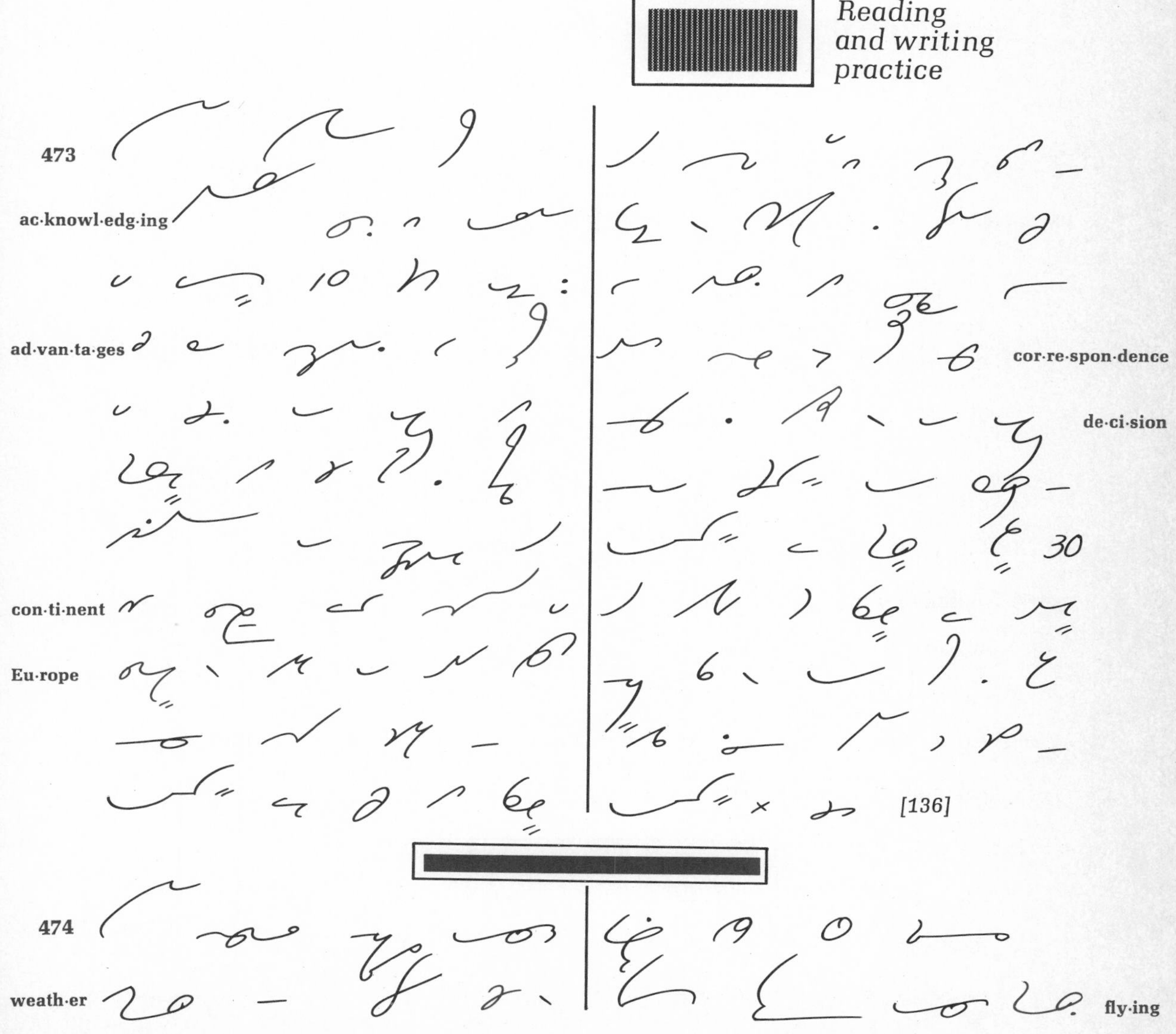

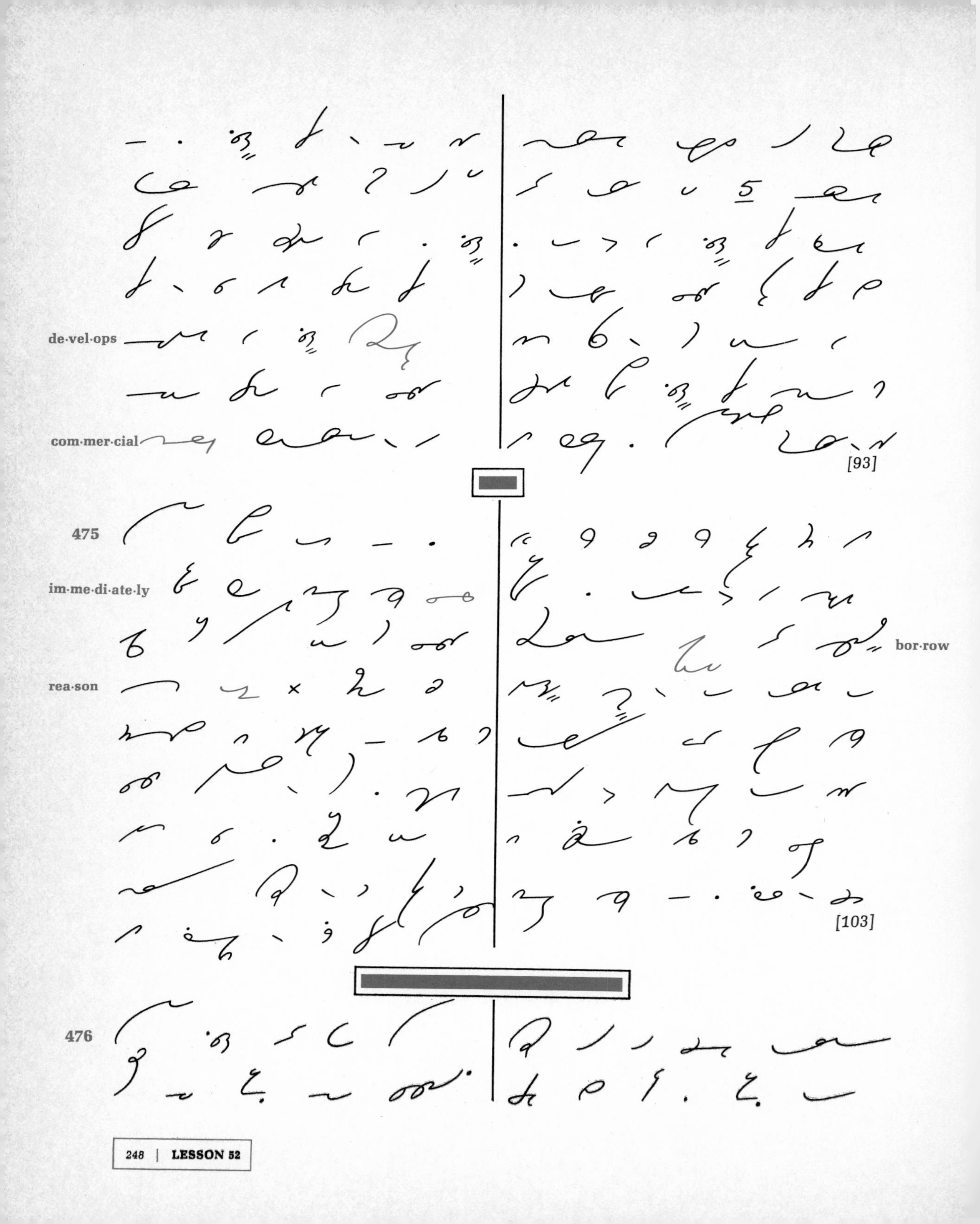

de·vel·ops

com·mer·cial

[93]

475

im·me·di·ate·ly

bor·row

rea·son

[103]

476

cor·re·spon·dent

[99]

477

re·plies

grat·i·fy·ing

ad·ver·tis·ing

[115]

SPELLING AND PUNCTUATION CHECK LIST

Are you careful to punctuate and spell correctly when—

- ☐ **1** You write your compositions in English?
- ☐ **2** Prepare your reports for your social studies classes?
- ☐ **3** Correspond with friends to whom you must write in longhand?

In short, are you making correct spelling and punctuation a habit in all the longhand writing or typing that you do?

The practice material in this lesson concentrates on the shorthand principles you studied in Chapter 5.

478 **BRIEF FORMS AND DERIVATIVES**

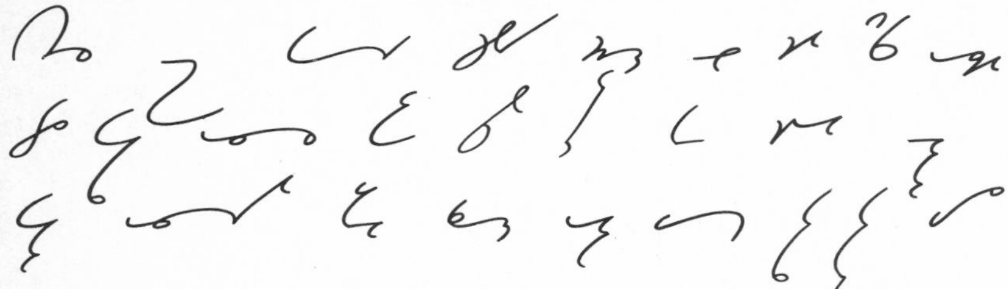

Difficulty, envelope, progressed, satisfied, successes, next, states, underpay, requests. Particularly, probably, regularly, speaker, ideas, subjects, upon, streets, newspapers. Purposes, regards, opinions, circulars, responsible, organization, publicly, publications, ordinarily.

Building transcription skills

479

Business vocabulary builder	**creative** Being able to produce something through imaginative skill. **extended** (*verb*) Made an offer to. **summarized** Presented briefly.

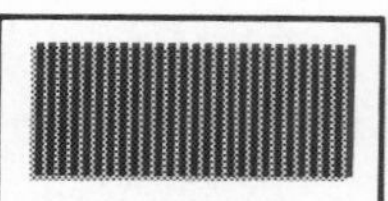

Reading and writing practice

480

sums

or·ga·ni·za·tion

wealth

cre·ative

[115]

481

re·spon·si·ble

di·rec·tors

speak·er's

[104]

482

in·ves·tor fac·tor

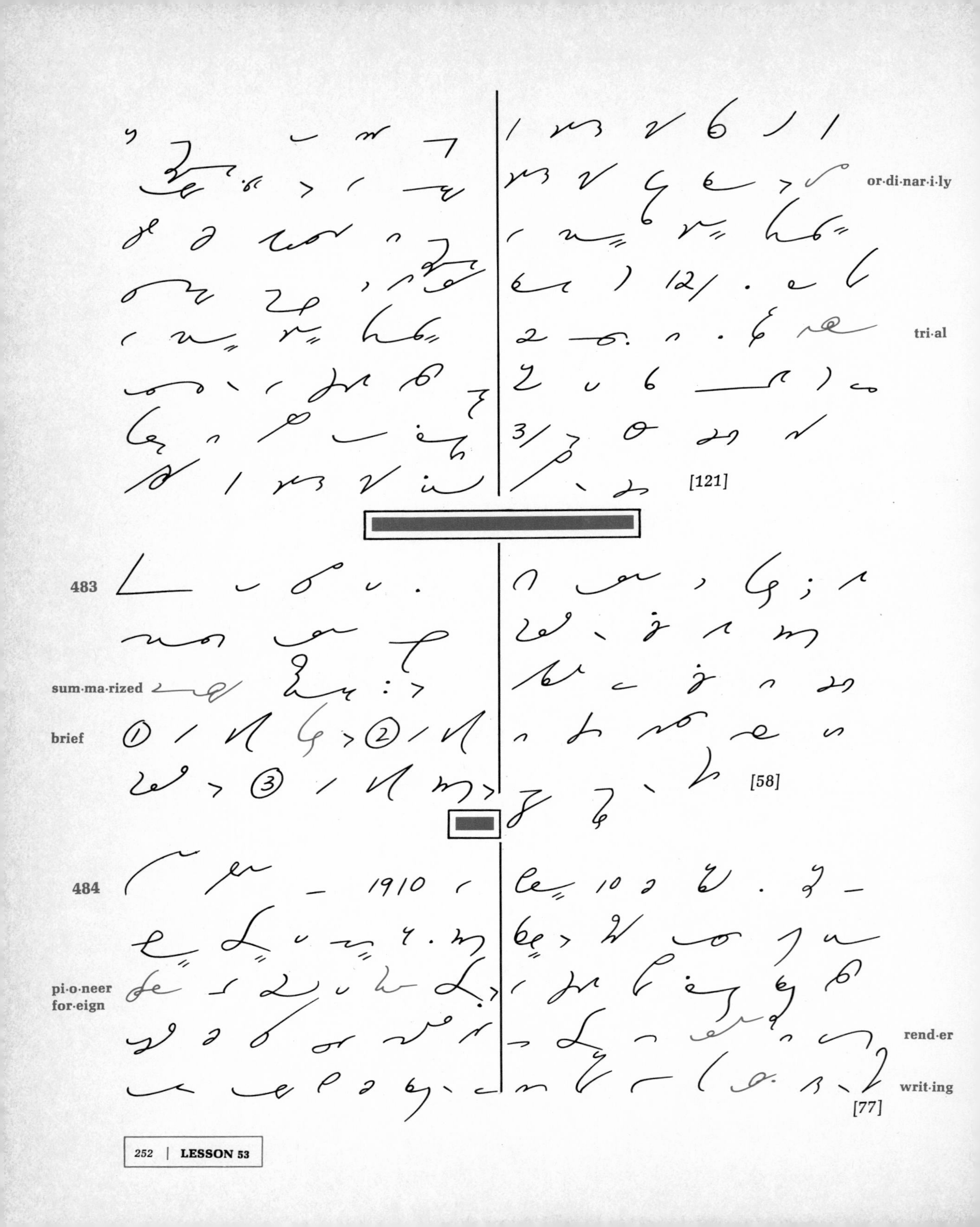

or·di·nar·i·ly

tri·al

[121]

483

sum·ma·rized

brief

[58]

484

pi·o·neer

for·eign

rend·er

writ·ing

[77]

The practice material in this lesson concentrates on the shorthand principles you studied in Chapter 6.

485 BRIEF FORMS AND DERIVATIVES

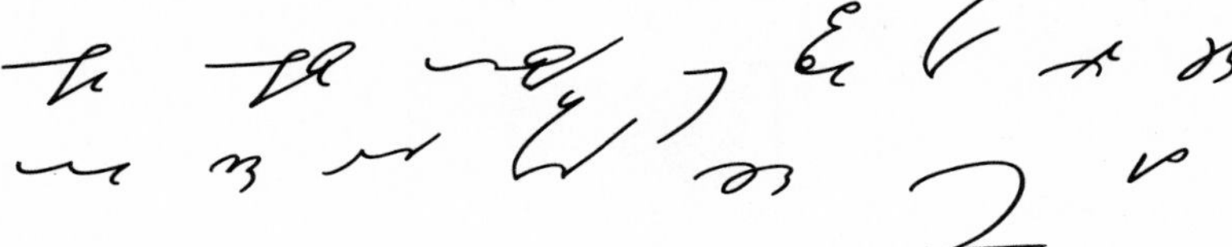

Merchants, merchandise, recognized, never, experiences, between, quantities, situations. Railroads, worlds, throughout, objected, characters, government, shortly.

Building transcription skills

486 SIMILAR-WORDS DRILL | weather, whether

weather State of the atmosphere with respect to wetness or dryness, cold or heat; climate.

You can take a good picture regardless of the weather.

The game was called because of the weather.

whether Indicating a choice (often followed by *or*). Also used to introduce an indirect question.

You can take a good picture whether *the sun is shining or* whether *it is raining.*

Let me know whether you will be free on Friday.

487

Business vocabulary builder	
	altered Changed.
	vouch for Give personal assurance; guarantee.
	settings Backgrounds.

Reading and writing practice

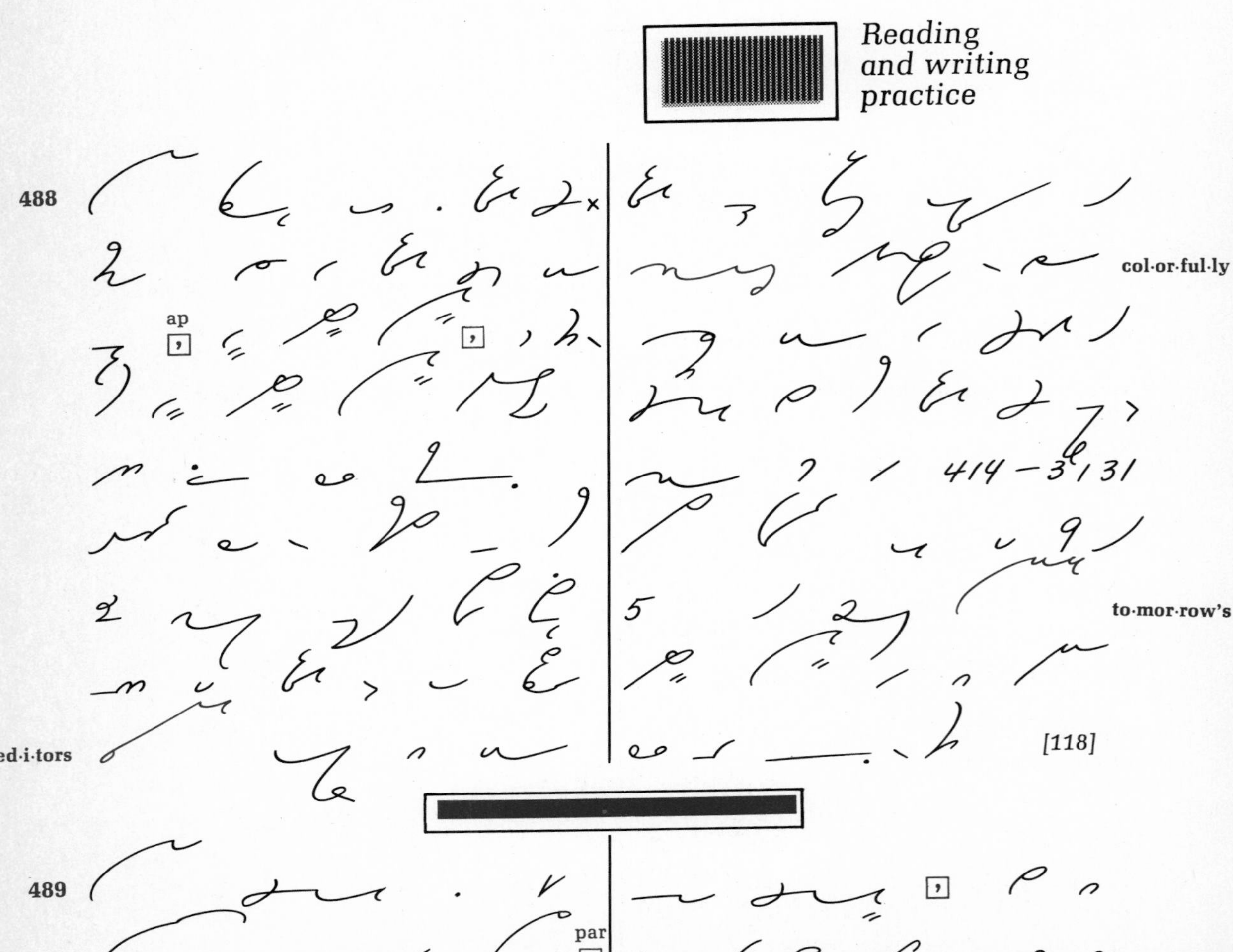

gov·ern·ment

phase

de·scribed

tech·ni·cal

vouch

ser

par

char·ac·ter ref·er·ence

ap

[109]

490

prac·ti·cal

weath·er

ser

ser

whether

cloudy

de·scrip·tive

ap

[113]

491

mod·ern

ad·vi·sors

ap

par

rec·og·nized

ser

pleas·ant

[127]

492 Car

[41]

SHORTHAND NOTEBOOK CHECK LIST

So that you can use your notebook efficiently, do you—

☐ **1** Write your name on the cover of your notebook?

☐ **2** Indicate on the cover the first and last days on which you used the notebook?

☐ **3** Place the date *at the bottom* of the first page of each day's dictation?

☐ **4** Place a rubber band around the completed pages of your notebook so that you lose no time finding the first blank page on which to start the day's dictation?

☐ **5** Draw a line through the shorthand notes that you have transcribed or read back so that you will know you are through with them?

The practice material in this lesson concentrates on the shorthand principles you studied in Chapter 7.

493 BRIEF-FORM DERIVATIVES

Greater, sooner, bigger, shorter, worker, sender, manufacturer.
Particularly, successfully, timely, immediately, partly, presently, gladly, purposely.
Suggested, corresponded, timed, progressed, organized, governed.

Building transcription skills

494 GRAMMAR CHECKUP | the infinitive

The infinitive is the form of the verb usually introduced by *to—to see, to be, to have, to do.*

Careful writers try to avoid "splitting" an infinitive, that is, inserting a word or phrase between *to* and the following word.

no

To properly do the job, you need better tools.

yes

To do the job properly, you need better tools.

no

He was told to carefully prepare the report.

yes

He was told to prepare the report carefully.

495

Business vocabulary builder	
	shabby Showing the effects of wear.
	gruff Deep and harsh.
	convey Get across.

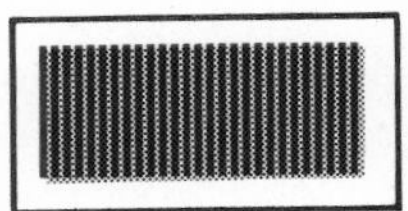

Reading and writing practice

496

when

shab·by

ser

if

fa·vor·ably im·pressed

if

intro

sub·stan·tial

intro

in·te·ri·or

dec·o·ra·tors

[145]

497

par

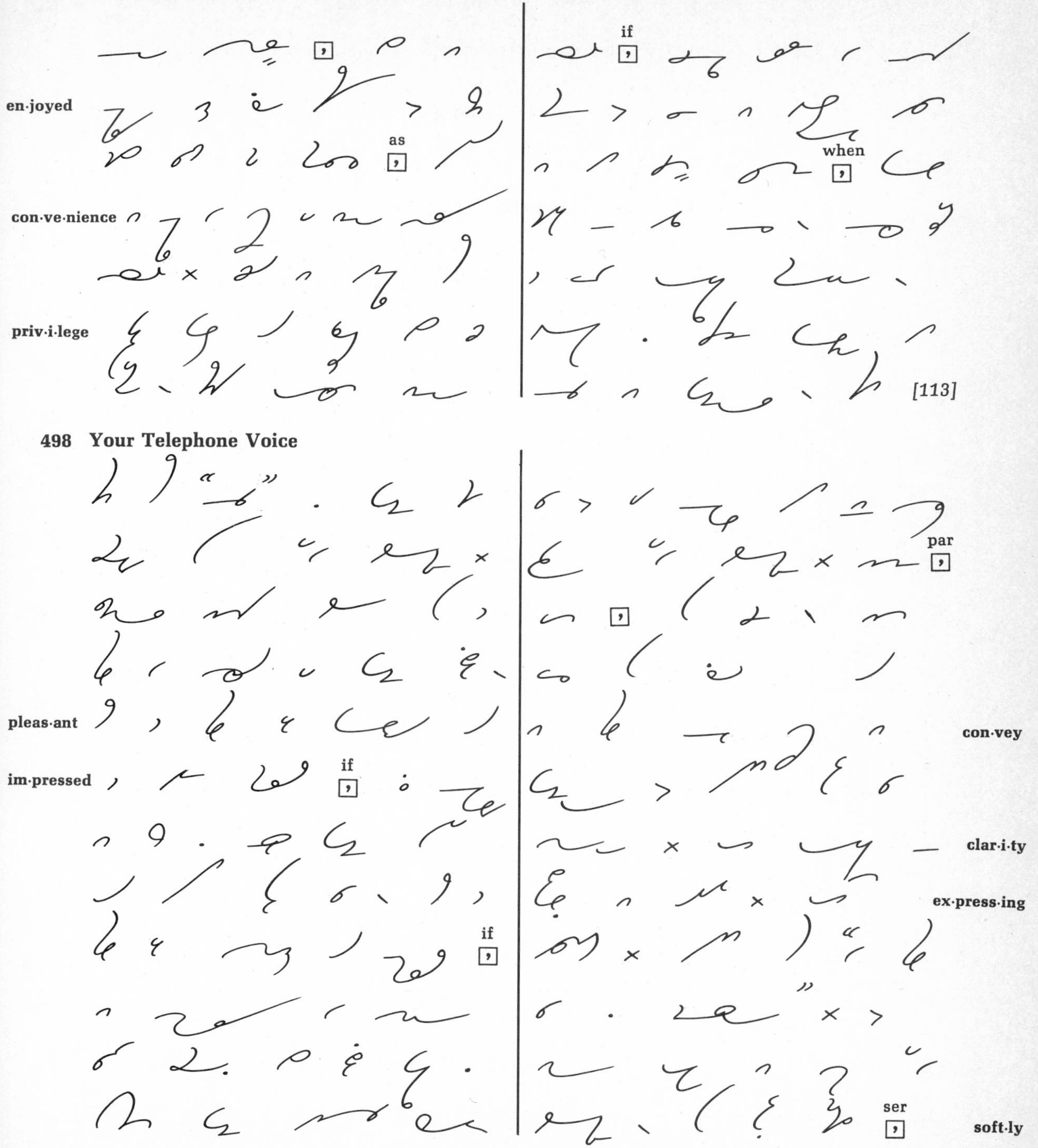

498 Your Telephone Voice

choos·ing

intro

[168]

499

intro

enough

conj

intro

ap

slop·py

when

[118]

500 **Doctor**

[47]

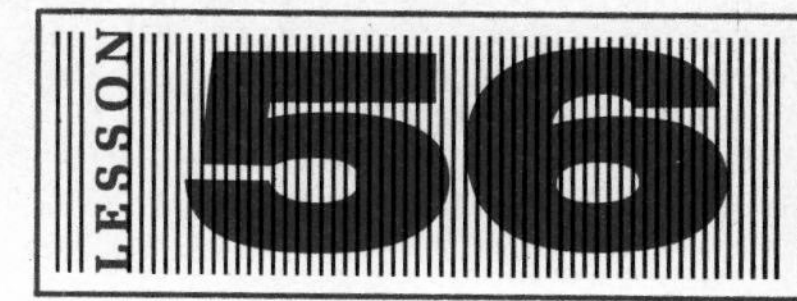

The practice material in this lesson concentrates on the shorthand principles you studied in Chapter 8.

501 BRIEF FORMS AND DERIVATIVES

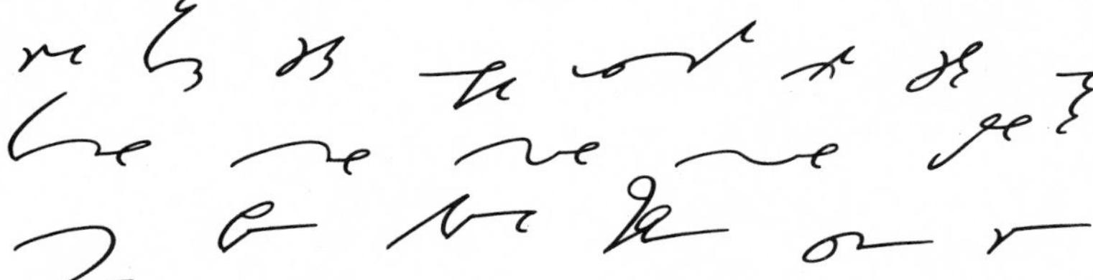

Streets, objects, situations, merchants, regards, quantities, satisfies, newspapers.
Bigness, goodness, greatness, gladness, orderliness.
Government, apartment, departments, advertisement, acknowledgment, statement.

Building transcription skills

502 COMMON PREFIXES | super-

Many words in the English language contain common prefixes. An understanding of the meanings of these prefixes will often give you a clue to the meaning of words with which you are unfamiliar.

Perhaps you never heard the word *posterity.* However, if you know that *post* means *after,* you may be able to figure out that *posterity* refers to those who come after, or descendants.

In each "Common Prefixes" exercise you will be given a common prefix, its meaning, and a list of words in which the prefix is used.

Read each definition carefully, and then study the illustrations that follow. A number of the illustrations are used in the Reading and Writing Practice of this lesson.

super- over, more than

supervise To oversee.

supervisor One who oversees.

superior Over in rank, higher.

supertax A tax over and above a normal tax.

503

Business vocabulary builder	
	self-service elevators Elevators on which there are no operators.
	executive Person charged with running a company or department of a company.
	simultaneously At the same time.

Reading and writing practice

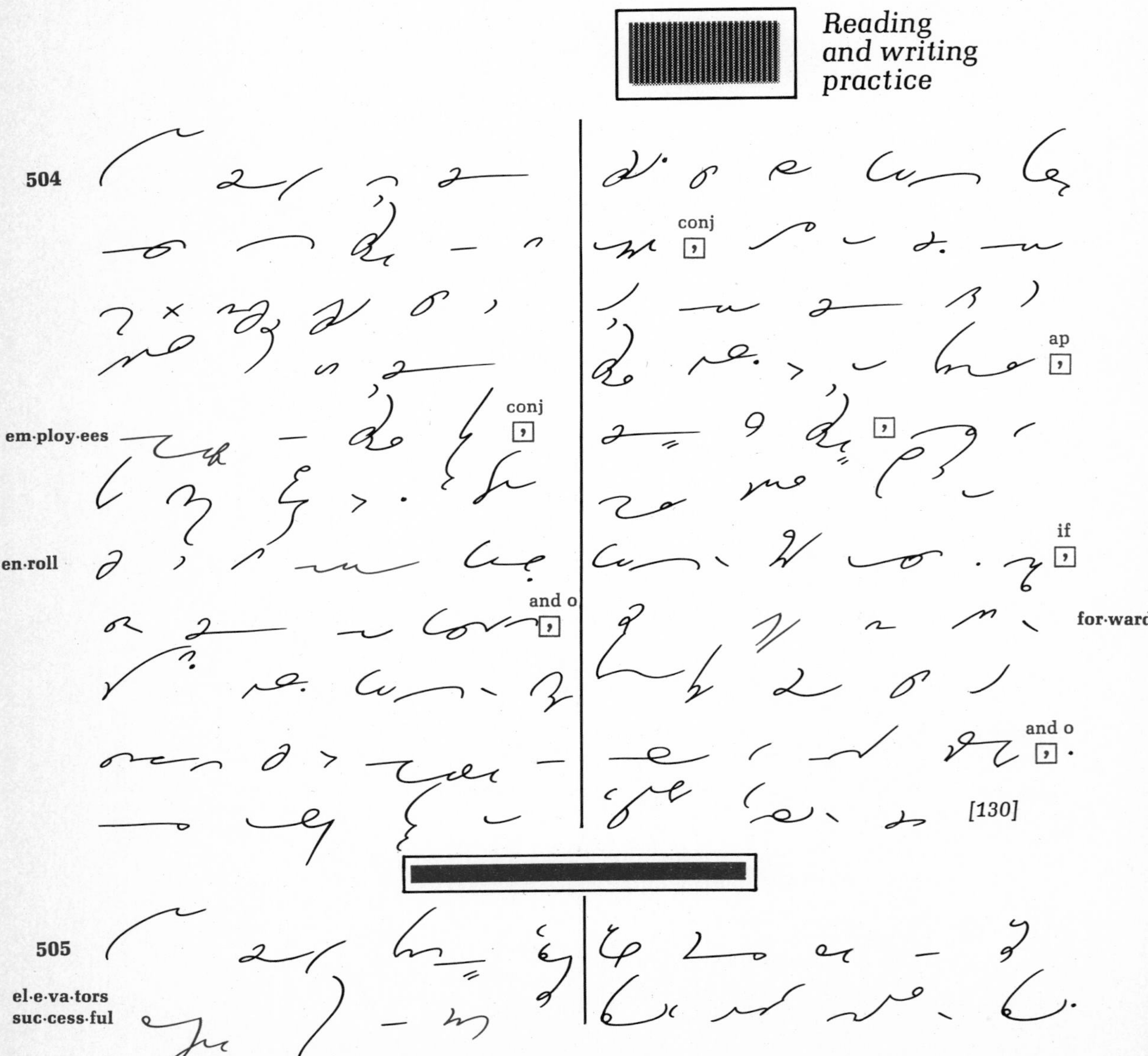

in·stal·la·tion

if

and o

worth·while

re·ceive

when

[117]

prompt·ly

506

ser

par

par

equip·ment

su·pe·ri·or

and o

shirk

when

su·per·vise
si·mul·ta·neous·ly

[144]

507

when

ma·jor

re·frig·er·a·tor

25

ser

intro

cur·rent

intro

and o

kilo·watt

ap

Con·sum·er

[130]

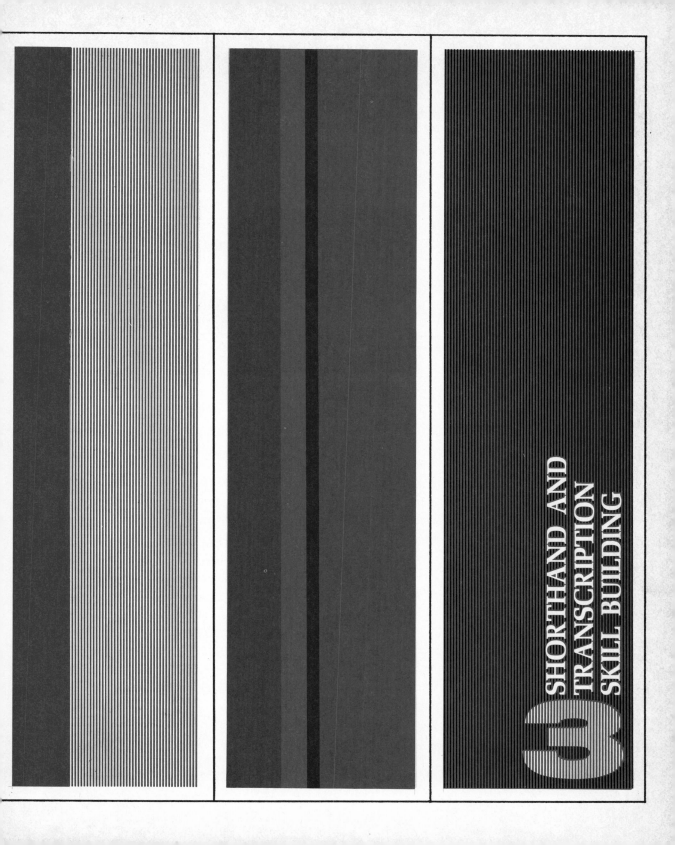

3
SHORTHAND AND
TRANSCRIPTION
SKILL BUILDING

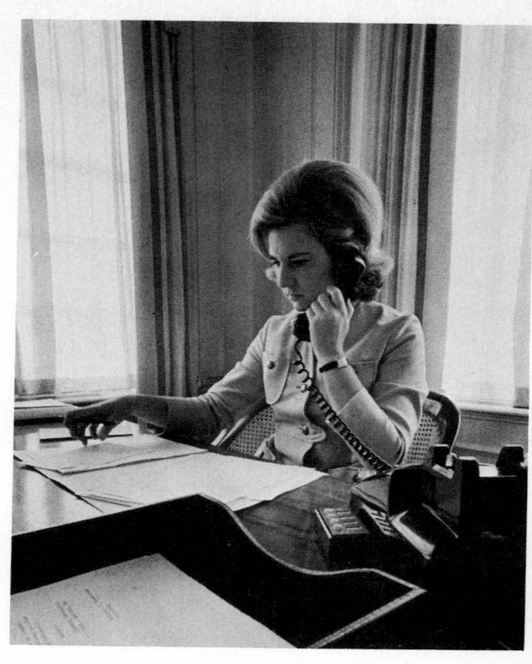

Chapter 10

The secretary moves up

The kind of job you will get and the progress you will make in it will depend almost entirely on you. Does this sound old-fashioned? Well, it is still true. Good looks and a sparkling personality are wonderful assets to anyone; if you are blessed with these gifts, make the most of them. But they are by no means everything. They are merely "frosting on the cake." If you manage to use your head and make the most of the talents, looks, and abilities you do have, your opportunities for promotion are great.

The business executive wants his secretary to have interest and ability. With those two qualities she can lick the world. Of course, he expects her to look smart, neat, and clean. Note that we did not say he insists that she be a raving beauty. While he is not averse to a sparkling personality and good looks, he can't afford to let these qualities influence his

decision in hiring and promoting.

In a secretarial position the opportunity to learn is unlimited. You will have an orchestra seat to all the important goings-on in your executive's domain. It has happened many times that the secretary moved into the boss's shoes when he was promoted.

Even if you don't aspire to the boss's job, your future will depend on how well he does his job. Are you skeptical? Let's examine this statement. In a typical company there are many executive promotions every year. Those promotions go to the people who have proved to be outstanding in their jobs and who "have a future." An executive can hardly be outstanding if he is saddled with inefficient secretarial help. Usually when he receives a promotion, his secretary gets one, too. Suppose he is a department head and is promoted to the position of vice-president. Automatically his salary is increased. And the secretary to a vice-president is a more important person than the secretary to a department manager; so she generally gets a salary increase, too. If the secretary is really good, she moves right up the ladder with her boss.

You and your boss will be a team. Your success will depend on his success. It's that simple.

The practice material in this lesson is "loaded" with brief forms and derivatives. Counting repetitions, it contains 317 brief forms and derivatives. If you gave proper attention to the brief forms as they were introduced, you should be able to complete this lesson in record time!

Building transcription skills

508 **SPELLING FAMILIES | silent e before -ment**

Words in Which Silent E Is Retained Before -ment

ad·vance·ment	**en·gage·ment**	**re·tire·ment**
ad·ver·tise·ment	**man·age·ment**	**re·quire·ment**
amuse·ment	**move·ment**	**state·ment**
en·cour·age·ment	**re·place·ment**	

Words in Which Silent E Is Omitted Before -ment

ac·knowl·edg·ment	**ar·gu·ment**	**judg·ment**

509 *Business vocabulary builder*

variety Collection of many different things.

speculates Wonders; thinks.

browse Examine casually merchandise offered for sale.

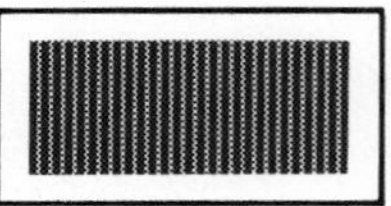

Reading and writing practice

510 **en·cour·age**

or·gan·ize

par

conj

be·com·ing

suc·cess

as

ser

[142]

511

ap

16

cor·res·pon·dence

re·ferred

conj

if

10 prob·a·bly

re·ceive

when

if

[99]

512

straight

conj

amuse·ment

judg·ment

intro

ap

513

conj

some·how
dif·fer·ent

sup·plied

intro

ser

plea·sur·able

prof·it·able

[123]

iden·ti·cal

conj

prompt·ly

conj

browse

hard·ware

fas·ci·nat·ing

[125]

514

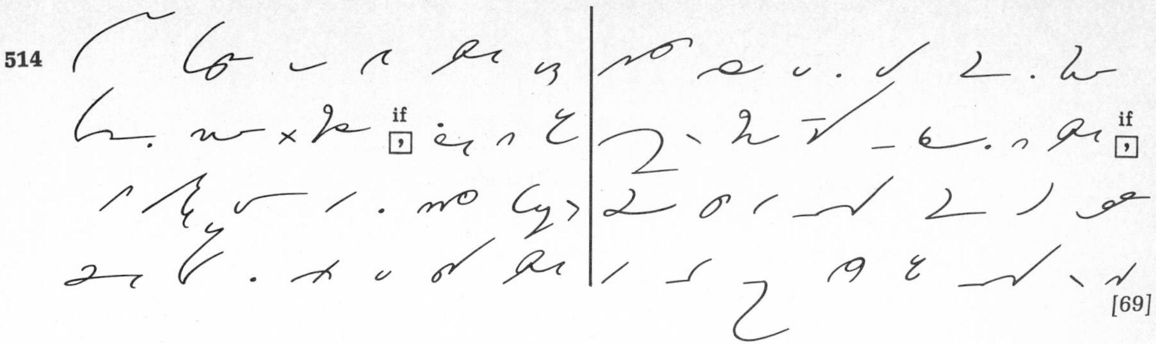

[69]

515 Transcription Quiz Beginning with Lesson 57, you will have an opportunity to see how well you have mastered the nine uses of the comma that were introduced in Chapters 6, 7, and 8. Lessons 57-69 contain one letter each that is called a "Transcription Quiz." It contains several illustrations of the uses of the comma that you have studied. The commas, however, are not indicated in the printed shorthand. It will be your job, as you copy the letter in shorthand in your notebook, to insert the commas in the proper places and to give the reasons why the commas are used. The shorthand in your notebook should resemble the following example:

▶ Caution: Please do not make any marks in your shorthand textbook. If you do, you will destroy the value of these quizzes to anyone else who may use the book.

The correct punctuation of the following letter calls for 4 commas—1 comma *as clause*, 2 commas parenthetical, 1 comma introductory.

[90]

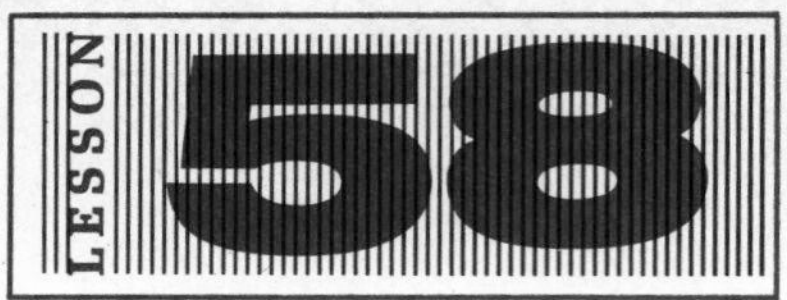

This lesson is designed to increase further your ability to use the frequent phrases of Gregg Shorthand. It contains several illustrations of all the phrasing principles. Altogether, there are 83 phrases, counting repetitions.

Building transcription skills

516 GRAMMAR CHECKUP | sentence structure

Parallel ideas should be expressed in parallel form.

no

I hope our relationship will be long, pleasant, and of profit *to both of us.*

yes

I hope our relationship will be long, pleasant, and profitable *to both of us.*

no

As soon as we receive the necessary information, your account will be opened and we will ship your order.

yes

As soon as we receive the necessary information, your account will be opened and your order will be shipped.

It is especially important to keep parallel all ideas in a tabulation.

no

Her main duties were:

1. *Taking dictation and transcribing*
2. *Answering the telephone*
3. To take care *of the files*

yes

Her main duties were:

1. *Taking dictation and transcribing*
2. *Answering the telephone*
3. Taking care *of the files*

517

Business vocabulary builder

adequate Sufficient.

expanding Getting larger.

solution Answer.

Reading and writing practice

518

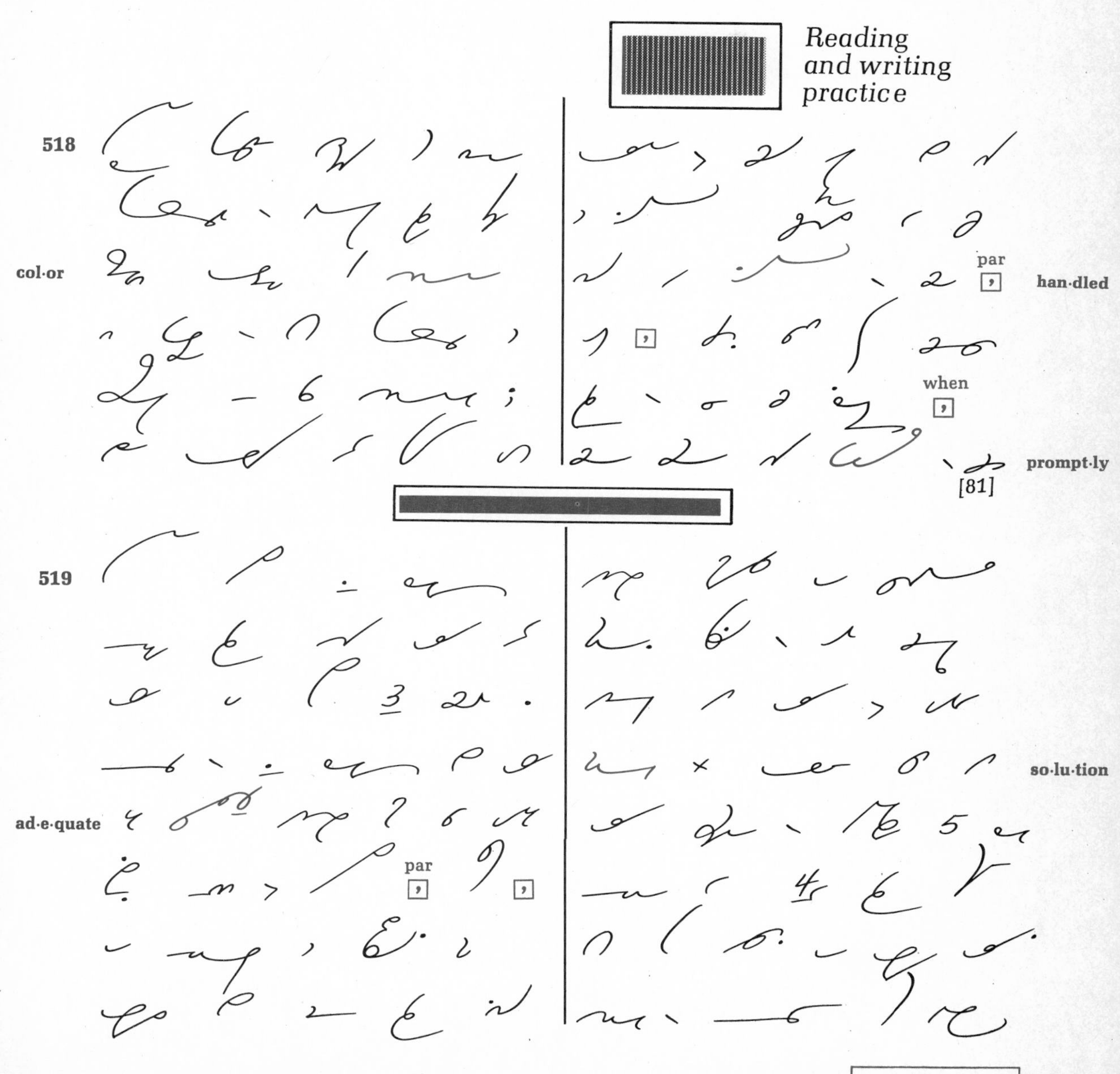

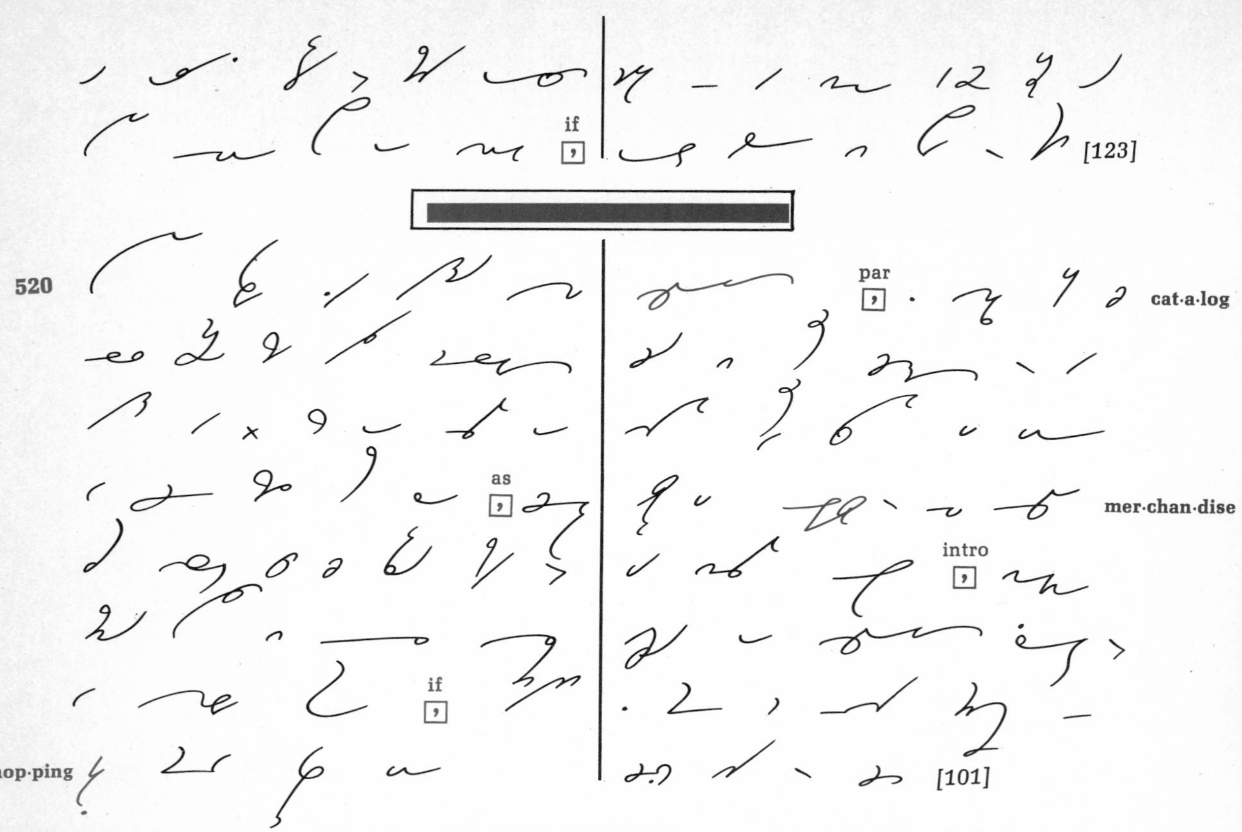

521 Transcription Quiz To punctuate the following letter correctly, you must supply 5 commas—1 comma conjunction, 2 commas series, 2 commas parenthetical.

No marks in the textbook, please!

[86]

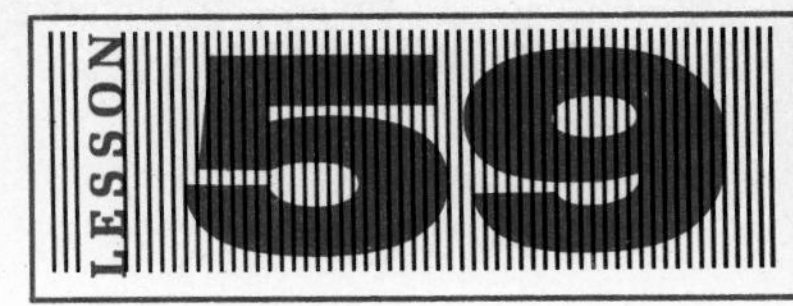

Are some of the joined word beginnings still a little hazy in your mind? The practice material in this lesson will help fix all the joined word beginnings more firmly in your mind. In this lesson you will find 61 joined word beginnings.

Building transcription skills

522 **SPELLING FAMILIES | -ence, -ance**

Words Ending in -ence

com·mence	**ev·i·dence**	**neg·li·gence**
con·fer·ence	**ex·is·tence**	**obe·di·ence**
con·fi·dence	**ex·cel·lence**	**oc·cur·rence**
con·va·les·cence	**ex·pe·ri·ence**	**ref·er·ence**
con·ve·nience	**in·de·pen·dence**	**vi·o·lence**

Words Ending in -ance

abun·dance	**bal·ance**	**in·sur·ance**
ac·cep·tance	**cir·cum·stance**	**is·su·ance**
al·low·ance	**en·dur·ance**	**per·for·mance**
as·sis·tance	**ig·no·rance**	**re·li·ance**
as·sur·ance	**in·stance**	**sub·stance**

523 *Business vocabulary builder*

formerly In the past.

encounter Meet.

incurred Brought upon oneself.

minor Of little importance.

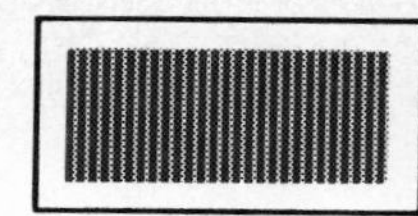

Reading and writing practice

524

em·bar·rassed

fur·ther·more intro

ad

de·scrib·ing

when

lose

intro

al·ready

for·mer·ly

par

conj **ac·cu·rate·ly**

[128]

525

ap

in·con·ve·nience

ex·pe·rienced

flight

con·nec·tion

par

intro **oc·ca·sion·al·ly**

mi·nor

in·curred 380

ex·pense

[131]

526

priv·i·le·ges

and o

routes

80

intro

de·pos·it 250 conj 250

[99]

527 Transcription Quiz The correct punctuation of the following letter calls for 8 commas—1 comma conjunction, 2 commas series, 4 commas parenthetical, 1 comma *and* omitted.

[99]

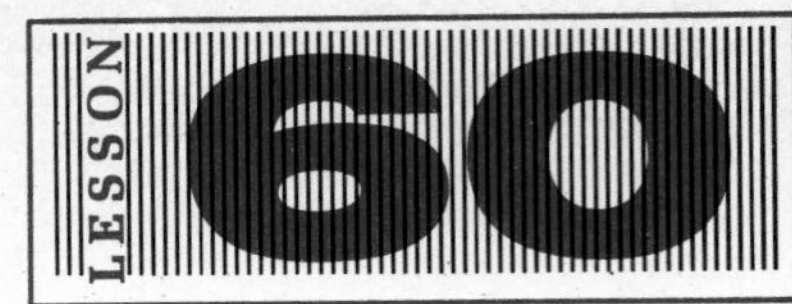

In this lesson you will "brush up" on joined word endings—there are 72 of them!

Building transcription skills

528 **COMMON PREFIXES | re-**

re- again

repack To pack again.

repeat To say again.

reconsider To take up again.

replenish To fill or supply again.

529

Business vocabulary builder	**impartial** Not favoring one side or the other; fair. **humid** Moist. **annual** Once a year.

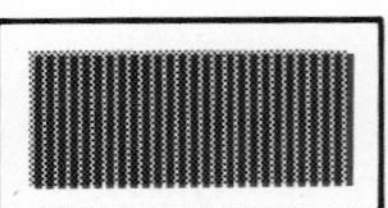

Reading and writing practice

Reading Scoreboard How much has your reading speed increased over your first score in Lesson 18? The table on the next page will help you determine your reading speed on Lesson 60.

Lesson 60 contains 601 words

If you read Lesson 60 in **13 minutes** *your reading rate is* **46 words a minute**
If you read Lesson 60 in **15 minutes** *your reading rate is* **40 words a minute**
If you read Lesson 60 in **17 minutes** *your reading rate is* **35 words a minute**
If you read Lesson 60 in **19 minutes** *your reading rate is* **31 words a minute**
If you read Lesson 60 in **21 minutes** *your reading rate is* **28 words a minute**
If you read Lesson 60 in **23 minutes** *your reading rate is* **26 words a minute**
If you read Lesson 60 in **25 minutes** *your reading rate is* **24 words a minute**

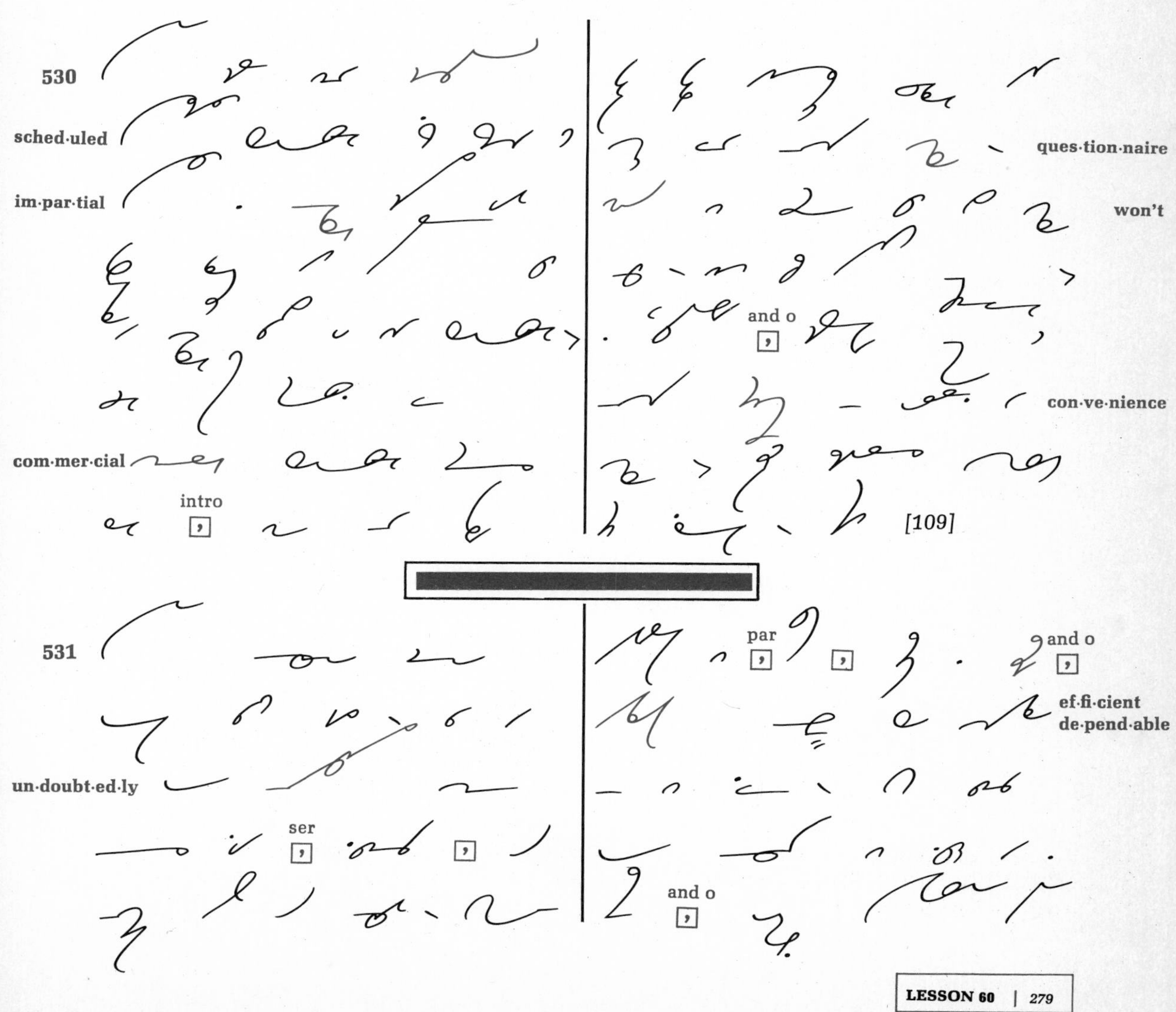

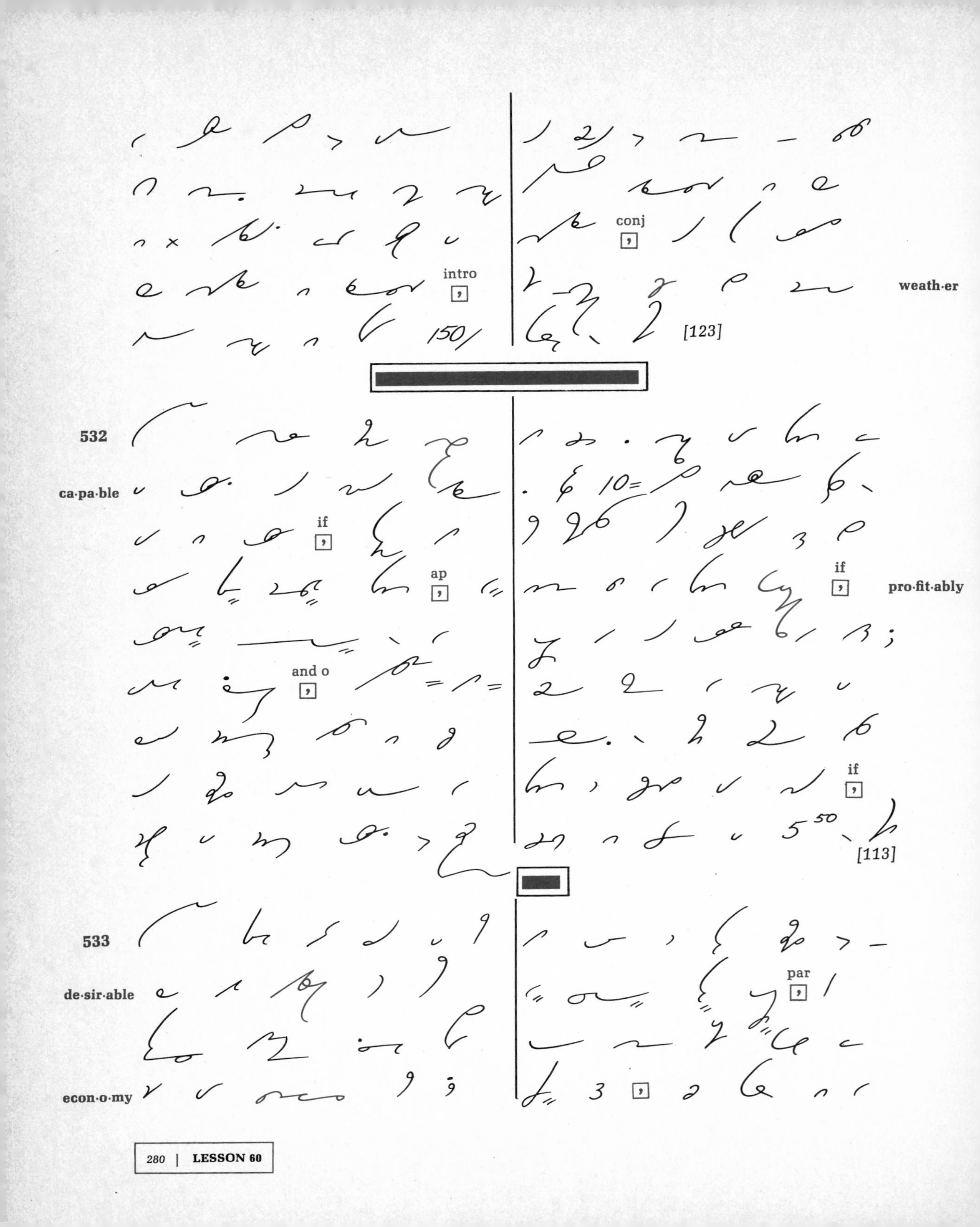

intro

conj

weath·er

[123]

532

ca·pa·ble

if

ap

and o

if

pro·fit·ably

if

[113]

533

de·sir·able

econ·o·my

par

whole

dis·cuss·es

conj

debt

conj

con·sump·tion

[137]

534 Transcription Quiz The correct punctuation of the following letter calls for 4 commas—1 comma apposition, 1 comma *and* omitted, 2 commas series.

As you copy the letter in your notebook, be sure to insert the necessary commas at the proper points and to indicate the reason for the punctuation.

[119]

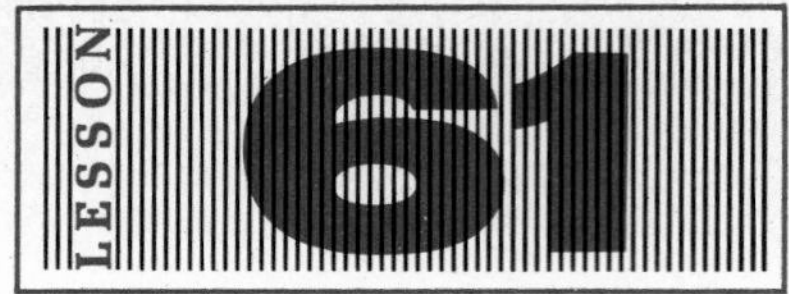

Disjoined word beginnings are given intensive treatment in this lesson. You will find 35 of them.

Building transcription skills

535 **GRAMMAR CHECKUP | comparisons**

The comparative degree of an adjective or adverb is used when reference is made to two objects; the superlative degree is used when reference is made to more than two objects.

comparative

Of the two boys, Jim is the taller.
Which boy is more efficient, Jim or Harry?
Is Mr. Smith or Mr. Green better qualified to do the job?

superlative

Of the three boys, Jim is the tallest.
Which of the boys is the most efficient, Jim, Harry, or John?
Is Mr. Smith, Mr. Green, or Mr. Brown the best qualified to do the job?

536

Business vocabulary builder	**transmit** Hand over to. **necessitated** Made necessary. **overall** Including everything.

Reading and writing practice

537

em·ploy·ee

al·ways

ar·eas

if

ed·i·tor

intro

wheth·er

par

thought·ful·ness

[106]

538

ap

trans·ferred

ne·ces·si·tat·ed

intro

sud·den·ness

over·all

[124]

539

par

mod·el

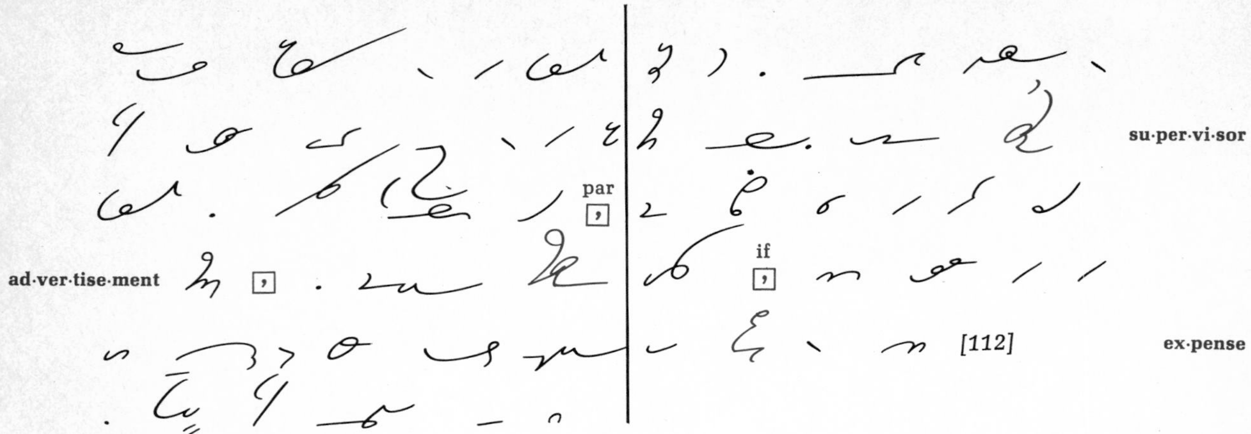

540 Transcription Quiz In the following letter you must supply 3 commas to punctuate it correctly—1 comma *when* clause, 2 commas series.

[109]

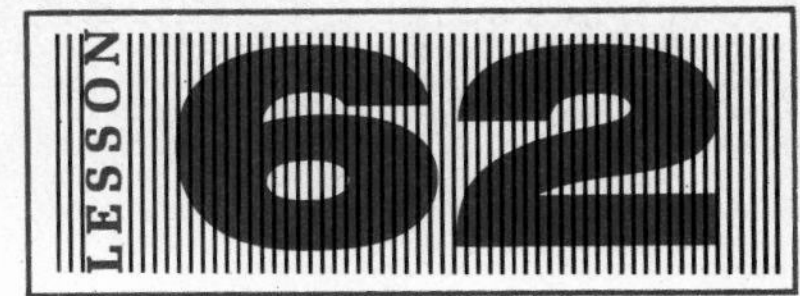

Do you find that you don't know the disjoined word endings as well as you would like? Then practice this lesson carefully. There are 33 disjoined word endings in it.

Building transcription skills

541 SIMILAR-WORDS DRILL | past, passed

past (noun) A former time. (*Past* is also used as an adjective.)

The program has been very successful in the past.

Please take care of your past-due *account.*

passed Went by; moved along; transferred.

I passed *him on the street.*

Before many days had passed*, he took care of his account.*

I passed *the report on to him.*

542

Business vocabulary builder

formulate Prepare; make.

potential In the making; possible.

with mixed feelings Be both happy and unhappy about the same situation.

Reading and writing practice

543

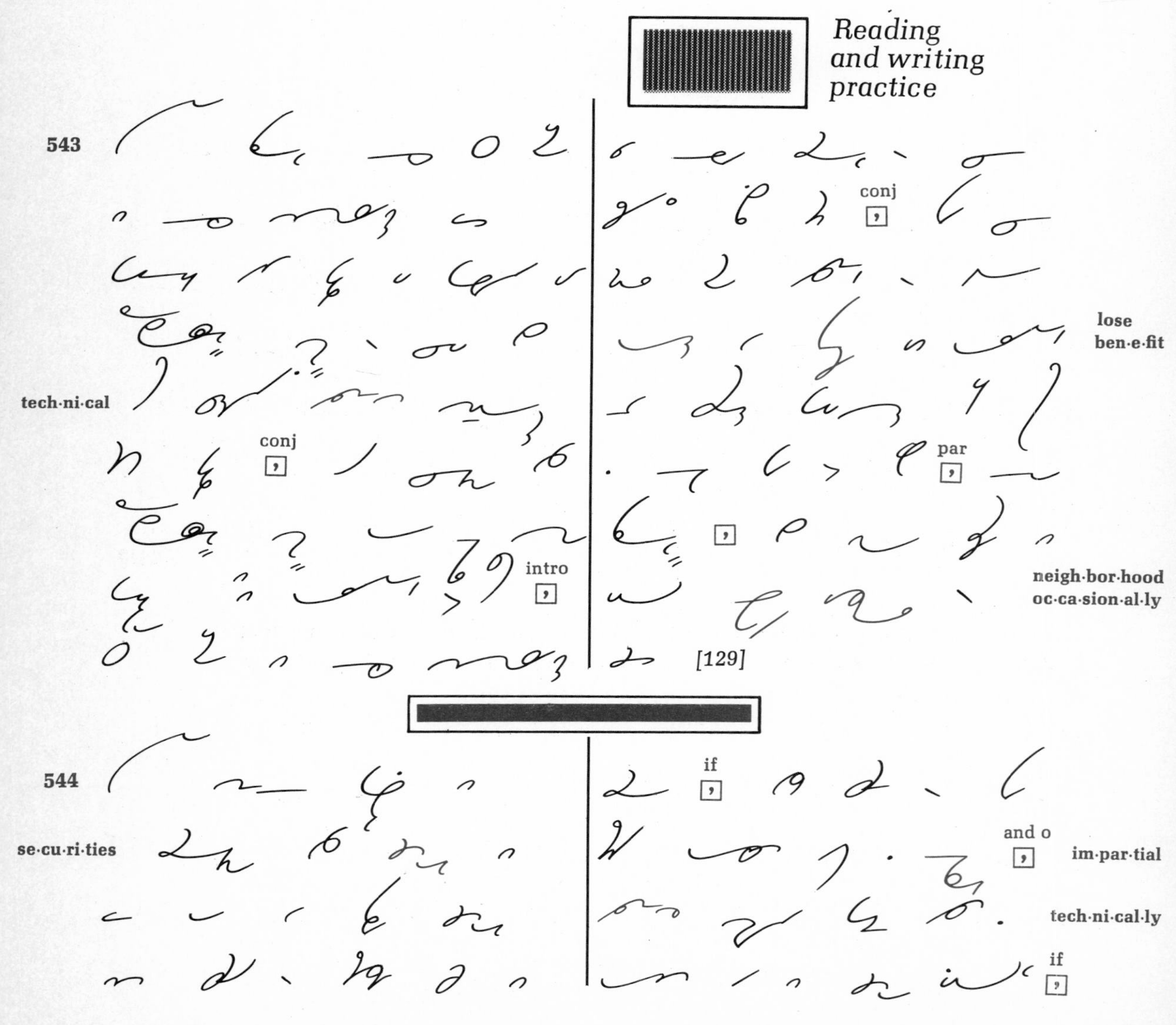

544

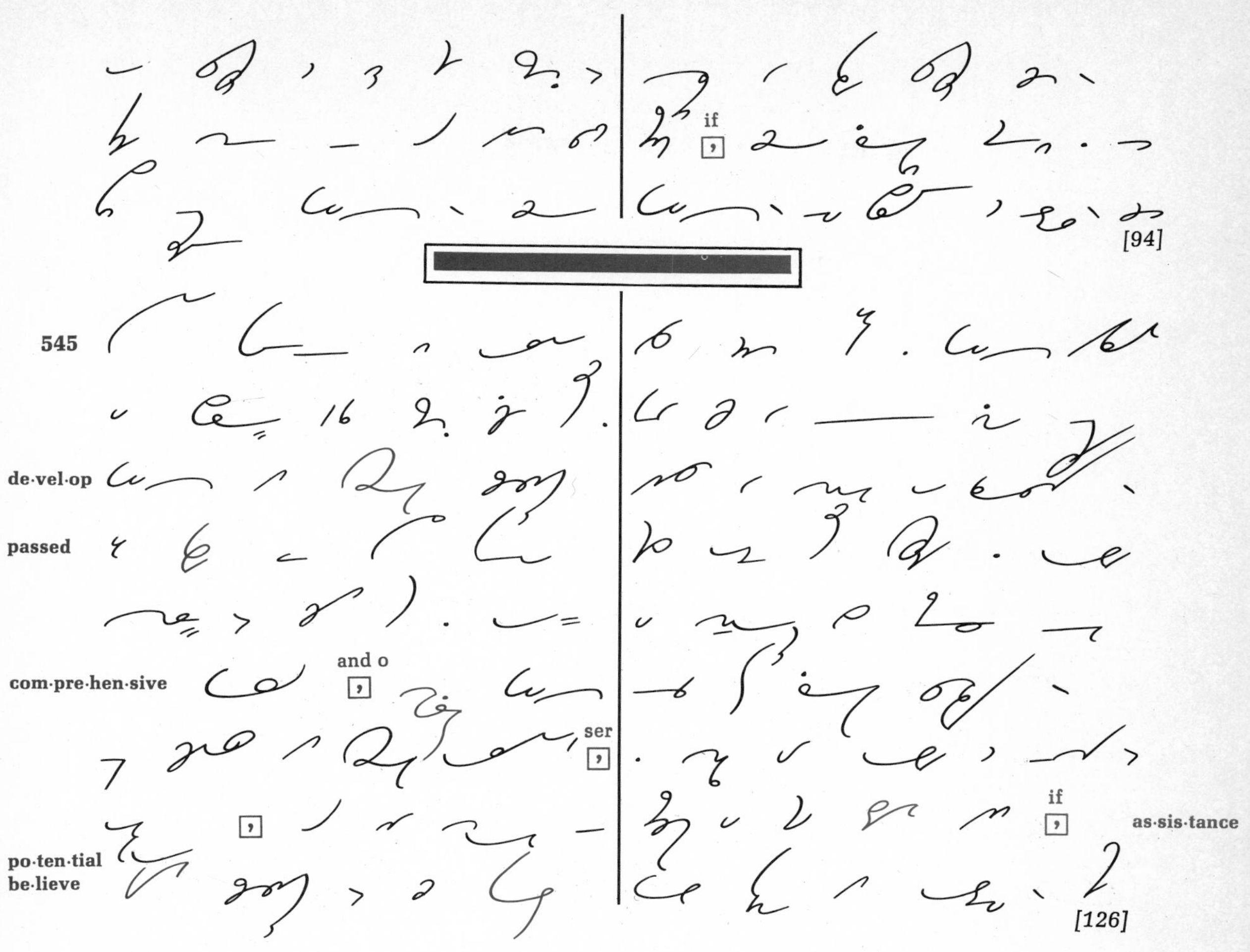

546 Transcription Quiz The following letter calls for 4 commas—1 comma introductory, 1 comma *when* clause, 2 commas parenthetical. Can you supply them?

[73]

Blends form a very important part of Gregg Shorthand. The material in this lesson reviews all the blends many times. In all, there are 71 words and phrases containing one or more blends.

Building transcription skills

547 COMMON PREFIXES ▌ co-

co- with, together, jointly

cooperation Act of working together.

coeducation Joint education; especially the education of boys and girls at the same school.

coordinate Bring together.

coherence A sticking together.

548

Business vocabulary builder

testimonial letter Letter expressing appreciation.

remedy (*verb*) Cure or correct.

exceeded Gone beyond.

net worth Difference between the total assets owned by a company and its total debts and obligations.

Reading and writing practice

549

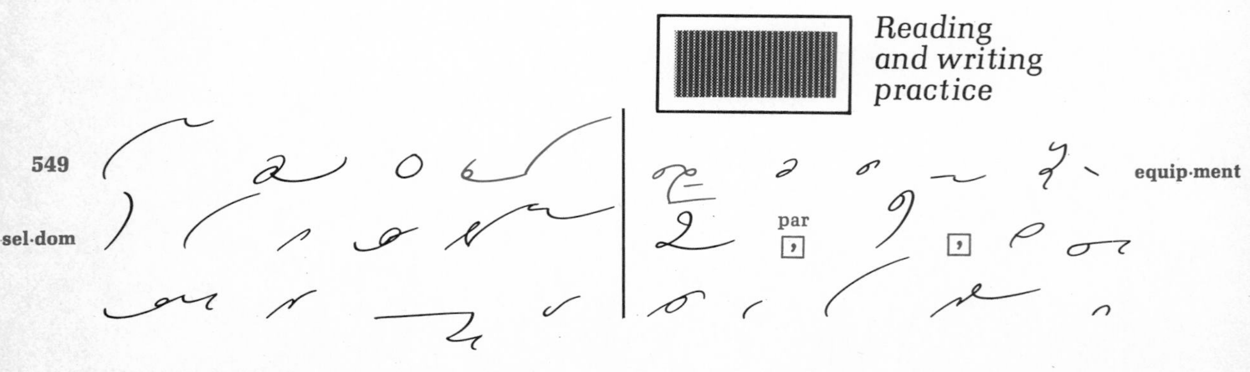

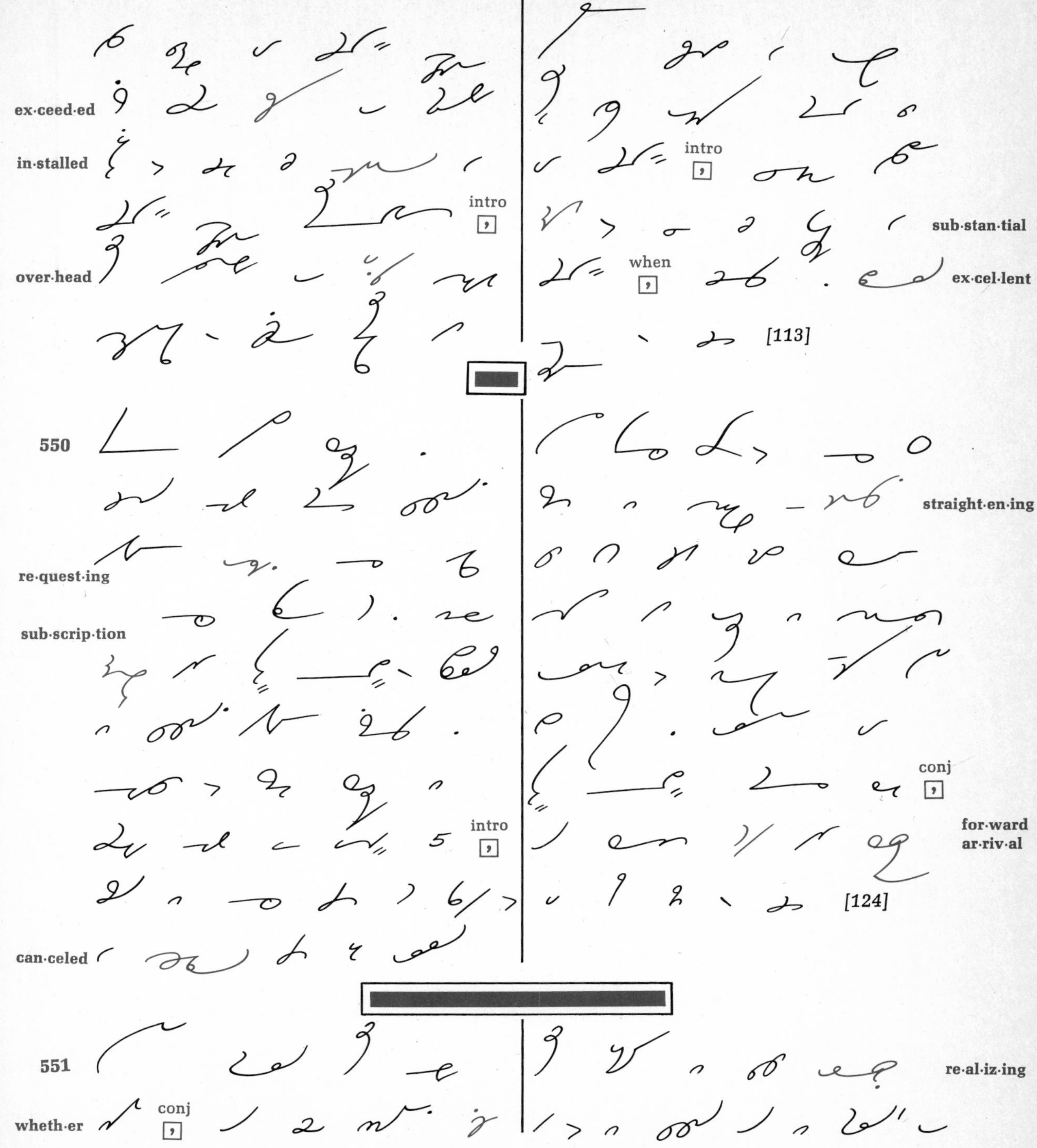

ex·ceed·ed

in·stalled

intro

over·head

intro

sub·stan·tial

when

ex·cel·lent

[113]

550

straight·en·ing

re·quest·ing

sub·scrip·tion

conj

intro

for·ward

ar·riv·al

[124]

can·celed

551

re·al·iz·ing

conj

wheth·er

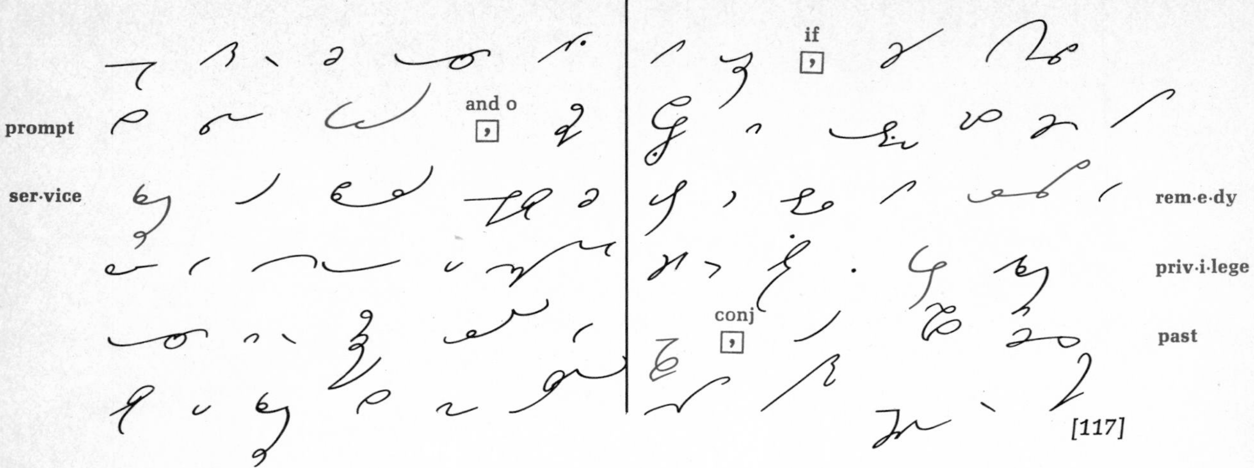

552 **Transcription Quiz** The following letter requires 6 commas to be punctuated correctly—2 commas conjunction, 2 commas parenthetical, 2 commas series. Remember to indicate these commas in your shorthand notes and to give the reason for their use.

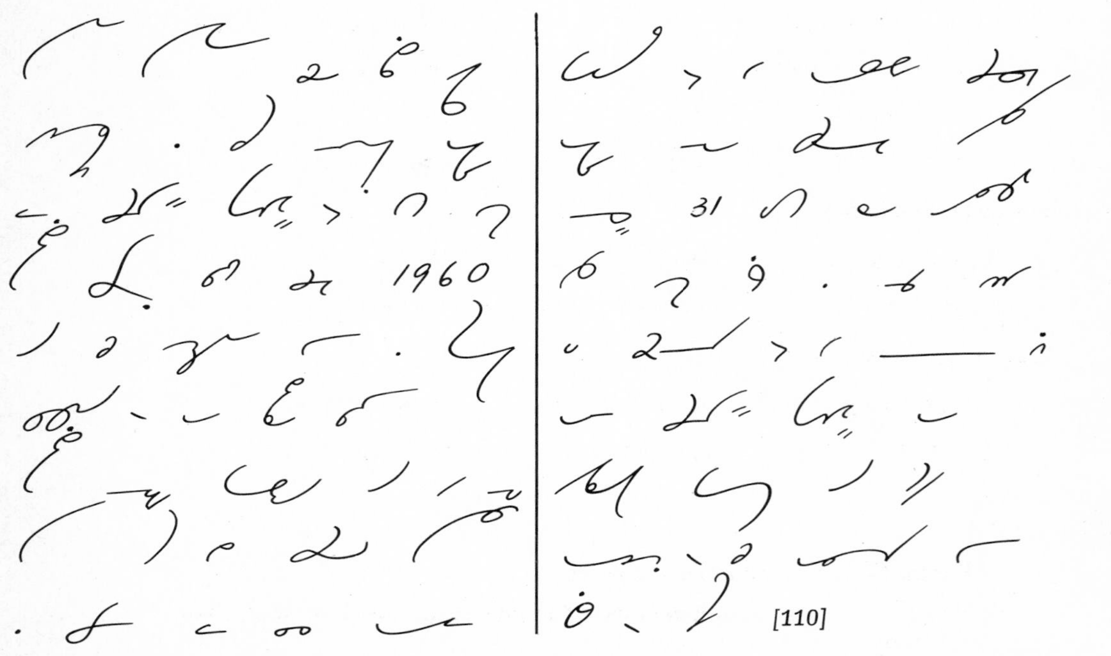

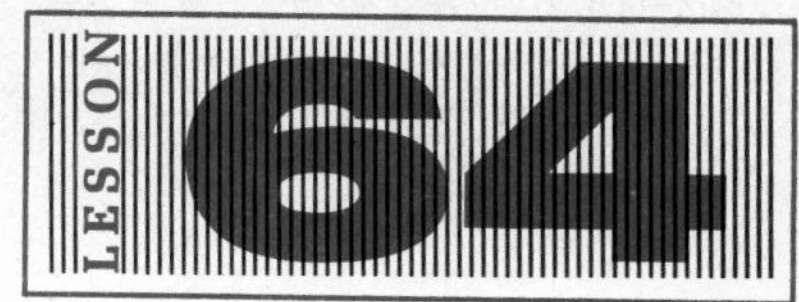

As you learned during the early stages of your study of Gregg Shorthand, vowels are omitted in some words to help gain fluency of writing. In this lesson you will find many illustrations of words from which vowels are omitted.

Building transcription skills

553 **SPELLING FAMILIES | -ary, -ery, -ory**

Words Ending in -ary

an·ni·ver·sa·ry	**el·e·men·ta·ry**	**sec·re·tary**
com·pli·men·ta·ry	**li·brary**	**sum·ma·ry**
cus·tom·ary	**nec·es·sary**	**tem·po·rary**
dic·tio·nary	**sec·on·dary**	**vo·cab·u·lary**

Words Ending in -ery

bind·ery	**mas·tery**	**re·fin·ery**
dis·cov·ery	**re·cov·ery**	**sce·nery**

Words Ending in -ory

di·rec·to·ry	**his·to·ry**	**ter·ri·to·ry**
fac·to·ry	**in·ven·to·ry**	**vic·to·ry**

554

Business vocabulary builder

situated Located.

complimentary Expressing approval or admiration; favorable.

customary Usual.

Reading and writing practice

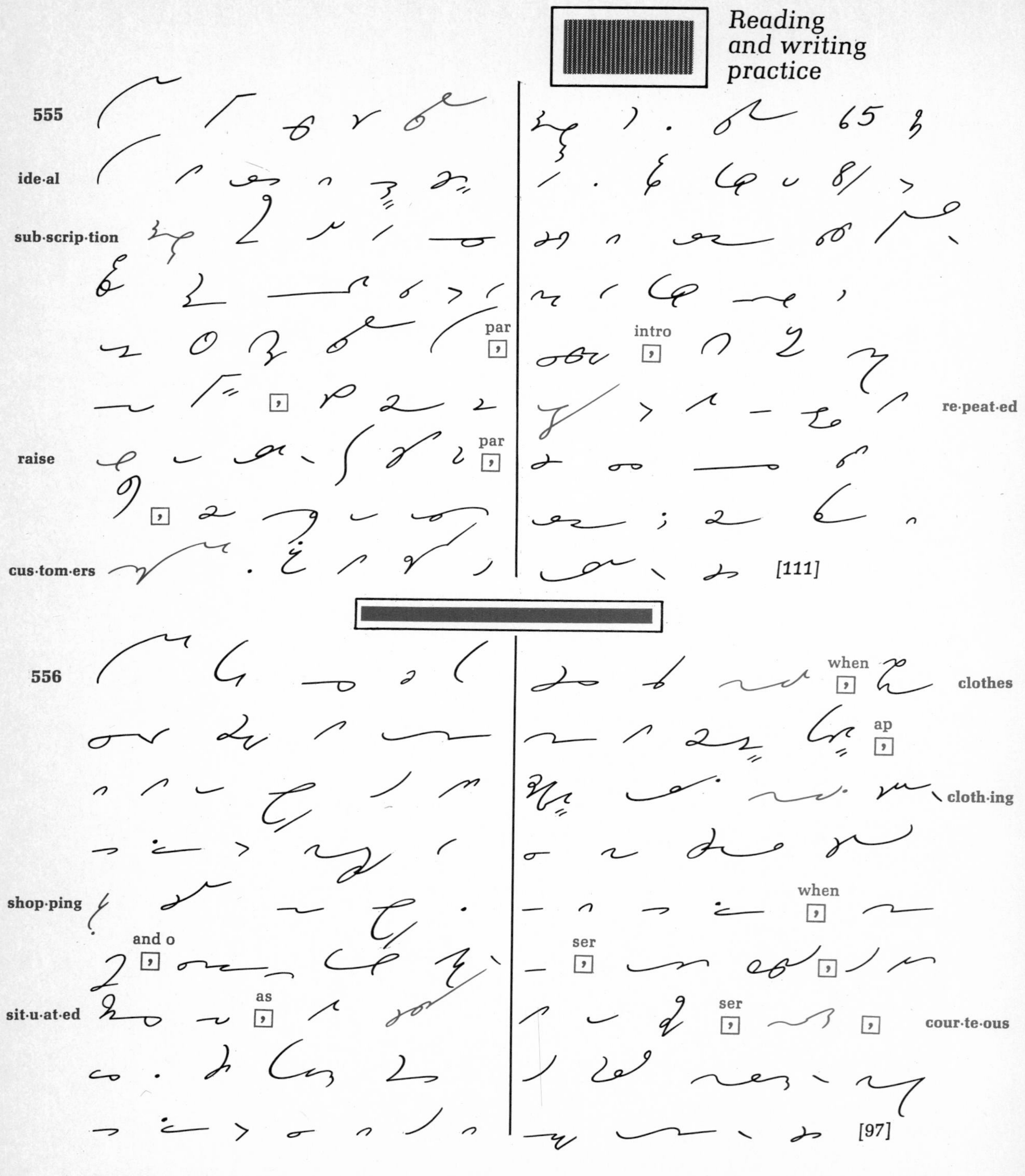

557

summary

career

par

utilize
excellent

ser

vacancy

if

par

intro

complimentary

[106]

558 **Transcription Quiz** For you to supply: 3 commas—2 commas introductory, 1 comma parenthetical.

[113]

You will frequently have to write numbers in business dictation. Because of the tremendous importance of accuracy in transcribing numbers, you must take special care to write numbers legibly in your notes. The material in this lesson will help you fix more firmly in your mind the various devices for expressing amounts and quantities in Gregg Shorthand.

Building transcription skills

559 **SIMILAR-WORDS DRILL** | **country, county**

country A nation.

He joined the armed forces of our country.

county A political division of a state.

Miami is in Dade County, *Florida.*

560

Business vocabulary builder	
exceeded	Went beyond.
pledges	Promises.
juvenile	Relating to children.

Reading and writing practice

561

Com·mu·ni·ty

ex·ceed·ed

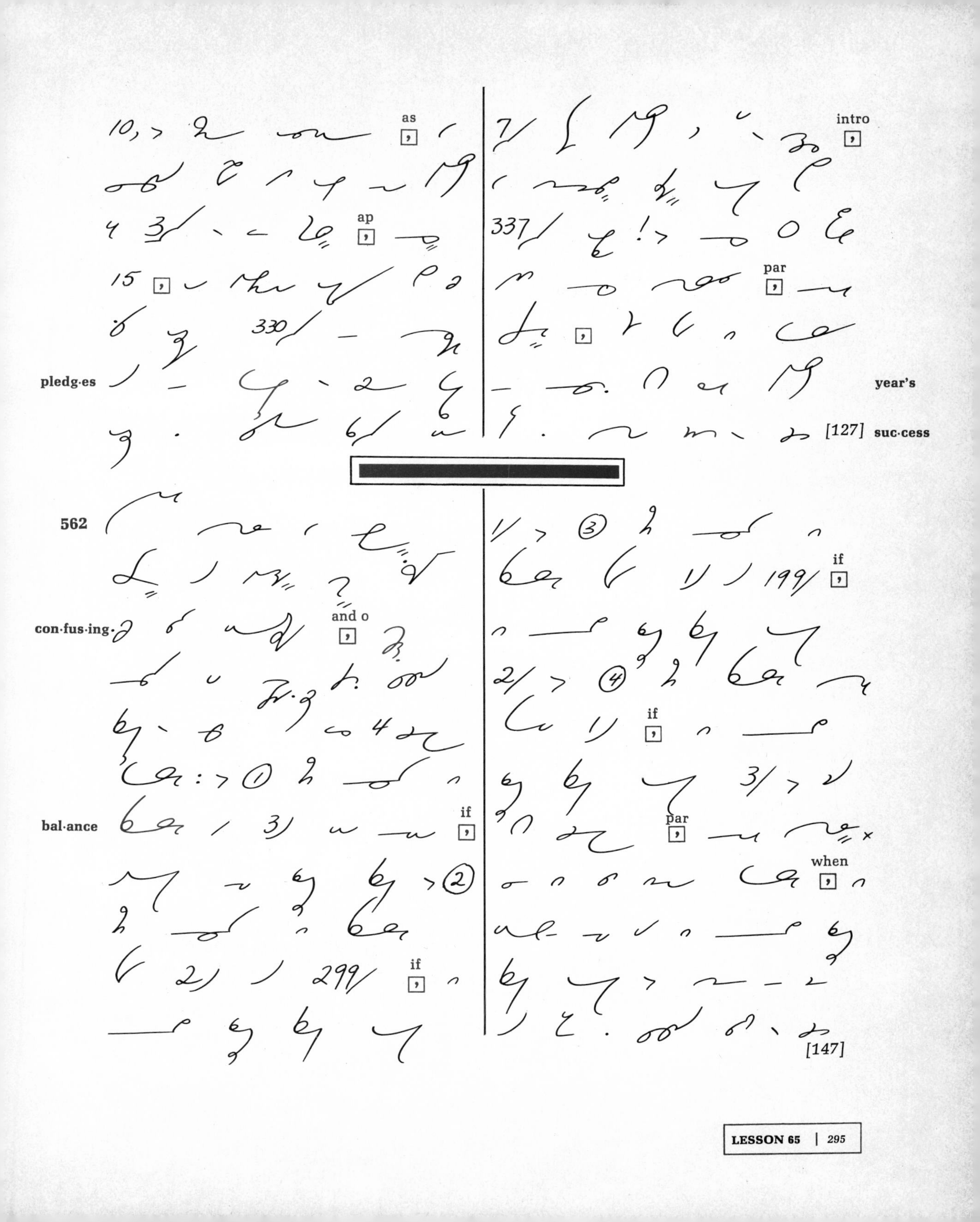

as

intro

ap

par

pledg·es

year's

[127]

suc·cess

562

con·fus·ing

and o

if

if

bal·ance

if

par

when

if

[147]

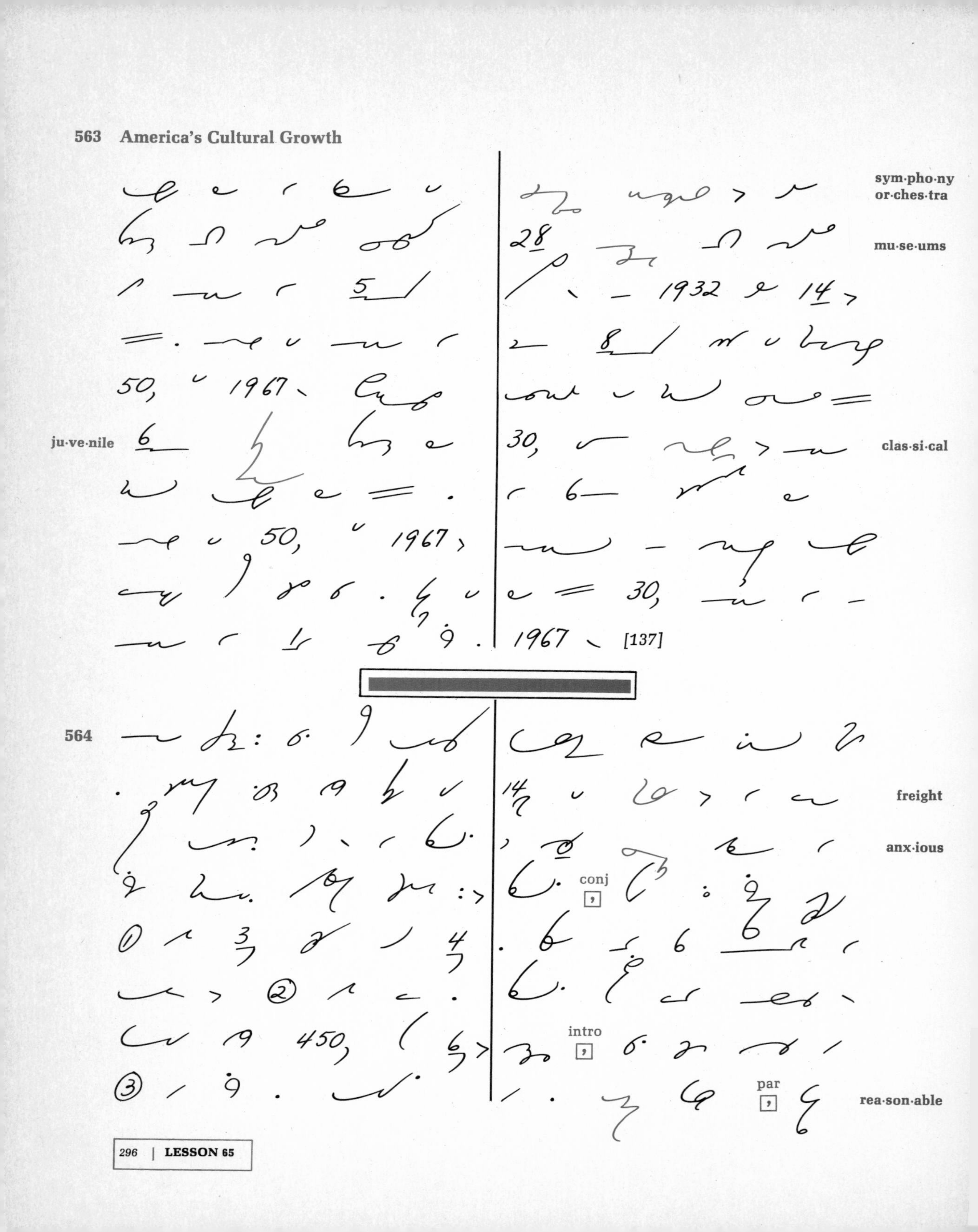

563 America's Cultural Growth

sym·pho·ny or·ches·tra

mu·se·ums

ju·ve·nile

clas·si·cal

[137]

564

freight

anx·ious

conj

intro

par

rea·son·able

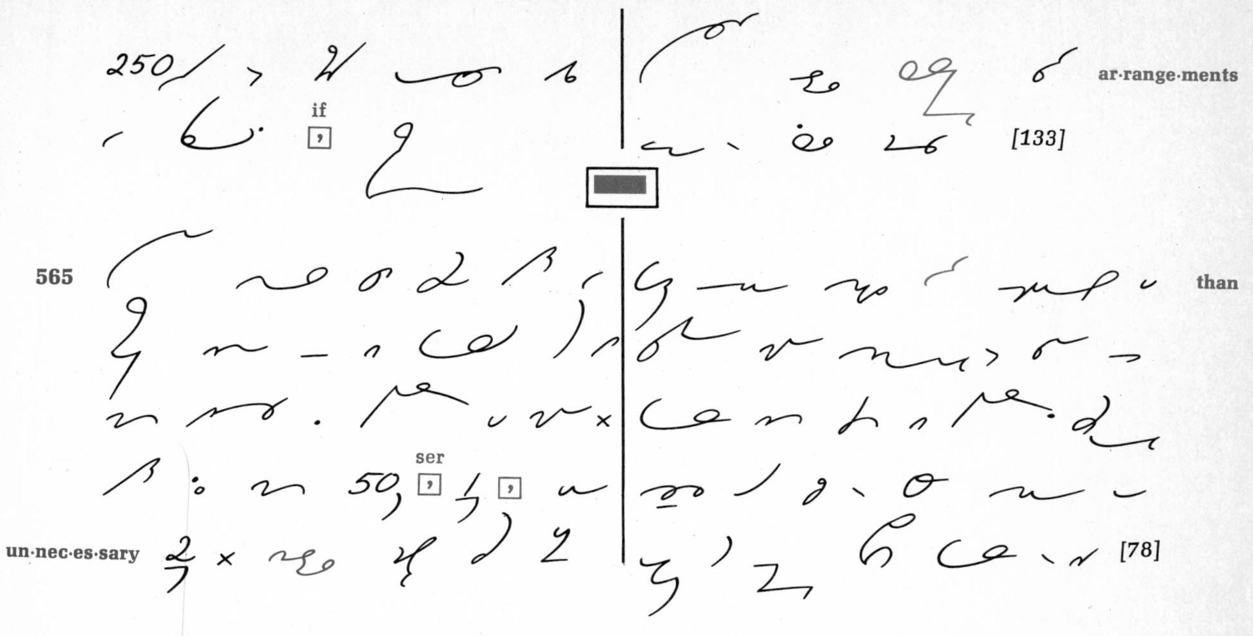

566 Transcription Quiz For you to supply: 8 commas—4 commas parenthetical, 1 comma introductory, 1 comma *and* omitted, 1 comma *if* clause, 1 comma apposition.

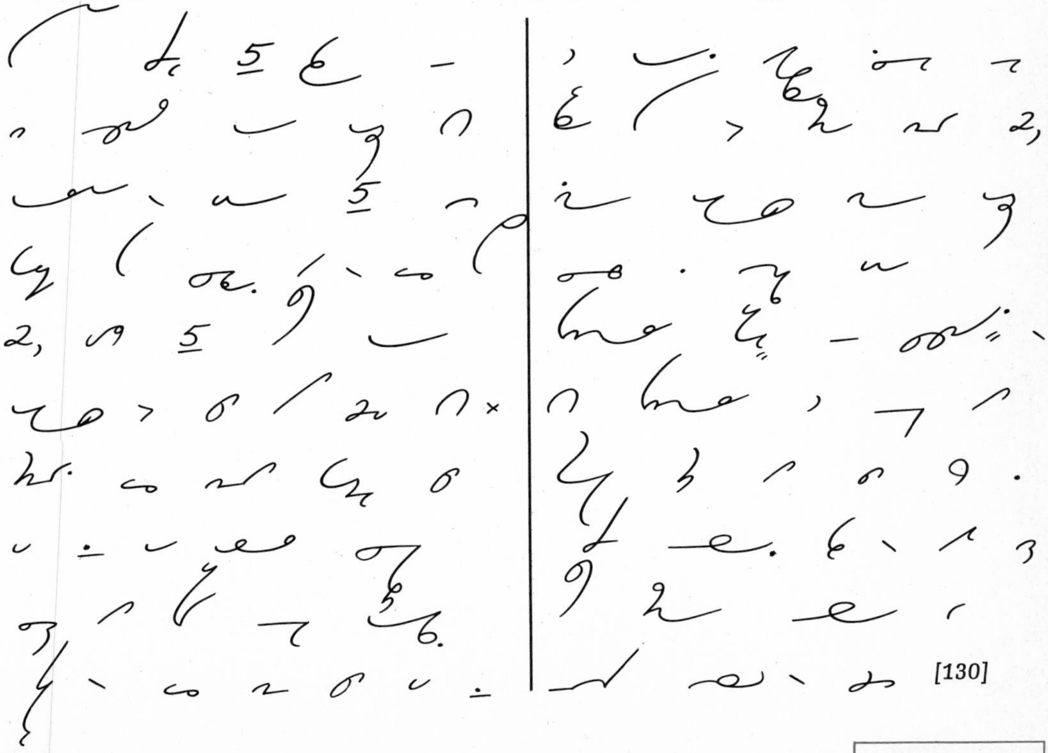

[130]

This is another lesson that concentrates on brief forms. Counting repetitions, it contains 206 brief forms and derivatives.

Building transcription skills

567 COMMON PREFIXES | un-

un- not

unusual Not usual; rare.

unnecessary Not needed.

unhappy Not happy; sad.

unsatisfactory Not satisfactory; bad.

568

Business vocabulary builder

fallout shelter A room, usually underground, that provides protection from the particles resulting from a nuclear explosion.

remiss Careless; negligent.

airfreight A method of shipping merchandise, usually heavy and bulky, by airplane.

Reading and writing practice

569

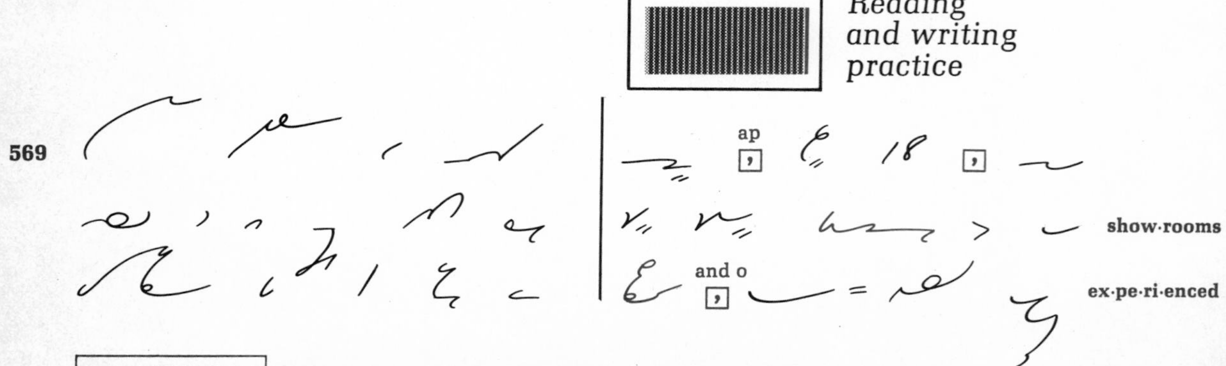

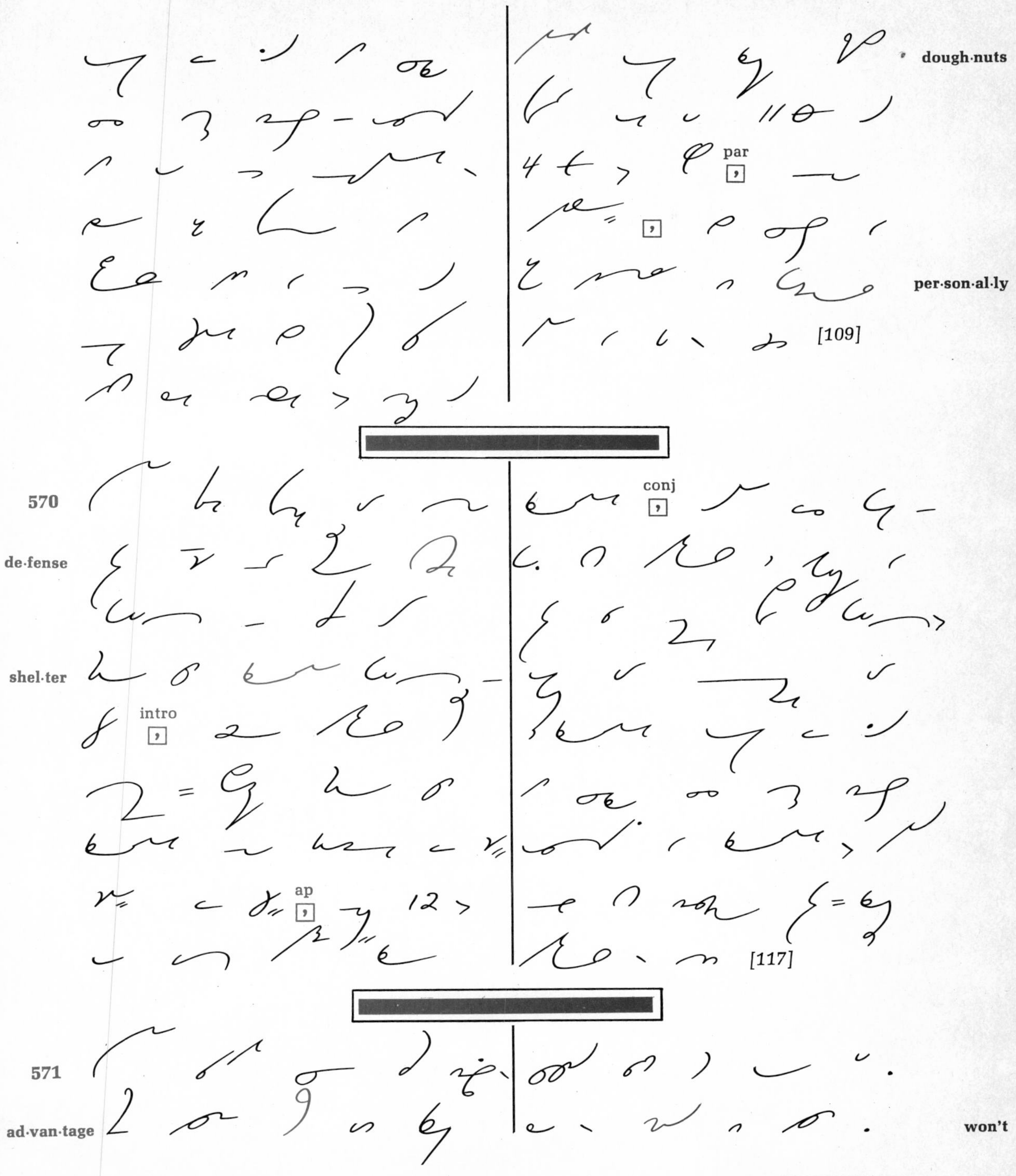
dough·nuts
par
per·son·al·ly
[109]
570
de·fense
conj
shel·ter
intro
ap
12
[117]
571
ad·van·tage
won't

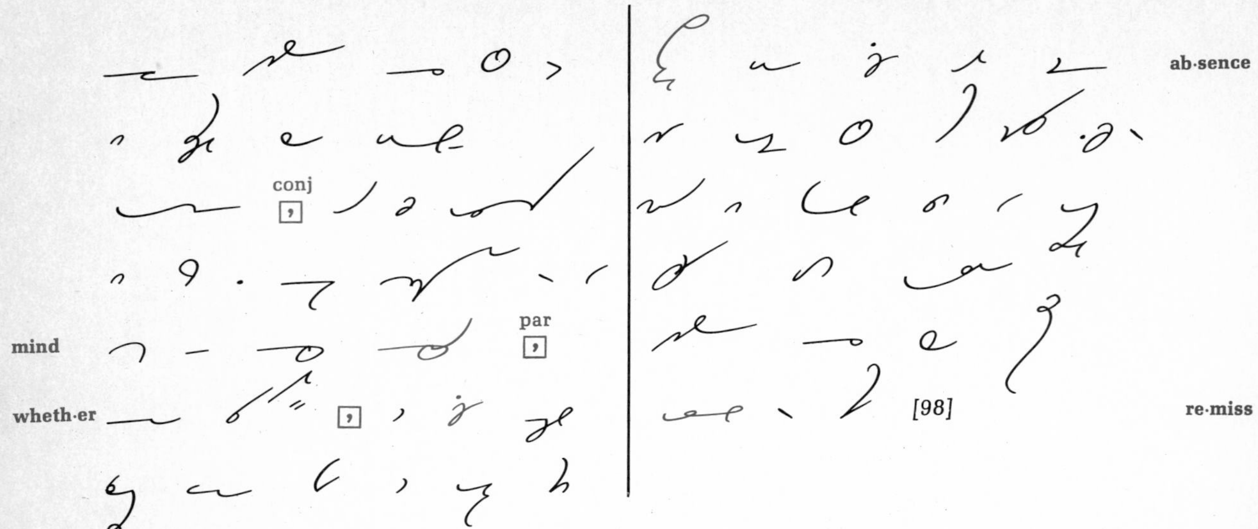

572 Transcription Quiz For you to supply: 4 commas—1 comma *when* clause, 2 commas series, 1 comma introductory.

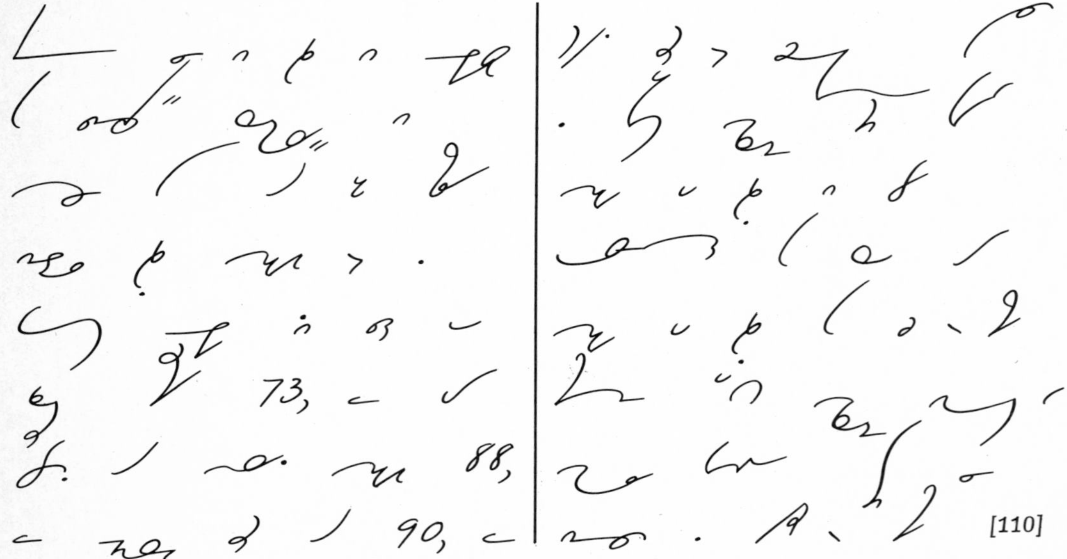

Here is another opportunity to check up on your phrasing skill. This lesson contains 119 phrases.

Building transcription skills

573 **GRAMMAR CHECKUP** ▌ **verbs—with "one of"**

1 In most cases, the expression *one of* takes a singular verb, which agrees with the subject *one.*

One *of the men on the staff* is *ill.*
One *of our typewriters* does not *work.*

2 When *one of* is part of an expression such as *one of those who* or *one of the things that,* a plural verb is used to agree with its antecedent in number.

He solved one of the problems *that* have been (*not* has been) *annoying businessmen for years.*
He is one of the men *who* drive (*not* drives) *to work.*

574

Business vocabulary builder	**comptroller** (pronounced *kon-tro-ler*) The officer of a company who has the responsibility for accounting and financial operations. **modernize** Bring up to date. **harassing** Worrying.

Reading and writing practice

575 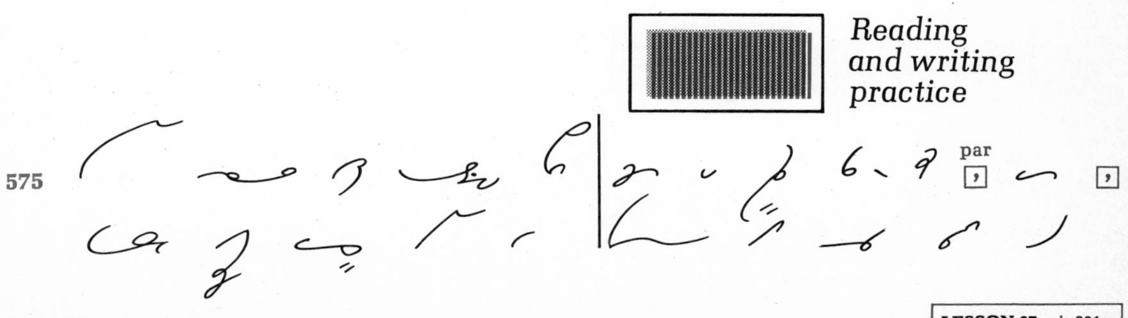

dis·cuss

intro intro

comp·trol·ler ap em·ploy·ees

par

[102]

576

if

wom·en if mod·ern·ize

proud

equal·ly sur·vey

kitch·en

intro

ap

intro

[113]

577

ser intro

sten·cils

ha·rass·ing

if

if

im·me·di·ate·ly

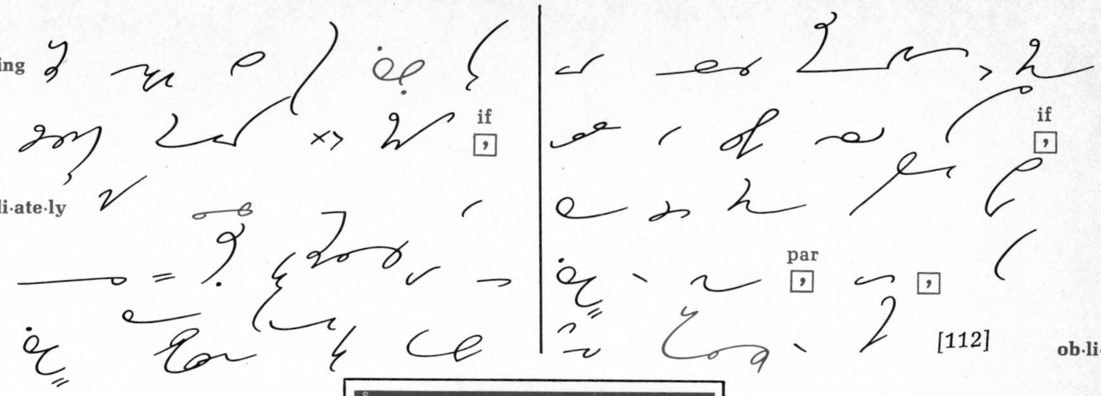

par

[112]

ob·li·ga·tion

578

as

conj

par

[52]

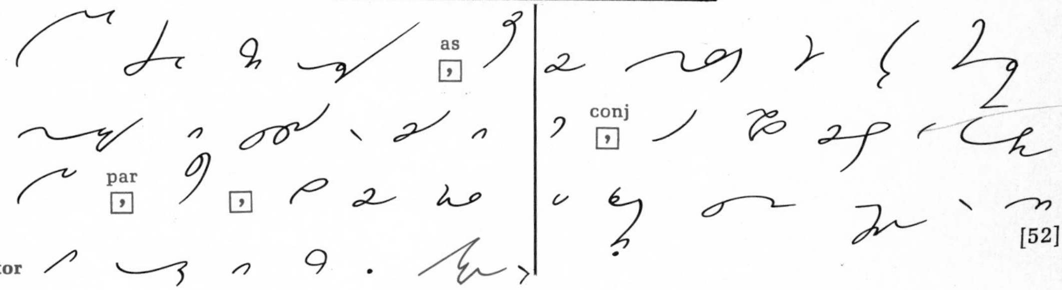

de·pos·i·tor

579 Transcription Quiz For you to supply: 5 commas—2 commas introductory, 1 comma *as* clause, 2 commas parenthetical.

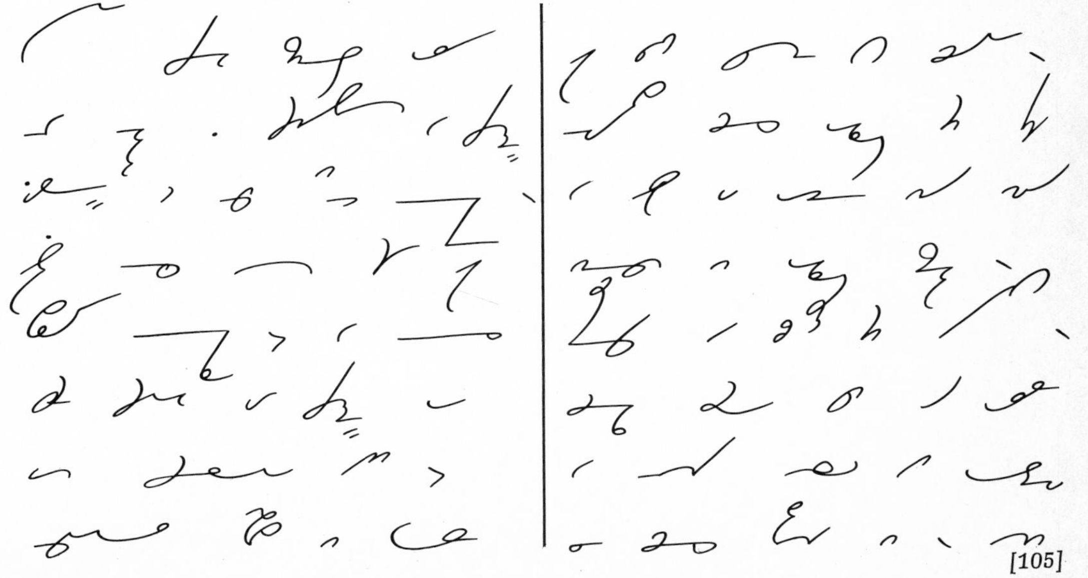

[105]

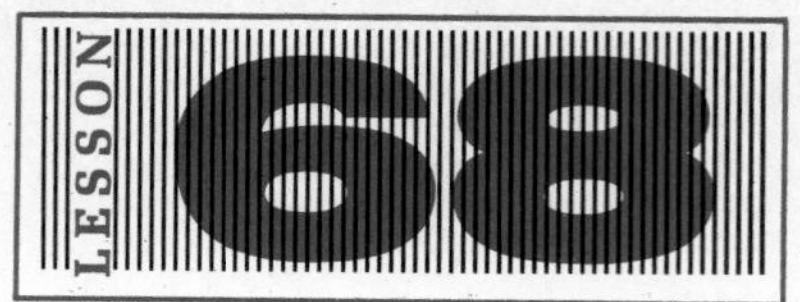

This lesson contains a general review of the major principles of Gregg Shorthand.

Building transcription skills

580 SIMILAR-WORDS DRILL | **assistance, assistants**

assistance Help.

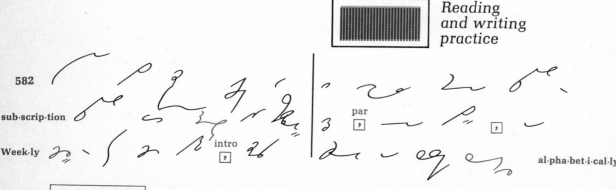

You will find many suggestions that will be of assistance *to you.*

assistants Helpers.

One of my assistants *tells me you will feature our line in your store.*

581

Business vocabulary builder	
	shortcomings Deficiencies; defects.
	fascinating Extremely interesting; charming.
	compensate Pay.

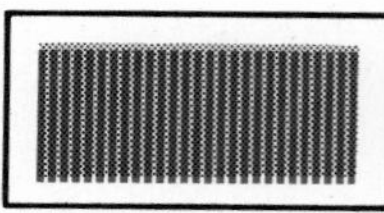

Reading and writing practice

582

sub·scrip·tion

par

Week·ly

intro

al·pha·bet·i·cal·ly

ser

as·sis·tance

in·for·ma·tion par [98]

re·ceiv·ing

583

and o

uti·liz·es

self-con·scious short·com·ings

fas·ci·nat·ing

intro

con·vinc·ing·ly

in·flu·ence if

[117]

584 par

as·sis·tants

plan·ning

suits

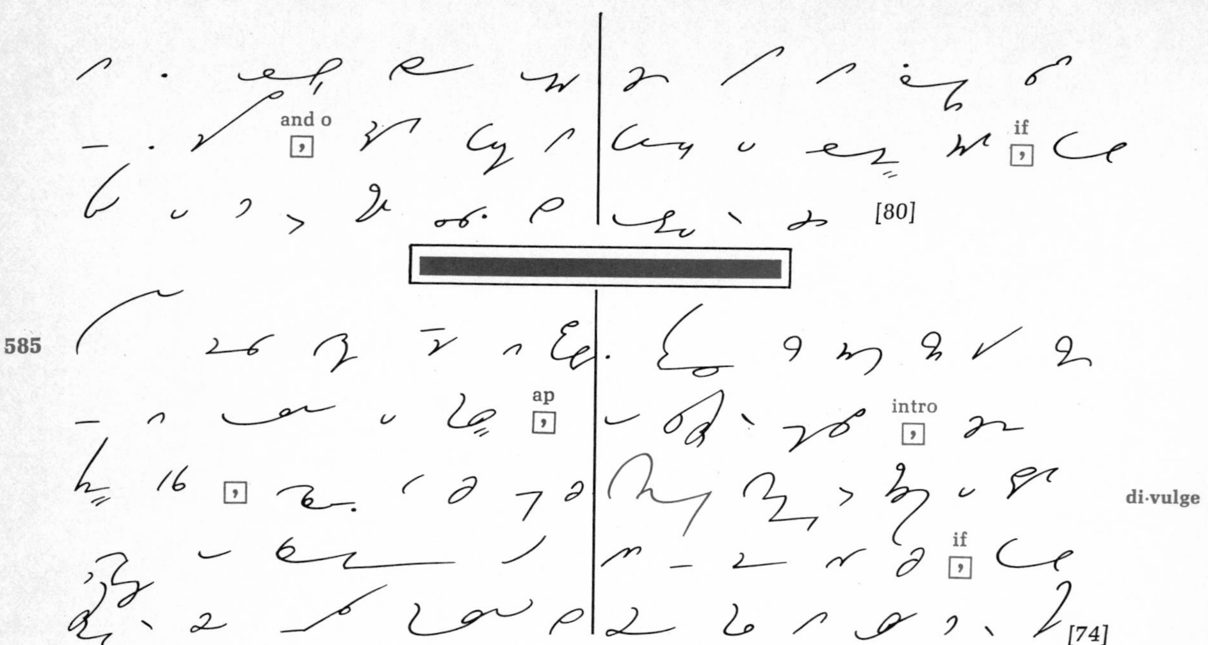

586 Transcription Quiz For you to supply: 5 commas—1 comma conjunction, 2 commas series, 1 comma introductory, 1 comma *when* clause.

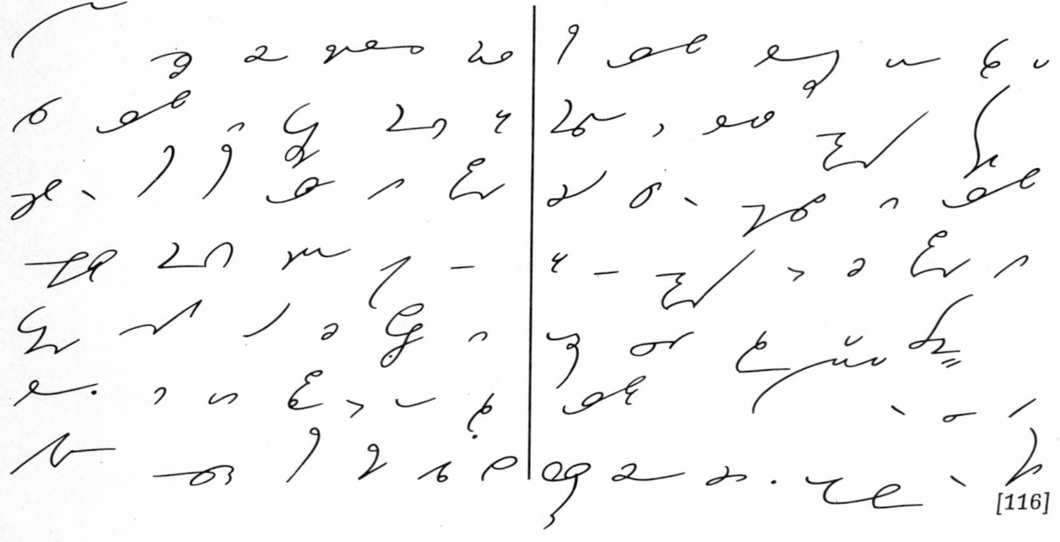

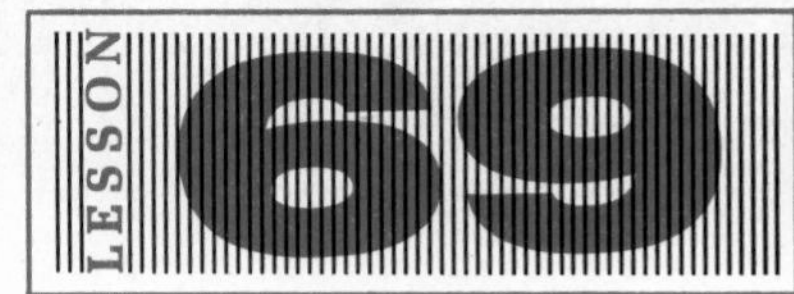

You won't be able to refrain from chuckling as you read the "hotel" letters in the Reading and Writing Practice of this lesson. They are an exchange of letters between a hotel manager and a guest.

Building transcription skills

587 COMMON PREFIXES | pre-

pre- before, beforehand

predict To tell beforehand; to prophesy.

preliminary Coming before the main business.

premature Happening before the proper time.

prearrange To arrange beforehand.

588

Business vocabulary builder

desolated Sad; unhappy; disappointed.

conceivably Possibly.

establishment Place of business.

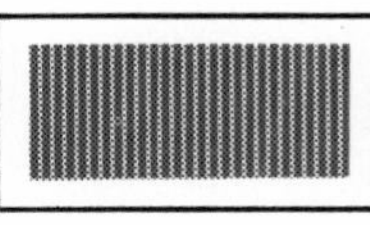

Reading and writing practice

589

intro

wool·en

par

oc·cu·pied

re·spect·ful·ly

intro

par

[93]

590

ap

par

par

intro

intro

catch

des·o·lat·ed

slight

sou·ve·nirs

vis·i·tor

con·ceiv·ably

oc·cu·pied

maid

when

if

gen·tle·man·ly
lan·guage

[254]

591 Transcription Quiz For you to supply: 6 commas—2 commas series, 1 comma introductory, 1 comma conjunction, 2 commas parenthetical.

[147]

The articles in this lesson contain information that will be of great help to you when you enter the business world. Read and study the articles carefully.

Building transcription skills

592 **SPELLING FAMILIES | past tense with r**

Past Tenses in Which R Is Doubled

blurred	**de·ferred**	**pre·ferred**
con·curred	**in·ferred**	**re·ferred**
con·ferred	**oc·curred**	**trans·ferred**

Past Tenses in Which R Is Not Doubled

cov·ered	**ma·jored**	**hon·ored**
dif·fered	**of·fered**	**suf·fered**

593 *Business vocabulary builder*

exerting Putting forth.

habitually Usually; by force of habit.

clue Hint.

dedication Devotion.

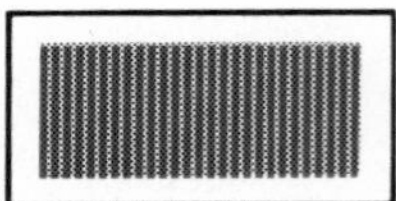

Reading and writing practice

Reading Scoreboard Now that you are on the last lesson, you are no doubt very much interested in your final shorthand reading rate. If you have followed the practice suggestions you received early in the course, your shorthand reading rate at this time should be a source of pride to you.

To get a real picture of how much your shorthand reading rate has increased with practice, compare it with your reading rate in Lesson 18, the first time you measured it.

Lesson 70 contains 452 words

If you read Lesson 70 in **9 minutes** *your reading rate is* **50 words a minute**
If you read Lesson 70 in **11 minutes** *your reading rate is* **41 words a minute**
If you read Lesson 70 in **13 minutes** *your reading rate is* **35 words a minute**
If you read Lesson 70 in **15 minutes** *your reading rate is* **30 words a minute**
If you read Lesson 70 in **17 minutes** *your reading rate is* **27 words a minute**
If you read Lesson 70 in **19 minutes** *your reading rate is* **24 words a minute**
If you read Lesson 70 in **21 minutes** *your reading rate is* **22 words a minute**

594 Names

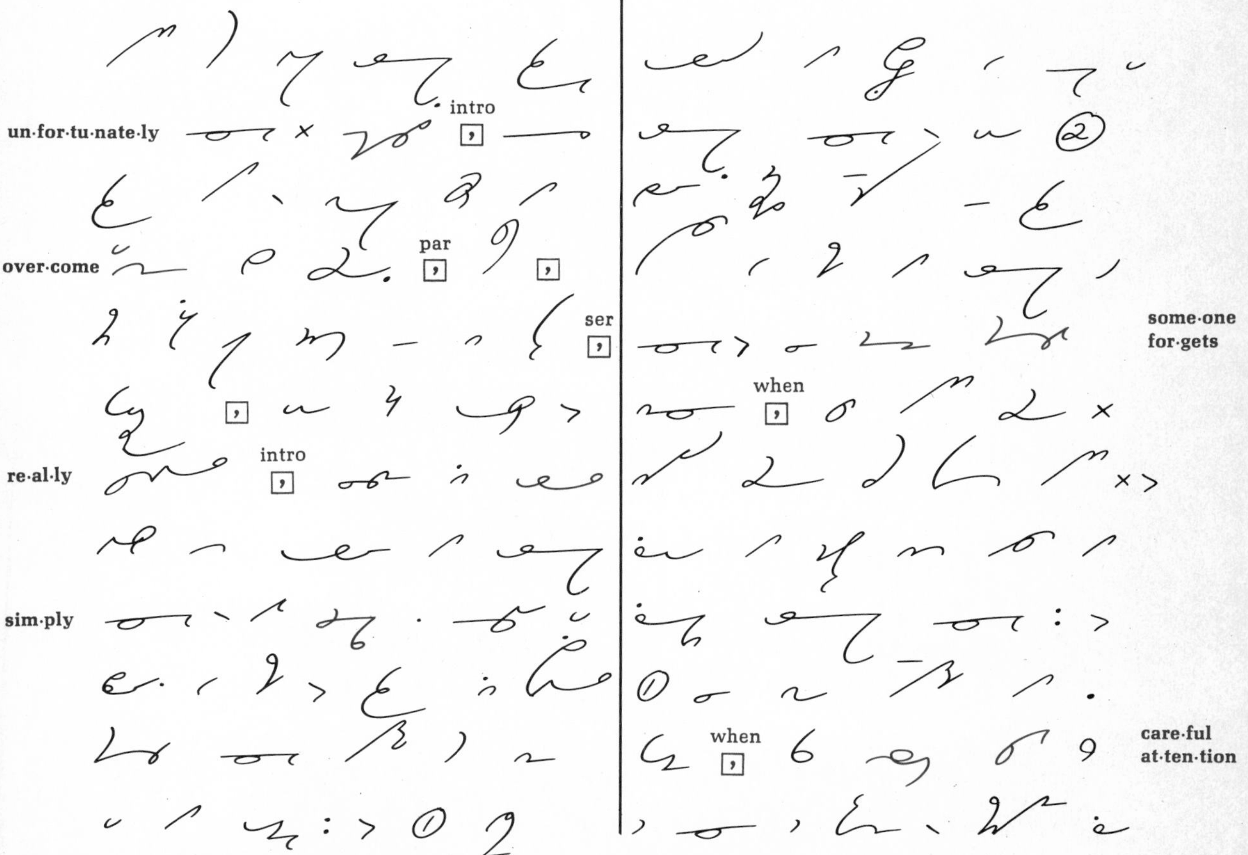

if

as·so·ci·ate ap

au·to·mat·i·cal·ly

gen·u·ine·ly

conj ex·treme·ly

[256]

595 Loyalty

par

fair

any·one

def·i·ni·tion conj

conj

re·ferred

pos·ses·ses

trait

ser

[196]

APPENDIX

States

The abbreviations in parentheses are those recommended by the Post Office Department.

Alabama (AL)

Alaska (AK)

Arizona (AZ)

Arkansas (AR)

California (CA)

Colorado (CO)

Connecticut (CT)

Delaware (DE)

Florida (FL)

Georgia (GA)

Hawaii (HI)

Idaho (ID)

Illinois (IL)

Indiana (IN)

Iowa (IA)

Kansas (KS)

Kentucky (KY)

Louisiana (LA)

Maine (ME)

Maryland (MD)

Massachusetts (MA)

Michigan (MI)

Minnesota (MN)

Mississippi (MS)

Missouri (MO)

Montana (MT)

Nebraska (NE)

Nevada (NV)

New Hampshire (NH)

New Jersey (NJ)

New Mexico (NM)

New York (NY)

North Carolina (NC)

North Dakota (ND)

Ohio (OH)

Oklahoma (OK)

Oregon (OR)

Pennsylvania (PA)

Rhode Island (RI)

South Carolina (SC)

South Dakota (SD)

Tennessee (TN)

Texas (TX)

Utah (UT)

Vermont (VT)

Virginia (VA)

Washington (WA)

West Virginia (WV)

Wisconsin (WI)

Wyoming (WY)

Principal cities of the United States

Akron
Albany
Atlanta
Baltimore
Birmingham
Boston
Bridgeport
Buffalo
Cambridge
Camden
Canton
Charlotte
Chattanooga
Chicago
Cincinnati
Cleveland
Columbus
Dallas
Dayton

Denver
Des Moines
Detroit
Duluth
Elizabeth
Erie
Fall River
Flint
Fort Wayne
Fort Worth
Gary
Grand Rapids
Hartford
Houston
Indianapolis
Jacksonville
Jersey City
Kansas City
Knoxville

Long Beach
Los Angeles
Louisville
Lowell
Memphis
Miami
Milwaukee
Minneapolis
Nashville
Newark
New Bedford
New Haven
New Orleans
New York
Norfolk
Oakland
Oklahoma City
Omaha
Paterson

Peoria
Philadelphia
Pittsburgh
Portland
Providence
Reading
Richmond
Rochester
Sacramento
St. Louis
St. Paul

Salt Lake City
San Antonio
San Diego
San Francisco
Scranton
Seattle
Somerville
South Bend
Spokane
Springfield
Syracuse

Tacoma
Tampa
Toledo
Trenton
Tulsa
Utica
Washington
Wichita
Wilmington
Worcester
Yonkers

Common geographical abbreviations

America
American
United States

England
English
Great Britain

Canada
Canadian
Puerto Rico

Index of Gregg Shorthand

In order to facilitate finding, this Index has been divided into six main sections—Alphabetic Characters, Brief Forms, General, Phrasing, Word Beginnings, Word Endings.

The first figure refers to the lesson; the second refers to the paragraph.

INDEX OF BRIEF FORMS

The first figure refers to the lesson; the second to the paragraph.

INDEX OF BUILDING TRANSCRIPTION SKILLS

The first figure refers to the lesson; the second figure to the paragraph.

COMMON PREFIXES

GRAMMAR CHECKUP

PUNCTUATION PRACTICE – COMMAS

SIMILAR WORDS

SPELLING FAMILIES